T0330427

Corporate Governance, Organization and the Firm

NEW PERSPECTIVES ON THE MODERN CORPORATION

Series Editor: Jonathan Michie, *Professor of Management and Director and Head, Birmingham Business School, University of Birmingham, UK*

The modern corporation has far reaching influence on our lives in an increasingly globalised economy. This series will provide an invaluable forum for the publication of high quality works of scholarship covering the areas of:

- corporate governance and corporate responsibility, including environmental sustainability
- human resource management and other management practices, and the relationship of these to organisational outcomes and corporate performance
- industrial economics, organisational behaviour, innovation and competitiveness
- outsourcing, offshoring, joint ventures and strategic alliances different ownership forms, including social enterprise and employee ownership
- intellectual property and the learning economy, including knowledge transfer and information exchange.

Titles in the series include:

Corporate Governance, Organization and the Firm
Co-operation and Outsourcing in the Global Economy
Edited by Mario Morroni

The Modern Firm, Corporate Governance and Investment
Edited by Per-Olof Bjuggren and Dennis C. Mueller

The Growth of Firms
A Survey of Theories and Empirical Evidence
Alex Coad

Corporate Governance, Organization and the Firm

Co-operation and Outsourcing in the Global Economy

Edited by

Mario Morroni

Department of Economics, University of Pisa, Italy

NEW PERSPECTIVES ON THE MODERN CORPORATION

Edward Elgar

Cheltenham, UK • Northampton, MA, USA

Published by
Edward Elgar Publishing Limited
The Lypiatts
15 Lansdown Road
Cheltenham
Glos GL50 2JA
UK

Edward Elgar Publishing, Inc.
William Pratt House
9 Dewey Court
Northampton
Massachusetts 01060
USA

A catalogue record for this book
is available from the British Library

Library of Congress Control Number: 2008939737

Mixed Sources
Product group from well-managed
forests and other controlled sources
www.fsc.org Cert no. SA-COC-1565
© 1996 Forest Stewardship Council

ISBN 978 1 84720 820 0

Printed and bound in Great Britain by MPG Books Ltd, Bodmin, Cornwall

Contents

Figures

Tables

Contributors

Patrick Cohendet, BETA University Louis Pasteur, Strasbourg, France, and HEC Montréal, Canada.

Mirella Damiani, Department of Economics, Finance and Statistics, University of Perugia, Italy.

Santi Furnari, CRORA, Bocconi University, Milan, Italy.

Carlo Gianelle, Doctoral School, University of Siena, Italy.

Anna Grandori, CRORA, Bocconi University, Milan, Italy.

Jackie Krafft, University of Nice Sophia Antipolis, CNRS-GREDEG, France.

Patrick Llerena, BETA Université Louis Pasteur, Strasbourg, France.

Massimiliano Mazzanti, Department of Economics, Institutions and Territory, University of Ferrara, Italy.

Claude Ménard, University of Paris (Pantheon-Sorbonne), Paris, France.

Sandro Montresor, Department of Economics, University of Bologna, Italy.

Mario Morroni, Department of Economics, University of Pisa, Italy.

Rafael Pardo, Department of Economics, CSIC (Spanish National Research Council), Madrid, Spain.

Paolo Pini, Department of Economics, Institutions and Territory, University of Ferrara, Italy.

Ruth Rama, Department of Economics, CSIC (Spanish National Research Council), Madrid, Spain.

Jacques-Laurent Ravix, University of Nice Sophia Antipolis, CNRS-GREDEG, France.

Andreas Reinstaller, Austrian Institute for Economic Research (WIFO), Vienna, Austria.

Giuseppe Tattara, Department of Economics, University of Venice, Italy.

Paul Windrum, Manchester Metropolitan University Business School, United Kingdom, and Max Planck Institute for Economics, Jena, Germany.

Acknowledgements

The participants in the international workshop on 'Internal Organization, Cooperative Relationships among Firms and Competitiveness', which took place in Lucca on 19–20 January 2007, are acknowledged for their contribution to stimulating discussions. The meeting was organized by the Department of Economics of the University of Pisa and generously sponsored by Fondazione della Cassa di Risparmio di Lucca and by the University of Pisa. Much credit for the workshop's success must go to Alga Foschi, Paola Giuri and Andrea Mangàni of the organizational committee. Particular thanks also to the keynote speakers Michael Dietrich, Richard Langlois and Claude Ménard, and to the discussants of the earlier version of papers published in this collection: Alberto Chilosi, Marco Furlotti, Anna Grandori, Riccardo Leoncini, Patrick Llerena, Paolo Mariti, Sandro Montresor, Vahagn Movsesyan, Jacques-Laurent Ravix and Alessandro Romagnoli. Finally, Rachel Costa and Heather Jones are gratefully acknowledged for skilful editorial assistance.

1. Introduction: Organizational variety and economic performance

Mario Morroni

1.1 AN INTERPRETATIVE FRAMEWORK

This book investigates the heterogeneity of organizational forms of business firms, offering a picture of recent advances in the analysis of different organizational settings adopted by firms in their endeavour to cope with increasing competitive pressure. The chapters of this book are derived from papers first presented at the international workshop on 'Internal Organization, Cooperative Relationships among Firms and Competitiveness', held in Lucca in January 2007. During the meeting a number of stimulating papers animated lively discussions, covering an extensive array of different theoretical and applied themes on the theory of the firm. The present selection contains the papers having direct relevance to the current debate on the emergent variety of organizational forms.[1] The papers have undergone a substantial revision that reflects the insights and comments from the participants in the workshop and the particular focus of this collection.

Applied studies show a widespread, profound and increasing heterogeneity across firms regarding strategy, organization arrangement and performance.[2] Different degrees of efficiency seem to bring about relatively persistent profitability differentials among firms, whilst there is no evidence of a link between profitability and the growth rate of firms. As is well known, growth rates tend to differ markedly among firms.[3] At the basis of inter-firm heterogeneity there is a complex set of links between basic conditions, decision-making mechanisms and organizational settings of the firms.[4] Efficiency and profitability of the firm depend on the organizational setting which, in turn, is influenced by basic conditions and internal decision making. Naturally, the causal chain also runs in the opposite direction: the competitiveness of a firm contributes to creating the basic conditions that shape internal decision-making processes. These links are outlined in Figure 1.1.

Basic conditions result from the interplay between the environmental conditions that business organizations face and the internal conditions

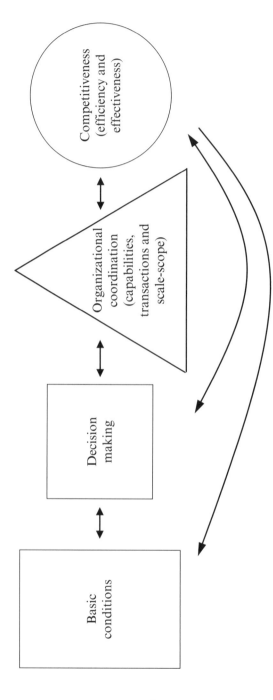

Figure 1.1   Basic conditions, decision making, coordination and competitiveness

created by business organizations themselves as a result of external constraints and opportunities. Basic conditions are mainly composed of the following interrelated features: (i) attributes of information, knowledge and available techniques and equipment, (ii) individual abilities, motivations and aims, (iii) degree of uncertainty, (iv) structural change and (v) institutional and market conditions.

Among important components that influence decision-making processes within the firm, property structures, control rights, aims of the firm, corporate culture, internal communication systems, incentive design, human resources practices and the kind of rationality (with reference to the level of uncertainty) occupy a salient position.

In industrialized countries a rich tapestry of ownership and governance structures can be observed. Mirella Damiani (Chapter 2 in this book) underlines that different property structures shape a variety of control devices and incentive arrangements across countries. Jackie Krafft and Jaques-Laurent Ravix (Chapter 3) convincingly argue that the adoption of an approach based on a unique and universal set of rules and arrangements neglects the heterogeneity of firms, the diversity of industries and the different stages of their life cycle, as well as the variety of institutional contexts.

Decision-making mechanisms are linked to a multiplicity of organizational practices aiming to pursue efficiency and effectiveness according to the multiplicity of basic conditions. As maintained by Anna Grandori and Santi Furnari (Chapter 4), the heterogeneity of organizational practices arises from the fact that they are the result of specific 'compositions' of different doses of elementary 'organizational elements' – just as different materials are the result of the combination of different qualities and doses of chemical elements.

Decision-making mechanisms and organizational practices affect the organizational coordination between (a) the development of capabilities, (b) the arrangement of transactions and (c) the design of the scale of different processes.

Developing capabilities means finding, interpreting and using knowledge on how to plan, organize and perform production processes. Dynamic capabilities consist of the firm's ability to integrate, build and reconfigure internal and external knowledge in order to address rapidly changing environments.[5]

The arrangement of transactions concerns decisions regarding the relationships with suppliers and customers. Firms that operate in the same sector of activity are often characterized by various levels of vertical integration and different outsourcing relations. This implies the existence of a large variety of hybrid arrangements that shape diverse forms of collaboration among firms. According to the definition provided by Claude

Ménard (Chapter 5), hybrids are understood as a mode of organization in which significant resources specific to the relationship among partners are shared while ownership remains distinct. Hybrids appear under many different guises: alliances, joint ventures, networks, long-term partnerships, franchising and so on. In recent years firms are no longer outsourcing peripheral activities alone (such as catering, security, distribution); but are instead increasingly outsourcing a wide range of activities encompassing more critical functions that contribute to their competitive position.[6]

In designing the operational scale of each process the firm has to balance the productive capacities of different inputs and intermediate stages. Extension of the boundaries of the firm implies learning how to solve problems of scaling up the processes of production by exploiting the properties of indivisible and complementary production elements (Chandler 1992, p. 84). One observes great variability in firm sizes among and within sectors, whereby the presence of many small firms may coexist with the presence of quite a few very large firms. Yet differences in size tend to persist over time notwithstanding the competition process. In other words, empirical evidence proves there is no tendency towards an optimal size.[7] Effectively, if we consider the possibility of informational asymmetries, the potential for learning processes within the firm leads to the logical impossibility of determining the firm's optimal size.[8] With asymmetric information and heterogeneous knowledge, different firms do not bear the same production costs nor do they exhibit the same learning ability. The increase in the whole size of the firm depends on the distinctive features which, in each individual firm, characterize the interaction among the three aspects of the firm's organizational coordination (namely, development of capabilities, arrangement of transactions and design of the scale and scope of processes).

As far as the relationship between the development of capabilities and the growth of the dimension of scale is concerned, applied studies demonstrate that success in innovative activity is a fundamental element that can account for the expansion of fast-growing firms. Not all firms that introduce innovation experience growth but almost all high-growth firms are innovative firms. Coad and Rao (2007) and Hölzl and Friesenbichler (2007) provide ample evidence that learning processes – linked with investments in innovative activity and in product diversification – are of great importance for high-growth firms.[9] Furthermore, Michie and Sheehan (2005, pp. 448ff.) show that the pursuit of quality and a strategy oriented towards innovation is positively correlated with a strategy of investment in progressive human relation practices that lead to higher levels of commitment and motivation among the members of the firm.

Elsewhere I have attempted to indicate the main conditions under which interaction between the three aspects of organizational coordination (capabilities, transaction and scale-scope) comes crucially into play (Morroni 2006a, 2007). For the sake of brevity, here it suffices to say that the interaction among these three aspects is intensely influential in determining the organizational boundaries whenever cognitive competence is limited, radical uncertainty is present,[10] some inputs and processes are indivisible and complementary, and some relevant knowledge is tacit, non-transmittable and characterized by set-up processes with high fixed costs. Under the above conditions, which are becoming increasingly important with the spread of the knowledge-based economy, the growth of the firm can be regarded as a consequence of managerial ability to set a strategy that exploits the mutually reinforcing advantages provided by the organizational coordination of capabilities, transactions and scale of processes, while limiting counteracting forces deriving from errors of strategy that are due to cognitive inertia and myopia, unclear allocation of rights and responsibilities, errors in identifying aims, imprecision in performance measuring, difficulty in focusing incentives, influence activities and problems of internal communication.

Basic conditions and decision-making mechanisms may bear consequences which shape and constrain future decisions of different business organizations. The growth of the firm is the result of a path-dependent process. Initial insignificant circumstances may turn out to be amplified: small causal events in history can thus become important.[11] Levinthal (1995, p. 26) has shown that even if all organizations face the same environment, they may be led, as a result of these different starting points, to adopt distinct organizational forms. Moreover, at each step, new events and the actions of agents, which may introduce some genuine novelty, could change the direction of path-dependent processes.[12]

With regard to market conditions, heterogeneity in customer preferences – involving such aspects as qualities and sales assistance – may favour the presence of diverse types of firms within narrowly defined industries.[13] The product of a large mass-production firm is very different, and meets different needs, from the analogous product supplied by a craftsman or by large-scale industrial flexible production. In a given sector of activity the coexistence of several firms of contrasting sizes is not a necessary consequence of the absence of significant economies of scale. It may instead arise from the specific benefits inherent in the small scale of production, which allows a rather different relationship between manufacturers and customers in terms of contractual advantages, flexibility and learning opportunities. Thus in spite of the significant economies of scale that characterize mass production, so highly prized is individual crafting that in many activities handicrafts have never been completely supplanted by cheaper industrial production, having instead survived alongside it. Analogously, just as traditional artisan production was not ousted by the rise of mass production in the twentieth century, it seems likely that mass production itself will not be doomed as a result of flexible industrial production (on a large or small scale): rather, the different forms meet quite different needs.

Nevertheless, there is no unequivocal relationship between the pursuit of greater flexibility and the size of production units or firms. In some cases new technology allows a high degree of flexibility in large-scale production, while in other cases it encourages the economic potential of small firms or production units. This results in the presence of a variety of technical and organizational structures.

The instability of demand, the saturation of numerous markets and rising competitive pressures call for diversification. Diversification usually takes place in areas in which the firm's capabilities or resources acquired in the past imply a competitive advantage in carrying out these new activities. Firms usually expand their scope following the development of capabilities in similar activities that need analogous abilities or complementary components or equipment.[14]

The process of growth of the firm takes time because firms have to develop the necessary capabilities both as a means to solve 'problems of scaling up the processes of production' (Chandler 1992, p. 84) and to create a demand for their commodities. For each given scale dimension achieved and technique that can be chosen by the production unit, there are different stages of the development of abilities that facilitate the use of specific machines and equipment. Moreover growth requires expansion of the management team, development of managerial capabilities and effort on the part of existing managers to train new managers. This entails adjustment costs. The pace at which the firm can develop its managerial capabilities sets a limit to its rate of growth (Penrose [1959] 1997, pp. 46–9; Lockett *et al*. 2007, pp. 5–6).

The innovative success of firms is generally rooted in product diversification.[15] The growth of the firm is linked to the expansion of its market share within a given market or creation of a new demand, thereby enlarging the market extension. Often the opportunity to exploit potential economies of scale is boosted by the success of a specific product, which is linked to the capacity to create a competitive advantage by exploiting technological opportunities in complementary commodities, matching potential demand and changes in consumer tastes and habits.[16] When information asymmetries are present, the development of an integrated set of dynamic capabilities through learning becomes an important basis for competitive advantage and therefore 'constitutes the foundation for continuing growth' (Chandler 2003, Chapter 1, pp. 7, 15). As argued by Cohendet and Llerena (Chapter 6), the formation of new capabilities is made possible by developing or tracking down new abilities and skills which are generated by the ability to utilize outside knowledge (absorptive capacity) and by intensive outside-inside interaction. Product differentiation is sustained by 'knowing communities' within and across firms that create opportunities for diversity and allow experimentation in product configurations.[17]

The achievement of technological progress produces, but at the same time requires, a high degree of variety and heterogeneous abilities among individuals. In economic systems variety springs from the existence of different abilities among individuals and from the fact that individuals are placed in different contexts. This implies potentially different patterns of connections between available bits of information, that is, individuals and organizations can interpret given information in a variety of ways. As Loasby puts it: 'incompleteness and dispersion of knowledge are a constant source of opportunities for creating new knowledge' (1999, p. 149). The ability to learn and innovate varies from one firm to another. The emergence and maintenance of diversity among organizations through innovative activity is favoured by the division of knowledge and is linked to accumulation of different individual abilities and the development of specific capabilities according to specific learning paths. Innovative activity broadens variety. Innovations are produced because firms deliberately seek to differentiate themselves from rivals and adapt to their external environment. Hence variety derives from the purposeful ability to introduce a genuine new idea, and purposefulness itself then plays a crucial role in the selection processes that take place in a social context.[18] Even more importantly, diversity constitutes a general condition for both the growth of knowledge and profit.[19] To sum up, there is thus a two-way relationship between innovative activity and heterogeneous abilities: innovative activity may create asymmetric information and heterogeneous abilities, while heterogeneous abilities explain why individuals may have a different propensity or ability to innovate.

The entrepreneurial firm builds a resource base to pursue opportunities. This Schumpeterian creative response generates innovation and diversity in organizational forms and products.[20] Accordingly, and in the wake of rapid technological change and global competition, firms tend to implement a very wide range of possible governance structures and organizational designs, leading to evolutionary outcomes whose specific traits may take very dissimilar forms in diverse types of firms. Furthermore, the 'entrepreneurial orientation' and the quality of managerial resources vary across firms and over time,[21] and the inevitably informal nature of the managing of relational agreements and the subjective and discretionary choices by management greatly affect the firm's revealed performance. This subjective element of managerial choice – which is influenced by the various basic conditions and the specific manner in which the different stakeholders' interests are weighed in decisions – moulds the specificity of each firm and yields a large variety of outcomes.

1.2   OUTLINE OF THE BOOK

The book is divided into two parts. The first addresses theoretical issues on corporate governance, organizational design and cooperative forms among firms, while the second part is dedicated to empirical research on outsourcing forms that are playing an increasing role as a consequence of globalization.

In Chapter 2 Mirella Damiani investigates the effects of diverse governance systems on corporate performance and on the ability to innovate. This chapter shows that various corporate governance systems prevail according to the specificities of the institutional and social environment leading to different forms of capitalism. In addressing the issue of stockholder versus stakeholder-oriented governance systems, Damiani stresses the increasing importance of human capital investments, analysing the complex interaction between labour relations and corporate governance mechanisms. The apparently good functioning of the market for corporate control may destroy long-term relationships and intangible assets, with negative side effects on the *ex ante* incentives of the potential stakeholders to invest in a specific relation. On the other hand, as Damiani writes in her enlightening chapter, the stakeholder perspective involves problems of incentive systems which may hide, instead of mitigating, managerial misconduct and moral hazard problems. This calls for an attempt to build up institutional complementarities capable of supporting the cooperative governance coalitions, while discouraging collusive alliances.

In the third and closely connected chapter Jackie Krafft and Jacques-Laurent Ravix analyse the governance of the knowledge-intensive firm in an industry life cycle approach, highlighting the crucial role of human assets in the growth of knowledge-intensive firms. They show that a mode of governance based on control of the manager's action in the interests of shareholders may not be the optimal solution, since this mode of governance favours short-term choices that may be detrimental to the development of innovation. Rather, within knowledge-intensive firms cooperation and assistance should be the key reference. Krafft and Ravix elaborate a novel interesting perspective on the governance of innovative corporations by defining the notion of 'corporate entrepreneurship' within which managers and investors are collectively involved in the coherence and development of innovative firms.

In Chapter 4 Anna Grandori and Santi Furnari observe that in dynamic and knowledge-intensive conditions firms are increasingly employing a mixture of organizational elements that are different in kind. They define four classes of organizational elements, distinguishing between market-like, bureaucratic, communitarian and democratic elements. The diversity of possible combinations among those elements is what accounts for the observed 'structural heterogeneity' among large sets of organization forms. Using a chemistry analogy, the chapter outlines a micro-analytic method for analysing organization forms as compounds of elements. The authors define some general 'laws of combinations' among such elements and investigate the effects of these combinations on performance functions under multiple contingencies, developing some formal examples of Boolean algebra applications. It is shown that more that one configuration may be effective under any given circumstance (equifinality). Grandori and Furnari's innovative methodology allows a more precise analysis of the variety of organizational solutions and is supported with references to several applied studies carried out by the two authors themselves, as well as by other scholars' research.

In Chapter 5 Claude Ménard offers a lucid and accurate account of the emergence of the concept of 'hybrid organizations' within transaction costs economics. Hybrid organizations are neither markets nor hierarchies: they are a combination of autonomy and mutual dependence among partners. As persuasively claimed by Ménard, hybrids depend upon the same attributes that explain the other organizational arrangements, that is, the degree of specificity of investments made in the context of the relationship and the uncertainty associated with contractual hazards. Ménard identifies three major dimensions of hybrids: the existence of specific contract laws; the presence of non-contractual modes of adaptation; and the complex nature and role of incentives in a structure in which autonomous holders of property rights develop interdependent activities. Examining systematically the representation of 'hybrids' developed by Oliver Williamson over 30 years, Ménard shows that transaction costs economics provides powerful tools for the understanding of 'hybrid organizations'.

The complex interaction between networks of firms and knowledge communities in a knowledge-intense context is the topic of the last chapter the first part of the book (Chapter 6). In this most interesting contribution Patrick Cohendet and Patrick Llerena explore the role of 'knowledge communities' as informal structures that create specialized knowledge within and across firms. Cohendet and Llerana maintain that the analysis of knowledge communities requires a theory of the firm able to consider simultaneously a transaction perspective, related to division of activities, and a capabilities-based perspective related to division of knowledge. The authors stress the difference between mass production and the information-intense production regime of growth. Mass production is characterized by standardized commodities produced by large firms in a relatively stable environment. Since variety in such a context is limited, specialization remains in the private domain of firms, whereas with the new knowledge-based regime of growth the challenge is to deal with increasing variety while maintaining economic efficiency under radical uncertainty. A wide range of products requires the differentiation of skills that are sometimes difficult to build up within the firm. Diversity among firms in their mix of specialized technological knowledge enables them to develop a full range of differentiated products. This new regime calls for cooperation within networks of firms, as cooperation fosters the development of skills in a mutually beneficial way, with each party specializing and agreeing to share learning.

The second part of the book adds significant empirical evidence on the various outsourcing and delocalization activities that, in recent years, have characterized the search for increased competitiveness in many industrial and service sectors.

In Chapter 7 Andreas Reinstaller and Paul Windrum look at the relationship between new internet-based information computer technologies, organizational innovation and outsourcing. They first undertake a useful review of recent empirical studies on the rapid growth in business service outsourcing over the last decade. Then Reinstaller and Windrum develop an original model of organizational innovation in which managers search for an organizational architecture that more effectively integrates the administrative routines of the firm. As part of the innovation process, managers can choose to carry out an administrative activity in-house or to outsource the given activity. A key factor influencing this decision is the relative information costs of organizing routines internally and the information costs associated with setting up and maintaining interfaces with external suppliers. Simulations conducted on this model enable the authors to consider the short- and long-run impact of outsourcing on administration overheads, and on long-term productivity growth. Outsourcing cuts labour costs but simultaneously reduces the scope for internal innovative activity and, hence, may result in being detrimental to long-run productivity gains. If so, there is the danger that managers may become locked into a low productivity growth trajectory. These findings accord well with the empirical data, and provide a salutary warning for managers and policy makers about the potential long-term implications of outsourcing.

In Chapter 8 Massimiliano Mazzanti, Sandro Montresor and Paolo Pini analyse theoretical correlations between outsourcing decisions and outsourcing variables, on the basis of a representative cross-sectional sample of firms of a local production system in Reggio Emilia (Italy). In this chapter the outsourcing firm is considered as a four-fold unit of analysis:

that is, as an organizational, production, industrial and innovation unit. The authors point out that outsourcing firms of the sample tend to avoid the danger – highlighted by Reinstaller and Windrum in the previous chapter – of being locked into a low productivity growth trajectory because of a myopic pursuit of a mere reduction of costs in the short run. Indeed, in the local production system the general profile of the outsourcing firms appears to be strategic rather than oriented to a short-run perspective, in the sense that tapping into the provider's resources and competences to eventually promote technological innovation seems more relevant than searching for lower costs by contracting out.[22]

The investigation carried out by Rafael Pardo and Ruth Rama in Chapter 9 examines vertical linkages between firms using a statistically representative sample of medium-sized and large companies in the Spanish automobile and electronics industries. Pardo and Rama explore whether the accumulated technological competence of a company is related to outsourcing networks. They conclude that there is ample evidence showing the coexistence of two different situations. For companies outsourcing some of their production, the propensity to network with other firms is positively linked to the technical capital possessed by the firm. In this case social capital and technical capital complement each other. For subcontractors, on the other hand, outsourcing relationships are negatively associated with technical capital possessed by the firm. In this second case social capital seems to be a substitute for the scarce technical capital available to the company. Consistently with the other applied analyses contained in this second part of the book, the variables most closely associated with networking are those indicating development of the internal capabilities of the company.

The last chapter by Carlo Gianelle and Giuseppe Tattara assesses the impact of the delocalization decision on a firm's value added, gross earnings and local employment in the footwear and clothing industries. This chapter presents important evidence based on a survey conducted on a group of final producers located in the north-east of Italy. Gianelle and Tattara consider direct investment, subcontracting and partnerships that materialize as product manufacturing abroad. In the 1980s local footwear and clothing firms reacted to the increased competition in the international markets by outsourcing to domestic subcontractors, while in the 1990s they transferred much of the previous outsourcing abroad, to low labour cost countries, mainly in Eastern Europe and East Asia. The investigation demonstrates that this strategy has been accompanied by a significant increase both in value added per capita and gross profit, giving new competitiveness to this traditional sector of activity.

To sum up, the chapters which are collected in this volume provide a broad range of illustrations of the multifarious nature of the firm. But notwithstanding the great variety of organizational solutions, the contributions stress the crucial and increasing role of a reorganization of production that can allow transmission, development and maintenance of productive knowledge in order to sustain a long-run competitive advantage.

NOTES

1. The theme of the heterogeneity of organizational forms is fascinating and one cannot but agree with Brian Loasby who argued that 'a theory which helps to explain why' firms do not behave in the same way in similar circumstances 'is perhaps to be preferred to one which asserts that they should' (1967, p. 167, quoted in Earl 2002, p. 1).
2. For discussion and bibliographical references on this point, see Dosi (2005, p. 20). On the increasing heterogeneity of Japanese firms since the beginning of the 1990s, see Lechevalier (2007, pp. 113ff.).
3. The significant heterogeneity of growth rates between firms, within the same sector, is highlighted in Bottazzi *et al.* (2007); Dosi (2005); Coad and Rao (2007); Baldwin and Gellatly (2006, pp. 7ff.); Hölzl and Friesenbichler (2007). In these applied studies the heavy-tailed nature of the growth rate distribution emerges clearly.
4. This interpretation is based on an analytical framework proposed in Morroni (2006a).
5. Teece *et al.* ([1997] 1998, p. 204); Loasby (1998, p. 176).
6. On this, see McIvor (2005, p. 8). The term outsourcing refers to the sourcing of intermediate goods and services, previously produced internally, from external suppliers.
7. On the wide variability in firm sizes, see Bottazzi *et al.* (2007); Bottazzi and Secchi (2006); Dosi (2005, pp. 3–4ff.). As argued by Dosi (2005), faced with the evidence that market selection does not seem to lead to an optimal size, the standard production theory centred around U-shaped cost curves loses much of its plausibility.
8. Foss (2002, p. 153). On this logical impossibility, see also Georgescu-Roegen ([1964] 1976, p. 296); Morroni (1992, pp. 141–2, 2006a, Chapter 6); Hodgson (1993, p. 856); Bianchi (1995, p. 187); Penrose ([1959] 1997, p. xii); Marris (2002, pp. 65, 71–2, 75).
9. Moreover, Coad and Rao (2007, p. 28) demonstrate that standard regression analysis on the growth of the mean firm could be misleading because it can be observed that a firm, on average, experiences only modest growth and the reasons for its growth may or may not be related to innovativeness. However, if one focuses on high-growth firms, strong evidence emerges on 'the importance of innovativeness over the entire conditional growth rate distribution'. Cf. Baldwin and Gellatly (2006, p. 25).
10. Lechevalier (2007, p. 128) focuses on the role of uncertainty in heterogeneity across firms. On the relationship between uncertainty and innovative activity, see Morroni (2006b).
11. Hodgson (1998, pp. 36, 47); Dosi and Metcalfe (1991, p. 133).
12. On this, see Antonelli (2004, p. 250); Loasby (2004, p. 271).
13. On the role of heterogeneity of demand and its effect on the industrial structure, see Bonaccorsi and Giuri (2003, pp. 59, 75ff.).
14. Richardson ([1972] 1996, pp. 139–40). Chandler (1992, pp. 83, 96) noticed that unrelated diversification tended quite often to fail 'in maintaining long term financial performance' because companies that move beyond the barriers created by their 'learned capabilities' could not capture 'economies of scale and scope to obtain lower unit costs'.
15. Fast growing firms are called gazelles by Hölzl and Friesenbichler (2007). These authors provide interesting empirical evidence of the fact that gazelles are more innovative than other firms.
16. See Rosenberg ([1969] 1976, pp. 111–2); Bianchi (1998, pp. 9–11).
17. Rosenberg (2002, p. 36) has called attention to the fact that 'in exploring unknown territory' a 'multiple source of decision making' enhances creative activities and the diversity of options necessary to provide highly differentiated products.

18. As pointed out in Hodgson and Knudsen (2004, pp. 283–4), artificial selection, particularly important in social contexts where purposefulness is important and acquired characters may be inherited, is consistent with Darwinian principles and can be regarded as a special case of natural selection. On the generation of novelty in the economic process, see Dopfer (1993, pp. 130ff).
19. Loasby (2002, p. 1234); Saviotti (1996, pp. 42, 111).
20. Garnsey (2007) discusses the role of entrepreneurial firms in the generation of diversity.
21. Lockett *et al.* (2007, pp. 25–6). On the heterogeneity of management practices and productivity, see Bloom and Van Reenen (2007). On firm-specific entrepreneurial knowledge and judgement, see Knight (1921, pp. 311–2); Penrose ([1959] 1997, p. 63); Ricketts (2002, pp. 232ff.).
22. Reinstaller and Windrum's results are consistent with those provided by Michie and Sheehan (2005, pp. 445ff., 461) who demonstrate – on the basis of original data collected from a large sample of publicly quoted UK manufacturing and service sector firms with more than 50 employees – that for companies pursuing quality enhancement or innovation, it is internal or functional flexibility, within an investment in human resource practices, that is linked with such strategies, rather than external or numerical flexibility within a cost-based strategy.

REFERENCES

Antonelli, C. (2004), 'The system dynamics of localized technological change: ingredients, governance and processes', draft, Dipartimento di Economia, Università di Torino, Italy.

Baldwin, J.R. and G. Gellatly (2006), 'Innovation capabilities: the knowledge capital behind the survival and growth of firms', research paper, Statistics Canada, Micro-economic Analysis Division, Ottawa.

Bianchi, M. (1995), 'Markets and firms: transaction costs versus strategic innovation', *Journal of Economic Behaviour and Organization*, **28** (2), 183–202.

Bianchi, M. (1998), 'Introduction', in M. Bianchi (ed.), *The Active Consumer. Novelty and Surprise in Consumer Choice*, London: Routledge, pp. 1–18.

Bloom, N. and J. Van Reenen (2007), 'Measuring and explaining management practices across firms and countries', *Quarterly Journal of Economics*, **122** (4), 1351–408.

Bonaccorsi, A. and P. Giuri (2003), 'Increasing returns and network structure in the evolutionary dynamics of industries', in P.P. Saviotti (ed.), *Applied Evolutionary Economics: New Empirical Methods and Simulation Techniques*, Cheltenham, UK and Northamptom, MA, USA: Edward Elgar, pp. 50–93.

Bottazzi, G., E. Cefis, G. Dosi and A. Secchi (2007), 'Invariances and diversities in the patterns of industrial evolution: some evidence from Italian manufacturing industries', *Small Business Economics*, **29** (136), 137–59.

Bottazzi, G. and A. Secchi (2006), 'Explaining the distribution of firm growth rates', *RAND Journal of Economics*, **37** (2), 235–56.

Chandler, A.D. (1992), 'Organizational capabilities and the economic history of the industrial enterprise', *Journal of Economic Perspectives*, **6** (3), 79–100.

Chandler, A. (2003), *Inventing the Electronic Century: The Epic Story of the Consumer Electronics and Computer Science Industries*, New York: The Free Press.

Coad, A. and R. Rao (2007), 'Innovation and firm growth in high-tech sectors: a quantile regression approach', LEM working paper series, Sant'Anna School of Advanced Studies, Pisa, Italy, June.

Dopfer, K. (1993), 'The generation of novelty in the economic process: an evolutionary concept', in J.C. Dragan, E.K. Seifert and M.C. Demetrescu (eds), *Entropy and Bioeconomics*, Rome: Nagard, pp. 130–53.

Dosi, G. (2005), 'Statistical regularities in the evolution of industries. A guide through some evidence and challenges for the theory', LEM working paper series, Sant'Anna School of Advanced Studies, Pisa, Italy, June.

Dosi, G. and J.S. Metcalfe (1991), 'On some notions of irreversibility in economics', in P.P. Saviotti and J.S. Metcalfe (eds), *Evolutionary Theories of Economic and Technological Change: Present State and Future Prospects*, London: Harwood Academic Publisher, pp. 133–59.

Earl, P.E. (2002), *Information, Opportunism and Economic Coordination*, Cheltenham, UK and Northamptom, MA, USA: Edward Elgar.

Foss, N.J. (2002), 'Edith Penrose: economics and strategic management', in C. Pitelis (ed.), *The Growth of the Firm. The Legacy of Edith Penrose*, Oxford: Oxford University Press, pp. 147–64.

Garnsey, E. (2007), 'The generation of diversity and the rationale for the entrepreneurial firm', draft, Cambridge: University of Cambridge.

Georgescu-Roegen, N. (1964), 'Measure, quality and optimum scale', in C.R. Rao (ed.), *Essays on Econometrics and Planning Presented to Professor P.C. Mahalanobis on His 70th Birthday*, Oxford: Pergamon Press, pp. 231–56; repr. in N. Georgescu-Roegen (1976), *Energy and Economic Myths*, New York: Pergamon Press, pp. 271–96.

Hodgson, G.M. (1993), 'Transaction costs and the evolution of the firm', in C. Pitelis (ed.), *Transaction Costs, Markets and Hierarchies*, Oxford: Blackwell, pp. 77–100.

Hodgson, G.M. (1998), 'Evolutionary and competence-based theories of firm', *Journal of Economic Studies*, **25** (1), 25–56.

Hodgson, G.M. and T. Knudsen (2004), 'The firm as an interactor: firms as vehicles for habits and routines', *Journal of Evolutionary Economics*, **14** (3), 281–307.

Hölzl, W. and K. Friesenbichler (2007), 'Are gazelles more innovative than other firms?', Europa Innova, Innovation Watch, preliminary draft, Vienna.

Knight, F.H. (1921), *Risk, Uncertainty and Profit*, Boston: Houghton.

Lechevalier, S. (2007), 'The diversity of capitalism and heterogeneity of firms – a case study of Japan during the lost decade', *Evolutionary and Institutional Economics Review*, **4** (1), 113–42.

Levinthal, D.A. (1995), 'Strategic management and the exploration of diversity', in C.A. Montgomery (ed.), *Resource-Based and Evolutionary Theories of the Firm: Towards a Synthesis*, Boston: Kluwer, pp. 19–42.

Loasby, B. (1967), 'Management economics and the theory of the firm', *Journal of Industrial Economics*, **15**, 165–76; repr. in P.E. Earl (ed.) (1988), *Behavioural Economics*, 2 vols, Aldershot, UK and Brookfield, USA: Edward Elgar, vol. I, pp. 461–72.

Loasby, B.J. (1998), 'The concept of capabilities', in N.J. Foss and B.J. Loasby (eds), *Economic Organization, Capabilities and Co-ordination: Essays in Honour of G.B. Richardson*, London: Routledge, pp. 163–82.

Loasby, B.J. (1999), *Knowledge, Institutions and Evolution in Economics*, London: Routledge.

Loasby, B.J. (2002), 'The evolution of knowledge: beyond the biological model', *Research Policy*, **31** (8–9), 1227–39.

Loasby, B. (2004), 'Economics after Simon', in M. Augier and J.G. March (eds),

Models of Man: Essays in Memory of Herbert Simon, Cambridge, MA: MIT Press, pp. 259–78.

Lockett, A., J. Wiklund and P. Davidsson (2007), 'Organic growth and acquisitive growth: re-examining and extending Penrose's growth theory', paper presented at the Academy of Management 2007 Annual Meeting, Philadelphia, USA.

Marris, R. (2002), 'Edith Penrose and economics', in C. Pitelis (ed.), *The Growth of the Firm. The Legacy of Edith Penrose*, Oxford: Oxford University Press, pp. 61–80.

McIvor, R. (2005), *The Outsourcing Process. Strategies for Evaluation and Management*, Cambridge: Cambridge University Press.

Michie, J. and M. Sheehan (2005), 'Business strategy, human resources, labour market flexibility and competitive advantage', *International Journal of Human Resource Management*, **16** (3), 445–64.

Morroni, M. (1992), *Production Process and Technical Change*, Cambridge: Cambridge University Press.

Morroni, M. (2006a), *Knowledge, Scale and Transactions in the Theory of the Firm*, Cambridge: Cambridge University Press.

Morroni, M. (2006b), 'Innovative activity, substantive uncertainty and the theory of the firm', *Economia e Politica Industriale*, **23** (3), 47–75.

Morroni, M. (2007), 'Complementarities among capability, transaction and scale-scope considerations in determining organizational boundaries', *Technology Analysis & Strategic Management*, **19** (1), 31–44.

Penrose, E. (1959), *The Theory of the Growth of the Firm*, 3rd edn, Oxford: Blackwell, with a Foreword by the author 1995, Oxford: Oxford University Press, repr. in 1997.

Richardson, G.B. (1972), 'The organization of industry', *The Economic Journal*, **82** (327), 883–96, repr. in L. Putterman and R.S. Kroszner (eds) (1996), *The Economic Nature of the Firm. A Reader*, 2nd edn, Cambridge: Cambridge University Press, pp. 136–45.

Ricketts, M. (2002), *The Economics of Business Enterprise. An Introduction to Economic Organization and the Theory of the Firm*, 3rd edn, Cheltenham, UK and Northampton, MA, USA: Edward Elgar.

Rosenberg, N. (1969), 'The direction of technological change: inducement mechanisms and focusing devices', *Economic Development and Cultural Change*, repr. in N. Rosenberg (1976), *Perspectives on Technologies*, Cambridge: Cambridge University Press, pp. 108–25.

Rosenberg, N. (2002), 'America's university/industry interfaces', draft, Department of Economics, Stanford, California.

Saviotti, P.P. (1996), *Technological Evolution, Variety and the Economy*, Cheltenham, UK and Brookfield, USA: Edward Elgar.

Teece, D.J., G. Pisano and A. Shuen (1997), 'Dynamic capabilities and strategic management', *Strategic Management Journal*, **18** (7), 509–33, repr. in D.J. Teece (1998), Strategy, *Technology and Public Policy: The Selected Papers of David J. Teece*, vol. 2, Cheltenham, UK and Lyme, USA: Edward Elgar, pp. 197–221.

PART I

THEORETICAL ASPECTS

2. The stakeholder corporate governance view revisited[1]

Mirella Damiani

2.1 INTRODUCTION

New theories of the firm suggest 'an alternative view in which the relationships among the people who participate in the production activity of firms are at the heart of the definition of the firm itself' (Blair 1995). Along similar lines, a broader definition of the firm as a nexus of specific physical and human capital investments has been recently proposed by Rajan and Zingales (1998, 2001). In this broader view the ownership of physical assets is not the only source of authority and an alternative mechanism to allocate power and to motivate specific human capital investments may be identified: access, that is, 'the ability to use, or work with, a critical resource' (Rajan and Zingales (1998, p. 388). But this novel view has not yet fully 'crystallized' in terms of an alternative definition of corporate governance. Even if the relevance of human capital is commonly accepted, only limited research systematically explores the related implications in terms of corporate governance institutions.[2]

This chapter is an attempt to examine the interplay of labour relations and corporate governance mechanisms prevailing in some varieties of capitalism around the world. This will be done by firstly reconsidering the role of the market for corporate control and, secondly, labour incentives, two main pillars of corporate governance. Both the perspectives will lead to examine the principal agent problem in an integrated framework where the position of labour as a stakeholder plays an increasing crucial role and where alliances and conflicts between owners of physical and human capital assets come to the forefront.

The ownership of unique, physical assets has long qualified the boundaries and the size of the firm itself. This definition is well founded on the property rights literature of Grossman and Hart (1986) and Hart and Moore (1990) where it is ownership of 'inanimate' resources that confers the residual rights of control over them.[3] In terms of corporate governance a well-known definition has been accepted: 'Corporate governance deals with the ways in which suppliers of finance to corporations assure themselves of getting a return on their investment' (Shleifer and Vishny 1997, p. 737).[4]

For instance, let us start from the preliminary point, the Berle and Means' problem of separation between ownership and control, and consider the story of one of the most successful firms of the new economy, Intel.

> Intel, the microprocessor manufacturer, was started . . . when Robert Noyce, the General Manager of Fairchild Semiconductor, and Gordon Moore, its head of R&D, walked out of Fairchild and set up their own firm Integrated Electronics. . . . Indeed, a scientist in Moore's department had discovered the silicon-gate technique to produce semiconductor memory devices. . . . Clearly, of all Fairchild's employees, Noyce and Moore had the greatest *access* to Fairchild's inventions, and at the very least, took a lot of *knowledge* and, equally important, *employees* with them to the start-up. Thus, Intel . . . is now one of the most profitable firms, while Fairchild Semiconductor is virtually a footnote in business history. (Rajan and Zingales 2001, p. 806)

This cautionary tale exemplifies many other situations where human capital plays a central role. Here, the regulation of access to critical enterprise resources (the 'silicon-gate' technique in our case) can induce specialized human capital investments and gives 'power' (Rajan and Zingales 1998). More generally, an idea, a customer relationship, a superior management technique or the ability to operate closely with an employee, confer the exercise of non-contractible rights rather than simple ownership. And this novelty prompts an amendment to the Berle and Means' problem in terms of 'separation between ownership, access and control'.

Many other approaches in the new theory of the firm have signalled the relevance of labour and the complex nature of labour relationships.[5] For instance, as suggested by Holmstrom and Milgrom (1994), a 'multitask principal–agent' model better represents the multidimensional tasks of employees. Furthermore, in this context, where institutional arrangements aimed at eliciting effort involve a high degree of complexities, the firm is better qualified as an 'incentive system' (Holmstrom and Milgrom 1994).

As suggested by the Intel story, incentive in a multi-task context design now faces a radically new problem: it must promote specialization of human capital to the critical resources, but it also has to avert competition from employees who have seized the specialization opportunity and have no difficulty in competing with the entrepreneur. After all, in the Intel case it is the 'agent' (Gordon Moore) who fires his own 'principal' (the Fairchild Semiconductor company) and sets up his own firm.

Some scientific evidence, more than a single anecdotal story, seems to confirm the relevance of these changes. First of all, one interesting point to emerge is the essence of internal organizations as a mechanism to offer employees differential access to critical resources; consequently, a 'flattening firm' can be observed. As found by Rajan and Wulf (2003), greater authority has been given to divisional managers, while 'the changing nature of corporate hierarchies implies that the number of layers separating managers from the CEO is decreasing, and *authority* is being pushed down the organization'[6] (*Ibid.*, p. 35).

Furthermore, the 'delayering' of corporate hierarchies (in our example a closer relationship between the general Manager of Fairchild Semiconductor, and the head of R&D Gordon Moore) is accompanied by new compensation rules. A growing and rich empirical literature has shown that American firms quite often offer 'incentives that do not have incentive effects' (Oyer 2004), give 'stock options to undiversified executives' (Hall and Murphy 2002) and in some cases even 'to all employees' (Oyer and Schaefer 2005). A potential explanation is that especially firms in the new economy have ranked employee retention as the most important objective of their compensation plans (Ittner *et al.* 2003), a plausible strategy to prevent events such as the Fairchild's misfortune.

Others, such as the 'entrenchment model' of Edlin and Stiglitz (1995), have suggested that access may cause new forms of abuse of power. In the same vein, it has been shown that managerial rewards may appear not as a solution, but as a manifestation of agency problems (Bebchuk and Fried 2003), and the pervasive nature of rent seeking behaviour has been stressed. Finally, some other studies point to the role of internal incentive structures founded on notions, rarely admitted in traditional economic theories, such as fairness, trust and equity (Baker *et al.* 1988).

It must be added that even in the traditional approaches two different options in terms of corporate governance can be adopted: the corporation belongs to stockholders and must be run in their interest; the corporation must be managed in the interest of stakeholders and, as the interests are various and contradictory, a compromise should be found. However, in the new firm a clear distinction between the shareholders' and stakeholders' views is less evident, at least regarding the position of those particular stakeholders represented by employees.

One of the problematic aspects of the stakeholders' versus shareholders' view is whether in the new enterprise coalitions between managers and employees – the latter now being more powerful actors in terms of non-contractible right – reflect collusive strategies (Hellwig 2000; Pagano and Volpin 2005), or permit the transmission of valuable information inside the firm (Freeman and Lazear 1994).

While these themes assume increasing contemporary relevance, it must be acknowledged that, up to now, labour participation and corporate governance have remained separate fields of research, while the changing nature of the modern firm requires that attention be paid to new corporate governance institutions. Indeed the role of organizations cannot remain a working field of research restricted to sociologists in a world where access (more than simple ownership) gives new rationales to an (inherent) incompleteness of contracts.

2.2 TAKEOVERS AND THE MANAGEMENT-LABOUR RELATIONSHIP: COOPERATION OR COLLUSION?

As well known, the various corporate institutional systems prevailing in different countries may be seen as different solutions to the problem of the separation of ownership and control. Some recent contributions, such as Gugler (2001) and Becht *et al.* (2003), offer a detailed documentation of these 'varieties' of capitalism. The Anglo-Saxon economies, characterized by dispersed ownership, are systems where individual investors have little incentive for active governance. However, in these economies where the single owner has insufficient power or incentive to detect and contrast inefficient management, alternative forces may play a disciplinary role. Takeover threats, managerial incentives and effective boards may mitigate the moral hazard problems affecting corporations (Shleifer and Vishny 1997).

But are these mechanisms a solution to the new problem of the separation of ownership, access and control? And how do these mechanisms work in aligning the interests of stakeholders and those of their agents?

Many studies have stressed, but only in a shareholders' perspective, the crucial relevance of the external threats from raiders as a means to induce greater loyalty from managers and favour an alignment of interests with their 'principals', especially when dispersed ownership impedes a direct monitoring over the 'agents'. In the Anglo-Saxon type of system, where it is not individual owners but market mechanisms that ensure efficient managerial conduct, and where a larger fraction of firms are widely held and market capitalization is higher, the incidence of hostile bids is more significant. This indicates that the dominating force which shapes the governance mechanisms is not the individual controlling shareholder, but the market. For instance, as shown in Rossi and Volpin (2004), for the years 1990–2002, hostile bids, as a percentage of total deals, were less than 1 per cent in Germany, and 6.34 per cent and 4.39 per cent in the USA and UK, respectively.

Misconduct by managers who waste resources and pursue unprofitable projects is reflected in declining share prices, which favours hostile takeovers. Managers of a publicly listed firm, who know that the company may be subject to takeovers and in that case could be fired by the new owners, are encouraged to adopt profit strategies more oriented to maximize shareholders' wealth (Manne 1965). The threat of management replacement thus improves investor protection.

However, the effectiveness of a market-oriented device to reduce managerial discretion may not be ensured, in a shareholders' perspective, for a number of reasons, as reviewed in Damiani (2006).

First of all, in hostile takeovers a free riding problem emerges. In fact, 'if a shareholder thinks that the raid will succeed and that the raider will improve the firm, he will not tender his shares, but will instead retain them, because he anticipates a profit from their price appreciation' (Grossman and Hart 1980, p. 43). Secondly, there is an *ex ante* inefficiency: hostile takeover threats and rent expropriation may result in a sub-optimal level of investments. Fear of hostile bidding may lead to negative outcomes such as management entrenchment and short-term oriented behaviour. Thirdly, the beneficial effects of takeovers, as mechanisms to transfer control from an inefficient to an efficient management, may not be achieved when the primary reason for bidding is not efficiency improvement. In these cases, as suggested by Jensen (1986), takeovers solve free cash flow problems, but not the agency problem.

The relevance of these forces, which has long been evaluated in the intense debate on takeovers, may now be reconsidered in a stakeholder perspective.

Consider the following story (Hernández-López 2003). It refers to two well-known luxury goods firms, LVMH and Gucci, and involves LVMH's bid for Gucci, with Pinault-Printemps-Redoute serving as Gucci's white knight. In 1999 LVMH began its bid for Gucci, as Gucci had reached financial success and its popularity had climbed. Thus a rather different situation from the 'managerial misconduct' motivation suggested by Manne.

At first, LVMH explained its investments were 'passive,' 'strategic,' and did not represent a bid for Gucci . . . by January 26, 1999, LVMH reported to the SEC that it had invested $337.5 million to reach 34.4% of shares in Gucci . . . Knowing LVMH's reputation and because LVMH was its main competitor, Gucci interpreted LVMH's investment as a hostile bid . . .

On February 18, with an ESOP, the Gucci board issued 37 million common shares to Gucci employees. The effect of the issuance was to be an additional number of shares in Gucci's capital stock. Additional shares diluted LVMH's voting power. LVMH now only had a 25.6% stake in Gucci. Theoretically with the new shares issued, Gucci could mitigate the LVMH threat . . .

> LVMH responded by suing Gucci . . . The raider claimed that the ESOP was illegal, because the ESOP's only objective was to limit LVMH from obtaining more shares, and the ESOP provided no benefits for the employees. Gucci's legal defense was that the ESOP was enacted because the board feared for the company's 'future well-being, interests and independence of the company, its employees, independent shareholders and other stakeholders.' Issuing shares to the employees guaranteed employees received an interest in the company and control of the company lay with the interest of labor. (Hernández-López 2003, pp. 152–6)

The Gucci story shows that the assumed interest of the employees may be invoked as a deterrent to hostile bids, and that an instrument of labour relations such as ESOP may perform as a hidden new powerful anti-takeover device. As a coincidence, exactly at the time of the battle between the two luxury goods firms, in 2000 Hellwig wrote that managers and stake-holders may become indeed 'natural allies'.

Some years later this intuition led Pagano and Volpin (2005) to formal-ize a general model where anti-takeover alliances between all the agents (individual shareholders, management and workers) satisfy their incentive compatibility constraints. The authors show that the adoption of employee share ownership schemes, as well as the bargaining of generous long-term wage contracts, may reduce the attraction of hostile bids, thus rendering corporate control unassailable.

First of all, it must be noted, as explored in the efficiency wage litera-ture, that incumbent managers may elicit effort with two different strate-gies: generous wage payments or strict monitoring of workers' activities. But these two policies are very different in terms of managerial prefer-ences. The cost of the first strategy is borne by shareholders, whereas the monitoring cost is borne by the manager. Secondly, managers' optimal conduct, aimed at maximizing their private benefits, rather than share-holder value, is conditioned by the raider's choices and employees' reac-tions. Thus, the raider, who usually purchases a 'toehold', may succeed in acquiring the target firm by offering dispersed shareholders a bid-price at least equal to the after takeover price. The increase in the latter will be obtained by cutting wages as much as possible and increasing monitoring activity; therefore the raider may induce a substantial increase in the share price, and gains from possession of a toehold share. But this scenario, where employees' welfare deteriorates, induces workers to ally themselves with their incumbent management. Meanwhile, the owner of the target company tries to align the interests of management with their own inter-ests and thus provides incentives to executives via inside equity. However, if managerial private benefits obtained from wage concessions – and a quiet life – on one hand, and takeover costs, on the other, are sufficiently high, neither internal incentives nor takeovers may solve the moral hazard problem.

To summarize, three main elements are the ingredients of the 'natural alliance' between managers and workers. Firstly, wage bonuses and stable relationships transform employees into shark repellents, as Pagano and Volpin suggest, thus reducing the advantageousness of the bids for the potential raider. Under employment protection rules long-term labour contracts are signed and the raider cannot succeed in renewing these arrangements, and in wage cutting. Secondly, employees become 'white squires', since they assume an immediate interest in acting against hostile acquisitions, for instance, via strikes and a strong opposition to the deal, thus performing the same role of investors who, by purchasing an interest in the target of a hostile bid, may succeed in deterring takeovers. Finally, managers, by simply providing wage premiums and long-term contracts, may forgo the riskier and effort demanding strategies represented by investment, plant acquisitions and plant destructions, to cite just a few among the strategies of the empire-building models of managerial preferences (Baumol 1959; Marris 1964). A weakening of raiders' hostile activity permits high wages for employees and a lesser monitoring effort for their management, 'very much, as in Hicks's (1935) suggestion that the best of all monopoly profit is a quiet life', as pointed out by Bertrand and Mullainathan (2003, p. 1047).

This argument fits well with the Gucci story and can be formalized with an analytical model where entrenchment strategies may reveal credible threats. Furthermore, the same hypothesis can be tested, quite naturally, to explain the experiences recorded in the USA, where during the 1980s almost a quarter of the large US corporations suffered a hostile bid (Mitchell and Mulherin 1996). Moreover, the empirical analysis performed by Bertrand and Mullainathan (1998) for the years 1976–95 using COMPUSTAT and LRD databases shows that increased attention to employees does not improve the efficiency of American firms, especially for firms incorporated in states with anti-takeover laws. In contrast, it is exactly the approval of state-level anti-takeover provisions that permits an increase in average wages up to the figure of 4 per cent for white collars, without impact either on labour productivity or on investments and firm size. In sum, stakeholder protection does not 'pay for itself'. Such a result should call for a better regulation of hostile bids and for company laws more oriented towards preventing the adoption of anti-takeover devices, sometimes hidden under the umbrella of stakeholders' interests.

But now listen to a second story, as told by Shleifer and Summers (1987, p. 35):

> Carl Icahn takes over USZ. He closes down the corporate headquarters and lays off thousands of highly paid senior employees who had previously been promised lifetime employment by the now displaced managers. He also shuts down the factories which dominate several small towns. As a consequence numerous stores, restaurants and bars go bankrupt. The stock of USZ goes up by 25 percent . . . The gains to USZ shareholders are offset by losses incurred by laid off employees and by the firms with immobile capital whose viability depended on the factories remaining open. And other firms find that their workers, seeing what happened at USZ, become less loyal and require higher wages to compensate for a reduction in their perceived securities. They also find it more difficult to induce suppliers to make fixed investments on their behalf.

The above case is representative of the massive acquisitions wave undertaken in the 1980s in the USA. In that period the actions of raiders, such as Icahn, Boone Pickens, Goldsmith, Perelman and Campeau, motivated books like *Barbarians at the Gate* that turned into bestsellers (Tirole 2006, p. 43). In any case, a more serious approach, for instance, that promised by Jensen and Ruback (1983) in their paper 'The market for corporate control: the scientific evidence', reveals a recurrent feature of hostile bids. Takeovers do not create value but have distributive effects that favour target shareholders, without enhancing the acquiring shareholders and with ambiguous effects on social welfare. After all, as suggested by Shleifer and Summers (1987, p. 23), 'it is hard to believe that Carl Icahn simultaneously has a comparative advantage at running a railcar leasing company (ACF), an airline (TWA) and a textile mill (Dan River). It is more plausible that his comparative advantage is tough bargaining and willingness to transfer value away from those who expect to have it'.

The vast literature devoted to evaluating the takeover consequences has shown that in the USA the average premium returns of the target shareholders have been in the range between 15 to 30 per cent (Andrade *et al.* 2001). On the other hand, there have been negative or no significant effects on bidder returns (see Andrade *et al.* 2001; Stulz 1988). But these findings should be reconsidered in a more open perspective, where efficiency and welfare considerations are evaluated in the long term.

The mere calculations of the abnormal cumulative returns of price assets of target and acquiring firms may not capture the 'reputational externalities' associated with hostile takeovers and their serious allocative effects. This is true not only because stakeholder losses are harder to measure than shareholder gains, but also because in an extended view the firm is a sort of nexus of long-term contracts between shareholders and stakeholders. Many of these contracts are implicit and self-enforcing, since they rely on the mutual trust of parties and 'such trustworthiness is a valuable asset of the corporation', as pointed out in Shleifer and Summers (1987, p. 56).

In this context the apparently good functioning of a market for corporate control represents a menace for this valuable asset, since it destroys those nexuses of long-term relationships and intangible assets represented by the firm's reputation (Kreps 1984). In other words, a hostile bid may represent a breach of trust (Shleifer and Summers 1987), which is a more serious damage that does not only have *ex post* distributive effects, but may also reduce the *ex ante* incentives of the potential stakeholders (employees, suppliers, subcontractors) to invest in relation-specific capital.

This negative side effect of takeovers, as suggested in Chemla (2005), should be properly considered by seeing that in the absence of takeovers stakeholders' bargaining power increases their incentive to invest in the firm, even though, on the other hand, it may reduce owners' incentive. Direct evidence concerning the effect of takeovers on stakeholders' relationships is difficult to obtain; however the findings presented in Mayer (1990, p. 312) show that in Japan, where inter-firm and long-term relationships are more prevalent than in the USA and the UK, firms use more trade credit,[7] while in the USA and the UK the market for corporate control is more active.

Additional evidence is provided in Schmidt (2003). The author shows that in a stakeholder society, such as the German economy, corporate governance fosters long-term cooperation and encourages firm-specific investments by lenders, employees and large shareholders. In this context insiders are active monitors of management and this may explain why even if an active market for corporate control is absent, management turnover is not lower than in other comparable countries,[8] while Kaplan (1994) provides evidence that German supervisory boards are effective in removing managers when the firm performs poorly (Table 2.1).

As stated earlier, the majority of empirical studies on takeovers are capable of capturing *ex post* shareholders' gains and losses, but fail in estimating stakeholders' losses. In a recent work Bruner (2004, Chapter 3) has surveyed the vast empirical literature which has animated the value creation and value destruction debate on takeovers. What emerges, from our perspective, is that in none of the 130 studies covering the period 1971–2001 is it possible to obtain estimates of the benefits for stakeholders, for instance, in terms of lower prices or job creation. Many contributions on European countries, usually considered more oriented to a stakeholder perspective, have limited themselves to calculating the abnormally high returns reaped by target shareholders, as against the modest gains obtained by bidder shareholders, but there is no mention of related stakeholders' premiums, as in Martynova and Renneboog (2006).

Some interesting, albeit indirect, insights on stakeholders' returns can, however, be inferred from some contributions, such as Croci (2004), which extends the analysis to the long run. In this case the main findings are that

Table 2.1   Market for corporate control and executive turnover (various years)[a]

Countries	Number of hostile bids	Block transfers (%)[b]	Executive turnover (%)
Germany	4	10	12
France	n.a.	10	11
UK	148	9	9
USA	150	7	n.a.

Notes:
[a] Germany (1989–94), France (1989–91), UK (1989–94), USA (1980–89).
[b] Block transfers (exceeding 10 per cent of total equity).

Source: Schmidt (2003).

raiders do not stay in a company for a period more than, on average, 20 months and many equities are sold within one year from the announcement of the bid. Table 2.2 shows these results more precisely.

One of the conclusions reached by Croci (2004, p. 26) is that in any case 'raiders are not so prone to interfere with the target management and sometimes limit their action to just costless public statements'.

Some reflections, however, are induced by the new theories of the firm. Shleifer and Summers assume that the protection provided by ownership induces valuable specific investments, and therefore stakeholders should have explicit property rights. But, in a world where it is access and not only ownership that is relevant, greater property rights do not automatically assure the incentives of stakeholders to invest; furthermore 'the debate largely ignores conflict between stakeholders. Stakeholders may have stronger abilities to inefficiently dispossess each other, and ownership will give additional power to do so' (Rajan and Zingales 1998, p. 424).

In sum, the issue concerning the possible inefficiencies of takeovers is still open to debate. The available devices for aligning the interests of stakeholders and those of their agents, such as incentive plans, should also be considered.

2.3   INCENTIVES AND LABOUR RELATIONSHIPS: REMEDIES OR FAILURES?

Reliable measures of stakeholders' welfare are difficult to find, and the problem of providing explicit incentives to pursue the interests of a multi-

Table 2.2   Holding period of raiders' purchases: mean, median and holding period distribution in some European countries (1990–2001)

Holding period (years)		Holding period distribution (%)		
Mean	Median	Less than 1 year	Less than 2 years	Less than 3 years
1.71	1.23	43.42	68.42	82.89

Note. The data refer to UK (1990–2001), Germany (1993 2001), France (1993 2001), Italy (1990–2001), Switzerland (1993–2001).

Source: Croci (2004).

plicity of stakeholders seems to fit well, as noticed in Tirole (2001), with the multi-task agency model suggested by Holmstrom and Milgrom (1991). In this model each agent is engaged in many duties and a well-designed incentive system has to motivate the allocation of efforts among these different tasks. Since this balance is difficult, one possible solution is a fixed payment, independent of any measure of performance, thus avoiding the distortions that may induce effort in one task but indifference and sub-optimal strain in some other occupations.

These considerations gain relevance in a stakeholder perspective where 'managerial incentives should be designed so as to align the managers' incentives with the sum of the stakeholders' surpluses rather than just the equityholders' surplus' (Tirole 2001, p. 25). But management may rationalize any action by invoking its impact on the welfare of some stakeholders, even if these actions worsen the welfare of some others. Hence, in a stakeholders' economy a flat compensation system may be preferable, and in this perspective, 'there is some consistency between lenient views in the French, German, and Japanese populations toward the stakeholder society and the low power of the managerial incentive schemes in these countries' (*Ibid.*, p. 26). Indeed, as seen in Table 2.3, in the USA, that is, in the more shareholder-oriented system, the CEO's compensation is less flat than in the other countries.

In any case, even by adopting a flat remuneration system, some critical objections on the feasibility of the stakeholder view remain and the existing literature seems to present two opposite views. As Jensen (2001, p. 9) writes:

Whereas value maximization provides corporate managers with a *single* objective, stakeholder theory directs corporate managers to serve '*many*

Table 2.3   Flat CEO's compensation and stakeholder society: variable
*   remuneration as percentage of total remuneration in some*
*   countries*

	Variable CEO's remuneration component (%)			
Countries	1996	2001	2003	2005
France	29	26	29	41
Germany	12	36	51	52
Italy	24	33	30	35
Japan	8	18	19	22
UK	30	30	34	35
US	47	61	63	62

Source: Towers Perrin (2001–02, 1997, 2005), 'Worldwide remuneration data'.

masters.' And, to paraphrase the old adage, when there are many masters, all end up being shortchanged. Without the clarity of mission provided by a single-valued objective function, companies embracing stakeholder theory will experience managerial confusion, conflict, inefficiency, and perhaps even competitive failure. And the same fate is likely to be visited on those companies that use the so called 'Balanced Scorecard' approach – the managerial equivalent of stakeholder theory – as a performance measurement system.

The thesis advanced by Jensen (2001) has been proved with different tools, for example, the socio-political analysis proposed by Pistor (1999), the legal perspective advanced by Roe (1999) or the econometric evidence shown in Gorton and Schmid (2004), to name just a few of the prominent contributions playing in the arena.

In the socio-political perspective Pistor (1999) suggests that under codetermination labour representatives may be very active actors in extraordinary situations, such as those calling for takeover resistance, while exerting a less active role in day-to day governance. Employees' representatives do not 'specialize' in business strategies, but only in workplace and employment matters, notwithstanding the training programmes to support their professional competence, as those undertaken in Germany by the National Federation of Labour Unions.[9] In this context where multi-player coalitions are present, the option 'voice' remains partly unexploited and room for managerial failures is left open. 'The net beneficiaries are those who ought to be controlled: the company's management' (Pistor 1999, p. 192).

Analogous scepticism is put forward on legal grounds by Roe (1999), an impartial expert who has devoted much of his academic research to evaluating the parallel defects of the shareholder system prevailing in the USA (see Roe 1994). In his 1999 contribution emphasis is placed on showing how the German boardroom hampers the functioning of an efficient securities market, thus determining infrequent Initial Public Offering (IPO) and the presence of big block-holders, with the result that German firms remain 'semi-private companies'. One of the main reasons is that diffuse shareholders may be unable to enter into alliance and to create a balance of power as a counterweight to the employee block; consequently a German securities market does not develop (Roe 1999, p. 194–5).

Finally, let us consider the micro econometric evidence shown in Gorton and Schmid (2000). The authors pose two broad questions. Firstly, does high employee representation on the supervisory board affect the performance of the firm, possibly because labour alters the firm's objective function? Secondly, are shareholders able to offset these distortions – away from maximizing shareholder wealth – by taking countermeasures in attempting to offset the voting power of employee representatives? What they find by studying a sample of the 250 largest German public companies for the years 1989–93 is that when labour and capital have equal representation on the supervisory board (1/2 seats each), the companies' market to book values are lower in comparison to situations where labour representation is lower (1/3 of seats). And the losses do not reduce overtime, but range from 21 per cent in 1989 to 43 per cent in 1992. A rationale behind these results is that employees wield sufficient power to obtain private benefits of control and pursue this strategy by altering managerial remuneration, as confirmed by the weaker link, in cases of more extensive labour participation, between executive managerial compensations and company results. Moreover, employees' representatives aim at maintaining a high staffing level and resistance to corporate restructuring.

Let us now consider a more optimistic view following the comprehensive approach adopted by Hall and Soskice (2001a) and by the several contributions collected in the book they have edited and devoted to analysing the varieties of capitalism around the world (Hall and Soskice 2001b).

To briefly reconsider these studies, it is relevant to recall the relevance of the relational view of the firm, as the quality of the relationships the firm is able to establish is a crucial ingredient of its dynamic capability. From this perspective, as suggested by Hall and Soskice (2001a), a core distinction may be traced between two different kinds of relationships that seem to prevail in different systems, the coordinated market economies and the liberal market economies. This distinction shows some significant overlaps, as we shall see, with the difference between a 'broad' and a 'narrow view' of the firm.

In coordinated market economies, as in the German and in the Japan cases, extensive relational and incomplete contracting entails greater

reliance on collaborative relationship and on the exchange of private information. This is coherent with the view that 'when complete contracts are
too costly or impossible, parties settle for relational agreements that frame
their relationship over time' (Morroni 2006, p. 207).

In Germany this design is mirrored in moderate wage differentials across
firms and industries that reduce the propensity of employees to change jobs,
thus contributing to a compressed wage structure and to long employment
tenure. Employment stability is implemented, at least at a first glance,
through the functioning of two important labour market institutions. The
first is the industry-level wage bargaining that prevents intra-industry wage
differentials and generates low spreads by firm size, thus lowering voluntary
separation rates. The second is the legal institution of codetermination at the
level of the supervisory board and works councils. These arrangements, as
shown in Freeman and Lazear (1994), enhance the efficiency of the firm by
permitting the flow of communications between management and workers,
but give voice to employees in their demand for lower layoffs and lower labour
shedding in case of adverse shocks. In this framework, where an implicit
empowerment of labour is provided, the interplay of wage and labour setting
rules reveals a crucial factor (FitzRoy and Kraft 2005). That is to say, as the
study of Milgrom and Roberts (1990) has shown in a general context, insiders' involvement may generate lobbying and 'influence' costs, with negative
side effects that outweigh the efficiency gains obtained from better communication. One of these potential drawbacks could be a higher bargaining
power over the distribution of the company results, with sub-optimal outcomes. This has been well clarified by Freeman and Lazear (1994).

Let us assume, following these two authors, that assigning control and
information rights to workers' councils increases the firm's rent over the level
obtained without these organizations, but let us also assume that these rights
affect the division of rents. A clear trade-off arises as the firm observes that
higher works council power may enhance productivity and rents (a larger
pie), but reduces its own share (a smaller slice). The firm's choice is a lower
sub-optimal level of codetermination since it cannot fully appropriate all the
benefits from collaborative labour relations. An escape and solution to
the dilemma could be to separate the factors that affect the magnitude of the
surplus from those that have an impact on its division. As underlined by
FitzRoy and Kraft: 'the designers of co-determination seem to have been
aware of these problems, because collective bargaining is formally quite separate from all aspects of codetermination' (FitzRoy and Kraft 2005, p. 236).

Unlike Germany, in Japan long-term relations are enforced by long-term
incentives of internal promotion and by returns of seniority that magnify
the high commitment of employees to company success and promote lifetime employment, thus encouraging firm-specific investments in human

Table 2.4 Comparative features of labour relations in some countries: stability of employment, wage setting system and wage spread in Coordinated Market Economies (CME) and Liberal Market Economies (LME)

Countries	Separation rate (as % of new hires)	Employment tenure (average tenure-years)	Bargaining level (dominant form)	Wage spread (ratio of the ninth over the fifth decile)	Ratio of remuneration of manual workers to CEO (manufacturing) (%)
CME					
Germany	27.2	9.9	sectoral	1.64	7.6
Japan	n.a.	11.3	sectoral	1.73	8.6
LME					
USA	65.9	7.4	company	2.22	2.4
UK	42.9	7.8	company	1.99	3.9
Years	1990s	1990s	1990s	Early 1990s	2001

Source: OECD (various years), *Employment Outlook*; European Commission (2003); Towers Perrin (2005), 'Worldwide remuneration data'.

capital. By contrast, in Germany, as is well synthesized in Jackson *et al.* (2006, p. 89), 'training takes place within a multi-player and quasi-public system of occupational training. These skills are portable and related to broad occupations, rather than firm specific.' A synthetic representation of the different wage and employment setting rules in coordinated market economies, such as Germany and Japan, as compared to those adopted in liberal market economies (USA and UK) is offered in Table 2.4.

What complementary institutions are necessary to implement the stakeholders-labour governance? Are the labour regulation rules sufficient per se to explain the success of German and Japanese firms? Here the argument of the role played by institutional complementarities suggested by Aoki (1994) proves to be decisive. This underlines that the efficiency of one institution increases the efficiency of the others.

In particular, in coordinated market economies long-term employment relationships call for a 'financial system capable of providing capital on terms that are not sensitive to current profitability. It suggests that nations with a particular type of coordination in one sphere of the economy should develop complementary practices in other spheres as well' (Hall and Soskice 2001a, p. 18).

Table 2.5   Comparative features of corporate governance in the 1990s in Coordinated Market Economies (CME) and Liberal Market Economies (LME). Concentration of ownership and of voting rights, role of financial institutions and inter-firm relations

Countries	Concentrated ownership (average % of shares owned by the first 5 largest owners)[a]	Largest voting block (% of voting shares) (median)[b]	Financial institutions as principals (% of total outstanding shares)[a]	Inter-firm relations (% of common stocks owned by other non-financial enterprises)[a]
CME				
Germany	41.5	57.0	33.0	42
Japan	33.1	n.a.	38.5	22
LME				
US	25.4	5.4–8.6*	2.2	0
UK	20.9	9.9	0.7	1

Note: *The figures refer, respectively, to NYSE and NASDAQ.

Source: [a]Prowse (1995); [b]Barca and Becht (2001, Table 1.1) data for non-financial enterprises.

Also, the option voice which sustains long-term relationships is related to concentrated ownership which makes it possible to overcome the free-riding problem of dispersed ownership, since large investors are able and motivated to exercise control by obtaining significant gains through their monitoring activity. In addition inter-firm relations are significant and are achieved by cross-shareholdings in Germany, where more than 40 per cent of total shares of companies are owned by other non-financial enterprises, or by business networks built on keiretsu organizations in Japan.

Moreover, bank monitoring may be an essential element in relational financing. For instance, in Germany banks and client firms maintain long-term relationships since banks have access to information on the firm's financial conditions (Edwards and Fischer 1994). Thus they are able to distinguish between good and bad projects and may renegotiate with failing but efficient firms in difficulties, thus avoiding their premature liquidations and favouring their restructuring (see Table 2.5).

Summing up, the coexistence of concentrated ownership, long-term oriented strategies, bank financing, inter-firm relations, industry-level wage bargaining and small wage dispersions are all significant aspects of a variety of capitalism where there are relevant forces capable of implementing long-term relationships and the interests of a group of stakeholders. Furthermore, these coordinated economies are more oriented towards investing 'in *specific* and *co-specific* assets – i.e. assets that cannot readily be turned to another purpose and assets whose returns depend heavily on the active cooperation of others', as Hall and Soskice suggest (2001a, p.17). It is not by chance, as documented by the European Patent Office, that German firms specialize in sectors (mechanical engineering, product handling, transport, machine tools) characterized by incremental innovation, while lagging behind the USA in fields (biotechnology, semiconductors, telecommunications) where innovations are more radical and represent strong discontinuities.

By contrast, liberal market economies, featuring short-term relationships tend to invest more extensively in switchable assets (that is, assets whose value can be realized if diverted to other purposes). In this context institutional complementarities work in the opposite direction. In these economies corporate governance arrangements allow investors who seek an immediate assurance of return of their assets to freely exert the option exit. Such features are complementary to analogous market channels to obtain finance and are parallel to market relations and arm's-length exchanges of labour services. In these the distinctive features of labour relationships are wage patterns linked to labour market conditions, decentralized company level bargaining and, finally, no restrictions on labour adjustment. Moreover, market failures, such as moral hazard and selection adverse problems, are, at least partially, solved by explicit incentives including pay performance systems or employee share ownership schemes that are introduced to enhance wage flexibility.

A parallel interpretation of these findings is that remuneration schemes, for instance tools for corporate governance, emerge as an indirect control device under conditions of imperfect observability (Holmstrom 1979) and, therefore, when other direct control measures are absent. This proposition fits well with observed phenomena, as shown in Table 2.6.

The different remuneration levels among countries confirm that managerial incentives play a crucial role especially in Anglo-Saxon systems, since direct monitoring and incentive payment systems emerge as close substitutes. Furthermore, the composition of incentive schemes, as documented in the last Equity Report by Towers Perrin, shows that the US system tends to rely more on performance-based rewards and on long-term incentive plans, such as stock options or restricted stock, which represent explicit incentives to pursue firms' successful strategies. These payment systems, as shown in the recent literature on executive compensation summarized in Damiani (2006), have also been an essential selection and

Table 2.6   Remuneration and incidence of incentive systems in Coordinated Market Economies (CME) and Liberal Market Economies (LME)

Countries	Remuneration of CEOs (USA = 100) 2005	Percentage of firms that offer long-term incentives to CEOs 2005 (%)			Percentage of firms that use Profit Sharing (PS) and ESO schemes 1990s (%)
CME		Stock options	Restricted stocks	Bonus shares	
Germany	47.1	40	5	10	PS 13 ESO 4
Japan	44.2	35	0	0	PS 13 ESO 3
LME					
UK	54.4	80	0	60	PS 40 ESO 23
USA	100	85	35	35	PS 20 ESO 7.7*

Note: *Percentage of private sector employees participating in ESO schemes.

Source: Towers Perrin (2005), 'Worldwide remuneration data' and Equity Report; OECD (2003); Poutsma (2001); Kruse (2002).

retention tool in managerial labour markets, thus representing a very strategical tool in a context where short-term relations tend to prevail (Ittner *et al.* 2003; Oyer and Schaefer 2005). These considerations may explain why their relevance is still prominent today, even after the scandal and managerial failures that triggered the corporate governance reform undertaken in 2002 (Sarbanes Oxley Act). Moreover, their diffusion is accompanied by employee participation in profit and ownership. This is well documented in Poutsma (2001) and Kruse (2002), as shown in Table 2.6.[10]

However, if top executives exert their influence on compensation committees and adopt rent seeking behaviour, managerial rewards become not so much a solution, but a manifestation of agency problems as shown in Bebchuk and Fried (2003). In this context, all the other subordinate workers may share rent seeking behaviour and a pervasive inefficient compensation structure tends to prevail. This has serious negative implications, as suggested by Baker *et al.* (1988): 'The effect of structuring CEO contracts that are independent of performance is likely to cascade down the hierarchy – each successive layer has fewer incentives to structure effective contracts than the prior layer. The absence on incentives is pervasive, and it's not surprising that large organizations typically evolve into bureaucracies' (Baker *et al.* 1988, p. 614).

In Germany and Japan, where management control is easier and less expensive and lifetime commitment is higher, executive rewards are lower. Moreover, in these countries the lower level of managerial salaries is accompanied by a weaker link to company performance (Table 2.5) and the wide diffusion of stock options and bonus shares paid not only to CEOs but also offered to all 'agents' is absent. This wide diffusion is, on the other hand, very often recorded in the USA and the UK, where Profit Sharing and Employee Share Ownership schemes are paid to a broader base of dependent employees (Table 2.6). The above analysis confirms that the diffusion of forms of employee financial participation has not been a part of a 'package of participation' in control rights. This sort of bifurcation between payoff and control rights has been well documented by the vast participation literature (Uvalic 1991; Poutsma 2001; Pérotin and Robinson 2003; Uvalic 2006). As stressed in Uvalic (2006, p. 50):

> Although traditionally the main arguments in favour of financial participation were motivated by objectives such as greater equality in the distribution of income and wealth, and improving relations between workers and capitalists, today these schemes are considered as part of a new culture of industrial relations based on innovative managerial strategies and more flexible remuneration policies, which should ultimately result in increased enterprise efficiency.

The majority of studies in this field have shown how the wide diffusion of the several forms of employee financial participation has performed with the main aim of enhancing wage flexibility, achieving productivity gains and implementing a risk-sharing device. This evidence can explain why employee financial participation has found a natural space in liberal market economies, more than in coordinated market economies. However, employee participation should be considered in a broader perspective, as done in Gospel and Pendleton (2006), since management of labour is important for shaping corporate governance arrangements. In this broader standpoint various forms of participation are relevant, as suggested by Michie and Oughton (2003). First of all, it is because 'within the firm the agency problem is not confined to the relationship between owners and managers' and 'employee share *ownership* provides one of the mechanisms for aligning the interests of employees and owners and the interest of managers and non-managerial employees' (Michie and Oughton 2003, p. 17).

Secondly, as signalled by Blair (1995), human capital 'is at risk to the extent that the employees' productivity and the wage they command at other firms are significantly lower than what they can earn in that specific firm (Blair 1995, p. 15). In such circumstances employee participation in decision making should be naturally accorded since employees become new 'residual claimants'.

Finally, employee involvement may be justified by an extensive literature on human resource management (HRM) that breaks with the individual utility maximization behaviour and shows the relevance of cooperative attitudes and collective action.[11] These concerns open a natural space for investments in training and in the development of human resources that encourage longer-term relationships and alleviate the short-termism that afflicts the Anglo-Saxon economies.

In any case, the debate on advantages and disadvantages of employee financial participation, as overviewed in Uvalic (2006), has mainly concerned issues such as workers' incentives, wage moderation, promotion of firm-specific human capital investments – via long-term labour contracts, lower intra-firm conflicts – through fewer inequalities and risk sharing properties. But it must be admitted that this is a clear 'shareholder' perspective, one in which theoreticians and econometricians have the hard task to prove that 'wage premiums pay by themselves'. In contrast, in a 'stakeholder' view one of the main claims should be that 'if employees have no input into decision, they are exposed to moral hazard on the part of managers, who may make decisions that affect pay or wealth negatively. The problem is potentially more severe with employee share ownership than with simple profit sharing . . .' (Pérotin and Robinson 2003, p. 11).This is the preferential attitude declared, in 2004, by the OECD Principles of Corporate Governance where it is said that 'the corporate governance framework should permit performance enhancing mechanisms for stakeholder participation' (OECD 2004, Section IIIc) To what extent this participation has been reached may be, at least partly, assessed by the diffusion of the various forms of participation in the different countries (Table 2.7) as well documented in the 2003 OECD survey, one of the few that devotes a section to describing the diffusion of stakeholder protections.

2.4 CONCLUSIONS

The new theories of the firm are the premise for acknowledging that 'arrangements for governing the relationships among employees and the firm can no longer be treated as something separate from corporate governance' (Blair 1999, p. 86).

Moreover, in shaping governance and labour management, a whole set of institutional factors, rather more than the sole codetermination arrangements, are shown to be crucial.

In this context the role of institutional linkages and complementarities may offer a fruitful line of research, as this perspective leaves a natural space for reconsidering the full range of opportunities left to labour coalitions with the other two actors, capital and management. As noted by Pagano and Volpin (2005, p. 841), 'Labor economists view industrial relations as being shaped by the conflict between workers and management. Financial economists view corporate governance as the outcome of the diverging interest of shareholders and management. Actually, these two conflicts are present simultaneously and interact.'

Indeed, as seen in the previous sections, comparison among the various forms of capitalism reveals the potential drawbacks when workers are natural allies of managers and become accomplices of their misconduct. This implies that the traditional conflict between capital and labour may be replaced by a new conflict between strong insiders (management, employees, block-holders) and weak outsiders (small shareholders). In this scenario the 'broad view' of the firm does not represent a remedy to externalities and sub-optimal results, but on the contrary it may be at the origin of new failures. It should be noted that over the last decade the different economies, the coordinated market economies as well as the liberal market economies, have witnessed different forms of failures and scandals. However, they have shared a common feature represented by a badly performing function of their respective governance gatekeepers (Coffee 2005).

From this standpoint, where the eventual convergence towards a unique system of corporate governance may represent the menace of a convergence towards a uniform kind of failure, labour may assume a potential role as a natural guardian of the firm's accountability.[12] Control by empowered employee representatives could contribute to mitigating opportunistic behaviour and rent seeking by managers and to reducing private benefits of control accruing to block-holders.

In effect, if we conceptualize the firm as a set of multilateral contracts over time, and admit that employees sign implicit and explicit agreements with the other parties, their right to bargain over the distributive effects of these agreements must be acknowledged. In this context the condition of a fair contract is naturally required. As Freeman suggests in his 'stakeholder interpretation' of corporate governance, one device for obtaining fairness is the Rawlsian 'veil of ignorance':

Table 2.7 Control rights and payoff rights of employees in some OECD countries

Countries	Participation in monitoring functions Employees appoint some board members[a]	Participation in firm's choices Mandated Works Councils Statutory threshold[b]	Decision making power[c]	Diffusion of participation schemes[d] Percentages of private and public companies that adopt Employee Share Ownership (ESO) and Profit Sharing (PS)
Austria	Yes	5 employees*	Personal matters	ESO: small number of ESO PS: n.a.
Belgium	No	100 employees	Work regulations, recruitment, dismissals, welfare and holidays	ESO: selective application in specific companies PS: mainly by multinational firms
Denmark	Yes	35 employees	Working conditions, personnel policy and training	ESO: 6% PS: 10%
Finland	No	30 employees	None	ESO: n.a. PS: small number of companies
France	No	50 employees	Management of all company welfare schemes	ESO: 7% PS: 57%

Country				
Germany	Yes	5 employees*	Social welfare, personnel policies and economic affairs	ESO: 4% PS: 13%
Ireland	No	No	n.a.	ESO: 4 % PS: 8%
Italy	No	15 employees	None	ESO: 3 % PS: 4%
Japan	No	No	n.a.	ESO: 3 % PS: 13%
Netherlands	Yes	50 employees	Rules concerning, employees benefits working hours, holidays, health and security, recruitment, dismissals and training	ESO: 3% PS: 13%
Spain	No	50 employees	Collective agreements	ESO: 10% PS: 8%
Sweden	Yes	No	n.a.	ESO: 2% PS: 20%
UK	No	No	n.a.	ESO: 23% PS: 40%
USA	No	No	n.a.	ESO: 7.7%* PS: 20%

Note: *Percentage of private sector employees participating in ESO schemes.

Source: a, b, c: OECD (2003, pp. 47–50); d: EPOC Survey (1996); Poutsma (2001, p. 57); Kruse (2002, p. 67).

41

Our common sense notion of fairness is illustrated by the problem of dividing a cake into two pieces for two individuals. The 'fair' solution is for one individual to cut the cake and choose last, or put another way, to cut the cake without knowing which piece he will receive in the end . . . Interpreting fairness as taking place behind the veil of ignorance is consistent with the spirit of transaction cost economics, since it must take into account both ex post and ex ante perspectives. It would be irrational for stakeholders to give up the ability to participate in monitoring the actual effects of the firm on them. (Freeman 1990, p. 357)

NOTES

1. My greatest debt is to Alberto Chilosi who has helped me with valuable suggestions. I am also indebted to Milica Uvalic for her precious comments. However, I bear full responsibility for the contents of the present chapter.
2. A natural extension of this analysis is to investigate the implications of innovative processes on corporate arrangements, since, as noticed in O'Sullivan (2000), 'the leading theories of corporate governance – the shareholder and stakeholder theories – do not provide a systematic analysis of innovation in their analytical frameworks' (O'Sullivan 2000, p. 393). A comparative evaluation of corporate governance systems focused also on institutional mechanisms behind the innovation process and employee participation is provided by Lee *et al*. (2003). The main linkages between incentives (and more generally human resource management practices) and innovation are empirically explored, among others, in Michie and Sheehan (1999) for the UK, Kleinknecht (1998) for the Netherlands and Damiani (2000) for profit sharing in the Italian case.
3. In this view the property rights should be assigned, under contract incompleteness, to the party whose specific investments give the highest contribution to the creation of value. Blair (1999) offers a detailed overview and also reconsiders other approaches, such as the 'nexus of contracts' paradigm; the author compares 'old' and 'new' theories of the firm and explores the related implications in terms of governance structures. For a more comprehensive analysis on the current status of the theory of the firm, see Morroni (2006).
4. This perspective has been echoed in the growing 'law and finance' literature, inaugurated by La Porta *et al*. (1998), where the protection and the enforcement of shareholders' rights are the main pre-conditions for corporate value.
5. Some distinctions between the conceptualizations provided by Rajan and Zingales and Holmstrom and Milgrom should be made. In the former approach 'a nexus of specific investments' undertaken by individuals who have access to critical resources has a dominant role. In the latter approach the 'bundle' of institutional arrangements designed to provide appropriate incentives is relevant. A formalization of both models is illustrated in Damiani (2006, Appendix A.2.1 and A.6.1).
6. In over 300 large US firms, spanning a number of industries, the authors have found that from 1986 to 1999 the number of managers reporting to the Chief Executive Officer increased steadily over time from an average (median) of 4.4 (4) in 1986 to 7.2 (7) in 1999.
7. During the period 1970–85 the percentage of trade credit on the gross financing of non-financial enterprises was 18.3 per cent in Japan, and 2.8 per cent and 8.4 per cent in the UK and the USA, respectively (see Mayer 1990, p. 312).
8. However, as noticed by Schmidt (2003, p.18), the German system helps to create rents that in part may come 'from the "exploitation" of those shareholders who are not insiders, i.e. the small shareholders and possibly also some institutional investors'.
9. Pistor observes that the voice of labour may be not a single voice, as the mechanism of worker representation reveals conflicts of interests between white and blue collars, who in Germany elect in separate sessions their delegates for the designation of the supervisory board.

10. In the UK, of the top 1500 quoted companies, at least 80 per cent had introduced all-employee share schemes in 2000 (Michie and Oughton 2001).
11. See Becker and Huselid (2006) for an overview of directions of research of Human Resource Management literature.
12. The 'convergence' issue is still controversial and open to debate; for instance, for the German case, Jackson *et al.* (2006, pp. 117–18) stress that 'a more marketised role of capital has led to changes toward marketised employment relations in Germany'. However, the authors stress that 'the diffusion of shareholder value has not undermined the core institutions of German industrial relations, namely codetermination and collective bargaining'.

REFERENCES

Aoki, M. (1994), 'The Japanese firm as a system of attributes: a survey and research agenda', in M. Aoki and R. Dore (eds), *The Japanese Firm: Sources of Competitive Strength*, Oxford: Clarendon Press, pp. 11–40.

Andrade, G., M. Mitchell and E. Stafford. (2001), 'New evidence and perspectives on mergers', *Journal of Economic Perspectives*, **15** (2), 103–20.

Baker, G.P., M.C. Jensen and K.J. Murphy (1988), 'Compensation and incentives: practice versus theory', *Journal of Finance*, **43** (3), 593–616.

Barca, F. and M. Becht (2001), *The Control of Corporate Europe*, Oxford: Oxford University Press.

Baumol, W.J. (1959), *Business Behavior, Value and Growth*, New York: Macmillan.

Bebchuk, L.A. and J.M. Fried (2003), 'Executive compensation as an agency problem', *Journal of Economic Perspectives*, **17** (3), 71–92.

Becht, M., P. Bolton and A. Roell (2003), 'Corporate governance and control', in G.M. Costantinides, H. Milton and R.M. Stulz (eds), *Handbook of the Economics of Finance*, Amsterdam: North Holland, pp. 4–109.

Becker B.E. and M.A. Huselid (2006), 'Strategic human resources management: where do we go from here?', *Journal of Management*, **32** (6), 898–925.

Bertrand, M. and S. Mullainathan (1998), 'Executive compensation and incentives: the impact of takeover legislation', NBER working paper no. 6830.

Bertrand, M. and S. Mullainathan (2003), 'Enjoying a quite life', *Journal of Political Economy*, **111** (5), 1043–75.

Blair M M (1995), *Ownership and Control: Rethinking Corporate Governance for the Twenty-First Century*, Washington DC: The Brookings Institution.

Blair, M.M. (1999), 'Firm-specific human capital and theories of the firm', in M.M. Blair and M.J. Roe (eds) *Employees and Corporate Governance*, Washington, DC: The Brookings Institution, pp. 58–90.

Bruner, R.F. (2004), *Applied Mergers and Acquisitions*, New York: Wiley & Sons.

Chemla, G. (2005), 'Hold-up, stakeholders and takeover threats', *Journal of Financial Intermediation*, **14** (3), 376–97.

Coffee, J.C. (2005), 'A theory of corporate scandals: why the U.S. and Europe differ', *Oxford Review of Economic Policy*, **21** (2), 198–211.

Croci, E. (2004), 'The long run evidence about corporate raiders in Europe', EFMA 2004 Basel meetings paper.

Damiani, M. (2000), 'Profit sharing in a multiple bargaining system: the Italian case', *Economic Analysis*, **3** (2), 113–35.

Damiani, M. (2006), *Impresa e Corporate Governance*, Roma: Carocci.

Edlin, A. and J.E. Stiglitz (1995), 'Discouraging rivals: managerial rent-seeking and economic inefficiencies', *American Economic Review*, **85** (5), 1301–12.

Edwards, J. and K. Fischer (1994), *Banks, Finance and Investment in Germany*, Cambridge: Cambridge University Press.

Epoc Survey (1996), *New forms of work organisation: can Europe realize its potential? Results of a survey of direct employee participation in Europe*, European Foundation for the Improvement of living and working conditions, Office for Official Publications of the European Communities, Luxembourg.

European Commission (2003), *Employment in Europe, 2003 – Recent Trends and Prospects*, Brussels: Directorate General for Employment and Social Affairs.

FitzRoy, F.R. and K. Kraft (2005), 'Co-determination, efficiency and productivity', *British Journal of Industrial Relations*, **43** (2), 233–47.

Freeman, R.B. (1990), 'Corporate governance: a stakeholder interpretation', *Journal of Behavioral Economics*, **19** (4), 337–60.

Gorton, G. and F. Schmid (2000), 'Class struggle inside the firm: a Study of German codetermination', NBER working paper no. 7945.

Gorton, G. and F. Schmid (2004), 'Capital, labor and the firm: a study of German codetermination', *Journal of European Economic Association*, **2** (5), 863–905.

Gospel, H. and A. Pendleton (eds) (2006), *Corporate Governance and Labour Management*, Oxford: Oxford University Press.

Grossman, S.J. and O.D. Hart (1980), 'Takeover bids, the free rider problem, and the theory of corporation', *Bell Journal of Economics*, **11** (1), 42–64.

Grossman, S.J. and O.D. Hart (1986), 'The costs and benefits of ownership: a theory of vertical and lateral integration', *Journal of Political Economy*, **94** (4), 691–719.

Gugler, K. (2001), *Corporate Governance and Economic Performance*, Oxford: Oxford University Press.

Hall, B.J. and K.J. Murphy (2002), 'Stock options for undiversified executives', *Journal of Accounting and Economics*, **33** (1), 3–42.

Hall, P.A. and D.W. Soskice (2001a), 'Introduction', in P.A. Hall and D. Soskice (eds) *Varities of Capitalism*, Oxford: Oxford University Press, pp. 1–68.

Hall, P.H. and D.W. Soskice (eds) (2001b), *Varieties of Capitalism*, Oxford: Oxford University Press.

Hart, O.D. and J. Moore (1990), 'Property rights and the nature of the firm', *Journal of Political Economy*, **98** (6), 1119–58.

Hellwig, M. (2000), 'On the economics and politics of corporate finance and corporate control', in X. Vives (ed.), *Corporate Governance*, Cambridge: Cambridge University Press, pp. 95–136.

Hernández-López, E. (2003), 'Bag wars and bank wars, the Gucci and Banque National de Paris hostile bids: European corporate culture responds to active shareholders', *Fordham Journal of Corporate & Financial Law*, **9** (1), 127–90.

Holmstrom, B. (1979), 'Moral hazard and observability', *Bell Journal of Economics*, (**10**) 1, 74–91.

Holmstrom, B. and P. Milgrom (1991), 'Multitask principal-agent analyses: incentive contracts, asset ownership, and job design', *Journal of Law, Economics, and Organization*, **7** (1), 24–52.

Holmstrom, B. and P. Milgrom (1994), 'The firm as an incentive system', *American Economic Review*, **84** (4), 972–91.

Ittner, C.D., Lambert, R.A. and D.F. Larcker (2003), 'The structure and performance of equity grants to employees of the new economy firms', *Journal of Accounting and Economics*, **34** (1–3), 89–127.

Jackson, G., Höpner M. and A. Kurdelbusch (2006), 'Corporate governance and employees in Germany: changing linkages, complementarities, and tensions', in Gospel Howard and Andrew Pendleton (eds) *Corporate governance and labour management*, Oxford: Oxford University Press, pp. 84–121.

Jensen, M.C. (1986), 'Agency costs of free cash flow, corporate finance and takeovers', *American Economic Review*, **76** (2), 323–9.

Jensen, M.C. (2001), 'Value maximization, stakeholder theory, and the corporate objective function', *Journal of Applied Corporate Finance*, **14** (3), 8–21.

Jensen, M.C. and R. Ruback (1983), 'The market for corporate control: the scientific evidence', *Journal of Financial Economics*, **11** (1), 5–50.

Kaplan, S. (1994), 'Top executives, turnover and firm performance in Germany', *Journal of Law, Economics and Organization*, **10** (1), 142–59.

Kleinknecht, A. (1998), 'Is labour market flexibility harmful to innovation?', *Cambridge Journal of Economics*, **22** (3), 387–96.

Kreps, D.M. (1984), 'Corporate culture and economic theory', Stanford University Graduate School of Business, draft.

Kruse, D. (2002), 'Research evidence on the prevalence and effects of employee ownership', *Journal of Employee Ownership Law and Finance*, **14** (4), 65–90.

La Porta, R., F. Lopez-de Silanes, A. Shleifer and R. Vishny (1998), 'Law and finance', *Journal of Political Economy*, **106** (6), 1113–55.

Lee, S.H, J. Michie and C. Oughton (2003), 'Comparative corporate governance: beyond "shareholder value"', *Journal of Interdisciplinary Economics*, **14** (1), 81–111.

Manne, H.G. (1965), 'Mergers and the market for corporate control', *Journal of Political Economy*, **73** (2), 110–20.

Marris, R. (1964), *The Economic Theory of Managerial Capitalism*, London: Macmillan.

Martynova, M. and L. Renneboog (2006), 'Mergers and acquisitions in Europe', discussion paper no. 6, Tilburg University.

Mayer, C. (1990), 'Financial systems, corporate finance, and economic development', in G.R. Hubbard (ed.), *Asymmetric Information, Corporate Finance, and Investment*, Chicago, IL: University of Chicago Press, pp. 307–32.

Michie J. and C. Oughton (2001), 'Employee share ownership trusts and corporate governance', *Corporate Governance*, **1** (3), 4–8.

Michie J. and C. Oughton (2003), 'HRM, employee share ownership and corporate performance', *Research and Practice in Human Resource Management*, **11** (1), 15–36.

Michie, J. and M. Sheehan (1999), 'No innovation without representation? An analysis of participation, representation, R&D and innovation', *Economic Analysis*, **2** (2), 85–97.

Milgrom, P. and J. Roberts (1990), 'Bargaining cost, influence costs, and the organization of economic activity', in J.E. Alt. and K.A. Shepsle (eds), *Perspectives on Positive Political Economy*, Cambridge: Cambridge University Press, pp. 57–89.

Mitchell, M.L. and H.J. Mulherin (1996), 'The impact of industry shocks on takeover and restructuring activity', *Journal of Financial Economics*, **41** (2), 193–229.

Morroni, M. (2006), *Knowledge, Scale and Transaction in the Theory of the Firm*, Cambridge: Cambridge University Press.

O'Sullivan, M. (2000), 'The innovative enterprise and corporate governance', *Cambridge Journal of Economics*, **24** (4), 393–416.

OECD (2003), *Survey of Corporate Governance Developments in OECD Countries*, Paris: OECD.

OECD (2004), *Principles of Corporate Governance*, Paris: OECD.

OECD (various years), *Employment Outlook*, Paris: OECD.

Oyer, P. (2004), 'Why do firms use incentives that have no incentive effects?', *Journal of Finance*, **59** (4), 1619–49.

Oyer, P. and S. Schaefer (2005), 'Why do some firms give stock options to all employees? An empirical examination of alternative theories', *Journal of Financial Economics*, **76** (1), 99–133.

Pagano, M. and P.F. Volpin (2005), 'Managers, workers and corporate control', *Journal of Finance*, **60** (2), 841–68.

Pérotin, V. and A. Robinson (2003), 'Employee participation in profit and ownership: a review of the issues and evidence', working paper, Social Affairs Series, SOCI 109 EN, Luxembourg Parliament, Directorate-General for Research.

Pistor, K. (1999), 'Codetermination: a sociopolitical model with governance externalities', in M. Blair and M.J. Roe (eds), pp. 163–93.

Poutsma, E. (2001), *Recent Trends in Employee Financial Participation in the European Union*, Dublin: European Foundation for the Improvement of Living and Working Conditions.

Prowse, S. (1995), 'Corporate governance in an international perspective: a survey of corporate control mechanisms among large firms in the U.S., U.K., Japan and Germany', *Financial Markets, Institutions and Instruments*, **4** (1), 1–63.

Rajan, R.G. and J. Wulf (2003), 'The flattening firm: evidence from panel data on the changing nature of corporate hierarchies', NBER working paper no. 9633, rep. in 2006, *Review of Economics and Statistics*, **88** (4), 759–73.

Rajan, R.G. and L. Zingales (1998), 'Power in a theory of the firm', *Quarterly Journal of Economics*, **113** (2), 387–432.

Rajan, R.G. and L. Zingales (2001), 'The firm as a dedicated hierarchy: a theory of the origins and growth of firms', *Quarterly Journal of Economics*, **116** (3), 805–51.

Roe, M.J. (1994), *Strong Managers, Weak Owners: The Political Roots of American Corporate Finance*, Princeton, NJ: Princeton University Press.

Roe, M.J. (1999), 'Codetermination and German securities markets', in M. Blair and M.J. Roe (eds), *Employee and Corporate Governance*, Washington, DC: The Brookings Institution, pp. 194–205.

Rossi, S. and P.F. Volpin (2004) 'Cross-country determinants of mergers and acquisitions', *Journal of Financial Economics*, **74** (2), 277–304.

Schmidt, R.H. (2003), 'Corporate governance in Germany: an economic perspective', Center of Financial Studies, CFS working paper no. 36, p. 18.

Shleifer, A. and L.H. Summers (1987), 'Breach of trust in hostile takeovers', NBER working paper no. 2342, rep. in A.J. Auerbach (1988) (ed.), *Corporate Takeovers: Causes and Consequences*, National Bureau of Economic Research Project Report, Chicago: Chicago University Press, pp. 33–56.

Shleifer, A. and R. Vishny (1997), 'A survey of corporate governance,' *Journal of Finance*, **52** (2), 737–83.

Tirole, J. (2001), 'Corporate governance', *Econometrica*, **69** (1), 1–35.

Tirole, J. (2006), *The Theory of Corporate Finance*, Princeton, NJ: Princeton University Press.

Towers Perrin (various years), 'Worldwide remuneration data', www.towersperrin.com.

Uvalic, M. (1991), *The Pepper Report: Promotion of Employee Participation in Profits and Enterprise Results in the Member States of the European Community*, Social Europe Supplement, no. 3/91, Luxembourg Office for Official Publications of the European Communities.

Uvalic, M. (2006), 'Employee ownership – Western lessons for the Eastern new EU member states', in *The Pepper III Report: Promotion of Employee Participation in Profits and Enterprise Results in the New Member and Candidate Countries of the European Union*, Inter-University Center Split/Berlin, Institute for Eastern European Studies, Free University of Berlin, pp. 46–68.

3. The governance of the knowledge-intensive firm in an industry life cycle approach

Jackie Krafft and Jacques-Laurent Ravix

3.1 INTRODUCTION[1]

Today, a growing body of literature is developing the concept that different types of rules and norms should govern entrepreneurial and public firms differently, depending on the industry in which they operate and the stage of development of the industry (Fransman 2002; Lazonick and O'Sullivan 2002; Filatotchev and Wright 2004; Becht *et al.* 2005). The present chapter contributes to this new literature by adding the empirical dimensions that are pointed out in the industry life cycle (ILC) literature. The purpose is to investigate the nature of the governance of the knowledge-intensive firm as seen from the perspective of an industry life cycle approach. By knowledge-intensive firm, we mean that firms, independently of their age and size, may be involved in the creation of new knowledge and may be the key actors in the development of innovation processes. As we shall see, the ILC can provide an appropriate, though incomplete, approach to analyse this question. This approach explicitly considers that small new firms enlarge product characteristics and are thus the initiators of innovation in the phases of emergence and growth of the industry, while large mature firms continue the process of innovation by investing in process capacities in the phases of maturity and decline of the industry. In the meantime, this framework is silent on modes of governance of the firm in relation to the development of the industry. We thus believe it is important to understand how governance of the firm can stimulate the creation of new knowledge in the early phases of development of the industry, as well as contributing to maintenance of innovation in the late stages of development of the industry.

In Section 2 we show that when the two sets of literature – governance of firms and industry life cycle – are connected, the immediate result is that the governance of firms in the early stages of the life cycle should be different from the governance of firms in the late stages of the life cycle. When firms are in the early stages, in which they tend to be smaller and younger, they should benefit from a mode of governance based on cooperation and assistance to stimulate innovation, while a mode of governance based on control of the manager's action in the interest of the shareholders should be imposed when firms are in their later stages, because by this time they are often considered as larger, more mature and routinized. However, we claim that imposing the knowledge-intensive firms with a mode of governance based on control may not be the optimal solution, since this mode of governance is known to favour short-term choices that may be detrimental to the development of innovation. We advance the idea that new modes of governance should be based on the cognitive nature of the knowledge-intensive firm (large and small, young and old), considered as a distinctive category. In Section 3 we focus on corporate knowledge-intensive firms, the main problem of which is to maintain cognitive coherence on the activities both of knowledge coordination and knowledge creation. This coherence can be obtained through a mode of corporate governance that will be termed 'corporate entrepreneurship'. Its implications on the creation and coordination of new knowledge are analysed, together with its role in the validation or refutation of innovative conjectures. A general overview of the sum of our results is then provided, and some conclusions are drawn.

3.2 THE GOVERNANCE OF FIRMS IN THE INDUSTRY LIFE CYCLE

In this section we analyse the following series of questions: Should firms be owned and managed the same way at the time they emerge, grow, age and decline? Or should there be distinct types of governance along the phases of the ILC? On the one hand, the literature on start-ups and venture capital suggests that firms should be governed on the basis of a close cooperation between the founder entrepreneur (or professional manager) and the investor (business angel, venture capitalist). On the other hand, the literature on the governance of corporate firms generally supports the shareholder value vision in which the relationship between the manager and the investor are in terms of conflicting objectives, leading to a realignment of the manager's incentives in the investor's interests. The conclusion arising from these two trends of the literature is thus that there should be distinct modes of governance over the ILC, one dedicated to small, young firms, and based on cooperation; the other dedicated to older, large and mature firms, and based on control.

3.2.1   Cooperative Governance of Start-ups in the Early Stages of Development

The ILC gives small, new firms a key role in the impulse towards innovation: they are at the origins of a life cycle (see Klepper 1997; Gort and Klepper 1982).[2] The question of how these firms are financed during the seed phase is thus a key issue. Gompers and Lerner (2001) argue that a venture capital revolution has emerged for these firms. They maintain that (*Ibid*, p. 145): 'Venture capital is now an important intermediary in financial markets, by providing capital to firms that might otherwise have difficulty attracting financing. These firms are typically small and young, plagued with high levels of uncertainty and large differences between what entrepreneurs and investors know.'

This issue of 'what entrepreneurs and investors know' has long been treated in agency terms, that is, in a framework based on asymmetric information and complete contracts. The manager has important incentives to engage unproductive expenditure, since he does not bear the entire cost; or to develop an insufficient level of effort, since this level is not directly observable by the investor. These important information asymmetries between the entrepreneur and the venture capitalist can be solved (Jensen and Meckling 1976). The solution broadly lies in the investor's scrutinization of firms before providing capital and monitoring them afterwards, above all by being on the board of directors and defining compensation schemes (including stock options). However the outcome is, very often, highly complex venture capital contracts that may be very difficult to define and enforce in the real world (Gompers 1995, 1996; Kaplan and Stroemberg 2003, 2004).

New developments tend to recognize that the relation between the investor and the manager is necessarily based on incomplete contracts (Hart and Moore 1988). In that case, what entrepreneurs and investors know is highly dependent on their specific knowledge, skills, experience and practices (Audretsch and Lehman 2006). Since this knowledge is not easily transferable, the investor and the manager have to develop close connections in order to progressively share their respective knowledge. Close connection is partially necessary, since lenders are faced with evaluating innovative but less proven business concepts. Small, new firms do not generally demonstrate an established history of earning and financial stability. Also, for many start-ups the primary assets are intangible and difficult to value, thus failing to satisfy requirements for asset-based security. In such a case venture capitalists and business angels finance new and rapidly growing companies, and especially purchase equity securities. But, in order to embark on such an undertaking, they generally assist the development of new products or services, and add value to the company through active participation. They usually take higher risks with the expectation of higher rewards, and have a long-term orientation.

The nature of the relationship between the manager and the investor is thus based on cooperation and assistance: founder-entrepreneurs or professional managers have to disseminate their own knowledge on the characteristics of their innovation and market potentialities, while the business angel or venture capitalist has to propose different solutions to finance the initial step of elaboration of the innovative project, as well as its development over time.

3.2.2 Control-based Governance of Mature Firms in the Late Stages of the ILC

The ILC also views large firms as key actors in the development of innovation, especially by virtue of their greater capacity to invest in process innovation, based on the accumulation of knowledge and competences since their entry at the beginning of the life cycle. However negative effects may also be generated, such as inefficient choices by the manager in a situation where large size increases bureaucracy and decreases the intensity of competition. These effects are at the core of the literature on the governance of large, mature firms. In the big corporation the governance problem is essentially that of persuading the manager to behave fairly on behalf of the investor, and to avoid any discretionary behaviour. The general solution to this agency problem is to grant managers a highly contingent, long-term incentive contract *ex ante* to align their interests with those of principals (Schleifer and Vishny 1997). The formalization provides the essential requirements of corporate governance oriented towards shareholder value within a context of transparency of information and generalization of contractual relations in organizations. Managerial corrections may take various forms (board of directors, proxy fights, hostile takeovers, corporate financial structure), and are always oriented towards monitoring and disciplining management in the interest of shareholders and investors.

The nature of the relationship between the manager and the investor is based on control: the investor orientates and monitors the manager's choices. The investor, utilizing the information of key indicators such as Return on Investment, or Economic Value Added/Market Value Added, has the capacity to evaluate whether the manager has behaved fairly to shareholders or not. From these indicators, investors check whether managers have transformed their background knowledge into shareholder value maximizing strategies.

3.2.3   Governance of Firms Along the Different Stages of the ILC

Two sets of results are thereby derived: one related to the governance of firms in the early stages, where cooperation and assistance modes of governance should dominate, and one related to governance in the late stages that should be based on control and realignment of incentives (Figure 3.1).

In small, new, firms that operate in the early stages of the life cycle the manager is the innovator, the founder entrepreneur or a professional manager, whose role is to discover new technological and market opportunities. The investor is often a business angel or a venture capitalist who assists the development of new products, adds value to the company, takes higher risks with the expectation of higher rewards and has a long-term orientation. The governance is thus based on cooperation and assistance, and is supported by different structures, such as the development of scientific and R&D committees, to increase the long-term performance of the firm. In contrast, large and mature firms that dominate the late stages of development of the industry are governed by a board of directors that run the company in the interests of the shareholders. Very often these shareholders are institutional investors, such as pension funds, that tend to realign the managers' incentives, fight against manager's discretion and assess the value of the company on purely financial criteria. They are short-term and risk minimization oriented.

3.3   CORPORATE GOVERNANCE AND THE KNOWLEDGE-INTENSIVE FIRM

The results obtained in Section 2 on the governance of the firm along the different stages of the life cycle do not tell the complete story. They can be criticized for the following reasons. First, these results are based on an arbitrary vision of the firm, being highly knowledge-intensive at the beginning of their life, and much less as they age. There is no robust evidence on this: many industries are composed of old, large, but still highly innovative companies. Second, if these firms in the late stages of development of an industry are knowledge-intensive, then imposing on them a mode of governance based on control may not be the optimal solution. This mode of governance favours short-term choices that may be detrimental to the development of innovation. Third, the literature on the governance of start-ups has greatly changed over time, starting from basic control modes of governance inspired by agency theory, and ending up with more operational and pragmatic modes of governance based on cooperation and assistance. The recognition that the manager's knowledge was necessarily different from –

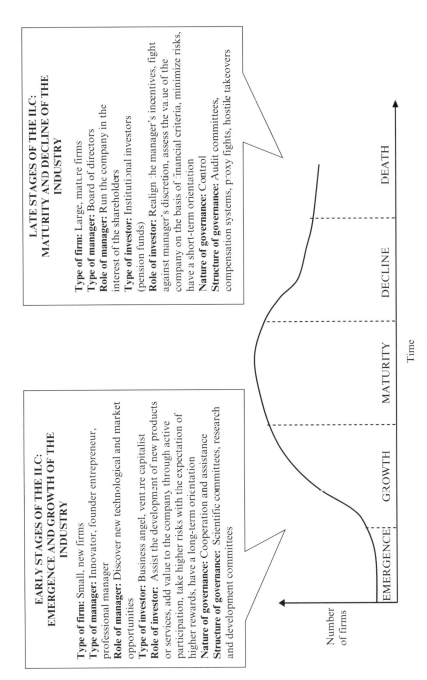

EARLY STAGES OF THE ILC: EMERGENCE AND GROWTH OF THE INDUSTRY

Type of firm: Small, new firms
Type of manager: Innovator, founder entrepreneur, professional manager
Role of manager: Discover new technological and market opportunities
Type of investor: Business angel, venture capitalist
Role of investor: Assist the development of new products or services, add value to the company through active participation, take higher risks with the expectation of higher rewards, have a long-term orientation
Nature of governance: Cooperation and assistance
Structure of governance: Scientific committees, research and development committees

LATE STAGES OF THE ILC: MATURITY AND DECLINE OF THE INDUSTRY

Type of firm: Large, mature firms
Type of manager: Board of directors
Role of manager: Run the company in the interest of the shareholders
Type of investor: Institutional investors (pension funds)
Role of investor: Realign the manager's incentives, fight against manager's discretion, assess the value of the company on the basis of financial criteria, minimize risks, have a short-term orientation
Nature of governance: Control
Structure of governance: Audit committees, compensation systems, proxy fights, hostile takeovers

Number of firms

EMERGENCE | GROWTH | MATURITY | DECLINE | DEATH

Time

Figure 3.1   Governance of firms along the different stages of the ILC

53

yet highly complementary to – that of the investor has been crucial in the change of vision. The argument could thus be logically generalized to the large knowledge-intensive firm.

In the following section we focus on the knowledge-intensive corporation. We argue first that the governance of large corporations involved in innovative activities and sectors cannot be adequately described in agency terms. The governance of knowledge-intensive corporations is mainly a matter of cognitive coherence of the firm. In a second step we generalize the argument made in Section 2 to show how the cooperation and control modes of governance should be implemented in the governance of knowledge-intensive corporations.

3.3.1   Governance and Cognitive Coherence of the Firm

The inadequacy of traditional agency problems
The distinction between information and knowledge can provide a new rationale to analyse how the predominant thesis on corporate governance based on control has developed, and how this thesis is contested today. The predominant thesis on corporate governance is that there should be a superior model promoting optimality by disclosure of information and transparency, and based on control of the manager's action and its realignment in the interest of shareholders. In this conventional vision of corporate governance, knowledge is assimilated to the managers' private information concerning their actions and efforts, which investors induce them to reveal by offering compensation schemes, for example, in the form of stock options. Monitoring by boards of directors and large shareholders, and the threat of proxy fights and hostile takeovers can also be implemented to discipline managers who otherwise might use this information to their own benefit at the expense of the shareholders. In terms of the innovative process, this conventional vision supports the belief that new activities and competences can mainly be acquired externally, for example, by means of mergers and acquisitions.

Today, this thesis is contested, since the adoption of a single and universal best practice model neglects the diversity and heterogeneity of firms and industries, as well as institutional contexts (Becht *et al.* 2005). Moreover, evidence shows that the conventional model of governance tends to generate major failures and turbulence, especially in knowledge-intensive industries (Fransman 2002; Lazonick and O'Sullivan 2002). Another strand of literature tends to show that this conventional model is not appropriate for the governance of knowledge-intensive firms: the cooperative theory of the Japanese firm argues that the manager is at the centre of the cooperative game relating shareholders and employees (Aoki 1984), the stakeholder perspective on corporations generalizes the argument to every partner enti-tled to be a residual claimant (Donaldson and Preston 1995; Blair 1995), the critical resource theory insists on the centrality of the manager as a coordinator of firm's activities (Rajan and Zingales 1998; Zingales 2000), and the entrepreneurial learning approach contrasts with the usual vision of the entrepreneur as an empire builder (Klein and Klein 2002; Ellig 2002).

We can surmise from this that agency problems based on the traditional ownership-control distinction and the need to monitor managerial discre-tion do not fit with knowledge-intensive firms for the following reasons: human assets are crucial in the development of knowledge-intensive firms whereas physical assets can be replaced easily; in knowledge-intensive firms the value of human capital is increasing, leading to greater independence for individual workers and more opportunity for job mobility, while financial innovations are enabling easier access to capital markets for indi-vidual entrepreneurs. Likewise, mergers and acquisitions, takeovers and LBOs are instruments for rationalizing the structure of the industry rather than mechanisms for disciplining managers or means for acquiring innov-ative activities and competences externally.[3]

The cognitive firm
However, the literature referred to above does not clearly identify corporate governance principles. Their identification calls for reference to a cognitive vision of the corporate firm (O'Sullivan 2000; Foss and Christensen 2001). This states that large, modern firms are mainly considered to be structures of innovative resource allocation and complementary knowledge assets involved in collective learning processes. Innovative resource allocation involves irreversible commitments of resources for uncertain returns, orga-nization of the collective learning process and strategic decisions as a cre-ative response to existing conditions (O'Sullivan 2000). Corporate firms have to solve two main problems: the problem of 'knowledge dispersal' among the different actors of the firm and the innovative problem of 'knowledge creation', which calls for new combinations of knowledge and learning (Foss and Christensen 2001, p. 222). When problems of change are awarded centre stage in the analysis, the real determinant of the governance of firms should be the presence or absence of innovation. The absence of innovation could legitimate the 'control' mode of governance in routinized firms, independently of their age or size, while the 'cooperation and assis-tance' mode must be the key reference when innovation is a central concern for the firm. A cognitive vision of the corporate firm leads to a new inter-pretation of the relationships among shareholders and managers, based on the notion of corporate entrepreneurship, in which the cooperation and control modes of governance intervene in a sequential timing.

Corporate entrepreneurship

Managerial control is useful in knowledge-intensive firms in so far as it is considered to be an entrepreneurial activity creating diversity, that is, creating new assets and competences in new businesses and experimenting in new directions in existing businesses. To focus on the cognitive coherence of the firm challenges the notion of corporate governance based on agency problems, that is, conflicts of interest involving members of the organization, especially owners and managers. When knowledge is a key element, the real determinant of the co-evolution of financial dynamics and industrial dynamics is how knowledge is coordinated among investors and managers, and how these actors arrive (or not) at cognitive coherence through corporate governance.

In knowledge-intensive firms both managers and investors are jointly committed to developing a mode of entrepreneurial behaviour favouring a long-term perspective, knowledge creation and coordination for innovative purposes, and implying the acceptance of greater uncertainty and higher risk taking. In such a perspective corporate governance is dedicated to the coordination of learning processes, meaning that corporate governance and the governance of knowledge are two facets of the development and coherence of the firm (Penrose 1959; Foss and Christensen 2001).

This mode of corporate governance has been analysed here by referring to the notion of 'corporate entrepreneurship'. We define corporate entrepreneurship as a hybrid form of corporate governance blending the cooperation and control modes described earlier in Section 2. Managers, by defining and selecting innovative processes, and investors, by determining the money that is invested to sustain these processes, both take part in the creation and governance of new knowledge by the firm. Cooperation must exist between managers and investors, since they collectively contribute to corporate development and coherence. Only in a second step does control occur: the investor reacts to the innovative choice, by endorsing or rejecting the innovative conjecture.

3.3.2 Cooperation and Control as Related Modes of Governance in the Knowledge-Intensive Firm

Cooperation for the creation and coordination of knowledge

Long-term innovation affects corporate coherence, since it involves important reconfigurations of resources and competencies over time (Chatterjee and Wernerfelt 1991; Foss 1993; Teece and Pisano 1994; Teece *et al.* 1997; Piscitello 2004). As argued above, in order to preserve corporate coherence in an innovation context, two sets of problems have to be solved (Foss and Christensen 2001). The first is that of knowledge creation, that is, how knowledge arises from new combinations, and from the discovery of new complementarities between existing stocks of knowledge and experimentation with new learning processes. The second problem is that of coordination of knowledge dispersal, which goes hand in hand with the specialization of tasks in large corporations, and involves efforts in constructing shared cognitive patterns.

The role of the manager is crucial in solving these two sets of problems. First, because managerial control has a basic facet of stimulating the entrepreneurial activity of the different stakeholders within the firm, but also among the network of innovation partners that favours knowledge creation. Second, because managerial control also involves command, management information systems, corporate routines and corporate cultures, which can act as knowledge coordination. In order to maintain corporate coherence, the manager has a key role to play in the achievement of a critical mass of stakeholders (at the level of the firm and also at the level of the network) by playing the long-term innovative strategy, while refraining from the temptation of predatory behaviour in the meantime.

The investor is also highly involved in the process. Investors face the task of developing new competences and experience in the evaluation of long-term innovative companies, since the usual market criteria essentially refer to tangible assets and require long-term track records that are often neither applicable nor available in highly innovative contexts. In that perspective, the valuation of intangibles by investors becomes a real issue: valuation is the outcome of a process of coordination of different elements of knowledge related to the perceived ability of the firm to create new technological and market opportunities; valuation is also a key element in sustaining some innovative projects (and not others) that shape the evolution of the industry.

Corporate entrepreneurship means that managers and investors are mostly intertwined *ex ante* in the process of solving corporate coherence problems in the modern cognitive firm. Each actor is endowed with a different aspect of knowledge that has to be recombined in a process of collective learning oriented towards corporate development. Managers bring their own competences to the development of learning processes by creating diversity, exploring new opportunities and providing continuity in innovation. Investors also contribute to the development of learning processes by providing the manager with their own skills and experiences regarding the financial feasibility of external restructurings (M&As, cooperation) or internal strategies (compensation plans, reporting activities, information systems). Cooperation between managers and investors favours the processes of creation and coordination of new knowledge that are engaged in a long-term innovative context. But the investor also has to control *ex post* the impact of innovative choices implemented in the company.

Control to endorse or reject the innovative conjecture
If initially long-term innovation greatly disturbs corporate coherence, one should expect over time that corporate coherence is improved. Here, therefore, control must be operated to guarantee that coherence is restored or at least evolves towards a reasonable level.

The manager must provide the investor with regular information (documents, reports and so on) explaining whether the innovative strategy impacts on corporate coherence and how. If after a sufficiently long time span the innovative strategy generates new but insufficiently coordinated knowledge, or if the critical mass of efforts is not obtained and that stakeholders massively adopt an alternative strategy, then the manager and the investor can jointly infer that erroneous decisions were implemented during the innovation process. The investor checks *ex post* that the manager implements the productive and organizational decisions (cooperation agreements or M&As within the innovation network) dedicated to sustaining the critical mass of efforts, and furthering the long-term innovative strategy. Contrary to shareholder value maximization principles, the problem of the investor is not to limit the discretionary power of the manager but, rather, to control this power. In particular, the investor has to assess the manager's trustworthiness, and possibly the propensity of the latter to engage in 'empire building', in reference to the manager's ability or inability to restore corporate coherence after embarking on a long-term innovative strategy. Thus, as far as innovation is concerned, the issue is not to impose drastic changes in strategies based on the belief that what the investor (or the manager) knows is always right. Rather, the issue is to control that innovation is developed and that corporate coherence is progressively restored.

The governance of knowledge-intensive firms along the industry life cycle
Corporate governance as well as the governance of small knowledge-intensive firms is thus constructed step by step with an *ex ante* process of collective learning, and an *ex post* process of control, in which each of the individual actors embodies an element of diversified and specialized knowledge related to their respective domains and fields of experience, which has to be recombined and used to stimulate corporate development. Figure 3.2 provides more details on the governance of knowledge-intensive firms.

Here the principles of governance concern knowledge-intensive firms, independently of their age and size. The manager has the double role of acting as a professional manager and as an entrepreneur, which means that a manager has to run the company in the interests of all the stakeholders who contribute to the value of the firm, and also to discover new technological and market opportunities by the active involvement of all stakeholders in learning processes. The investor has to develop a long-term

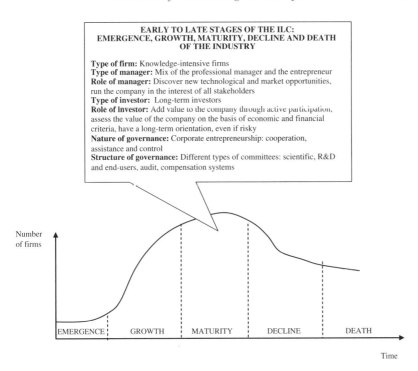

EARLY TO LATE STAGES OF THE ILC:
EMERGENCE, GROWTH, MATURITY, DECLINE AND DEATH
OF THE INDUSTRY

Type of firm: Knowledge-intensive firms
Type of manager: Mix of the professional manager and the entrepreneur
Role of manager: Discover new technological and market opportunities,
run the company in the interest of all stakeholders
Type of investor: Long-term investors
Role of investor: Add value to the company through active participation,
assess the value of the company on the basis of economic and financial
criteria, have a long-term orientation, even if risky
Nature of governance: Corporate entrepreneurship: cooperation,
assistance and control
Structure of governance: Different types of committees: scientific, R&D
and end-users, audit, compensation systems

Figure 3.2   The governance of the knowledge-intensive firm along the ILC

orientation, and is called upon to assess the value of the company on the
basis of economic and financial criteria. Cooperation and assistance
between the manager and the investor (business angel, venture capitalist or
major shareholder) must dominate, on the basis of specific structures of
governance favouring common learning processes. One could, for instance,
think of scientific, R&D or end-user committees as structures of governance of this kind. In the meantime, control also has to occur on the basis
of more traditional structures of governance, such as audit and compensation systems.

3.4   CONCLUSION

This chapter has analysed the governance of the knowledge-intensive firm
in an industry life cycle approach. It was shown that a simple connection
between the literature on the governance of firms and the industry life cycle
was not sufficient to analyse this question. The reason is that the outcome

of this simple connection promotes a mode of governance based on cooperation and assistance for small, young firms and a mode of governance based on control for corporate firms. We have demonstrated that this dichotomic model of governance is not appropriate for knowledge-intensive firms that stimulate the creation of new knowledge in the early stages of development of the industry, but still have to maintain innovation in the late stages of development of the industry. We argue that this cannot be guaranteed if the mode of governance is exclusively based on control. We thus elaborate new principles of governance for knowledge-intensive firms (that is, 'corporate entrepreneurship') that favour the cognitive coherence of their activities of knowledge coordination and knowledge creation.

NOTES

1. A preliminary version of this chapter was presented at the conference held in Lucca in January 2007. The work has been carried out with the scientific support of CNRS, and is part of a research project funded by Agence Nationale de la Recherche (contract number: ANR JCJC06_141306). The chapter draws on previous contributions: Krafft and Ravix (2005, 2007, 2008); Dietrich *et al.* (2008); Ravix (2008).
2. For surveys on the literature, see also Malerba and Orsenigo (1996); Dosi and Malerba (2002); Krafft (2006).
3. For a discussion of these questions, see also Chapter 2 by Mirella Damiani in this book.

REFERENCES

Aoki, M. (1984), *The Cooperative Game Theory of the Firm*, Oxford: Oxford University Press.
Audretsch, D. and E. Lehmann (2006), 'Entrepreneurial access and absorption of knowledge spillovers: strategic board and managerial composition for competitive advantage', *Journal of Small Business Management*, **44** (2), 155–66.
Becht, M., T. Jenkinson and C. Mayer (2005), 'Corporate governance: an assessment', *Oxford Review of Economic Policy*, **21** (2), 155–63.
Blair, M. (1995), *Ownership and Control: Rethinking Corporate Governance for the Twenty First Century*, Washington, DC: Brookings Institution Press.
Chatterjee, S. and B. Wernerfelt (1991), 'The link between resources and type of diversification: theory and evidence', *Strategic Management Journal*, **12** (1), 33–48.
Dietrich, M., J. Krafft and J.L. Ravix (2008), 'The governance and regulation of the firm – special issue', *International Review of Applied Economics*, **22** (4), 397–405.
Donaldson, T. and L. Preston (1995), 'The stakeholder theory of corporation: concepts, evidence and implications', *Academy of management Review*, **20** (1), 65–91.
Dosi, L. and F. Malerba (eds) (2002), 'Special issue: interpreting industrial dynamics 20 years after Nelson and Winter's Evolutionary Theory of Economic Change', *Industrial and Corporate Change*, **11** (4), 3–202.
Ellig, J. (2002), 'Telecommunication mergers and theories of the firm', in N. Foss and P. Klein (eds), *Entrepreneurship and the Firm: Austrian Perspectives on*

Economic Organization, Cheltenham, UK and Northampton, MA, USA: Edward Elgar, pp. 193–220.

Filatotchev, I. and M. Wright (eds) (2004), *The Life-Cycle of Corporate Governance*, Cheltenham UK and Northampton, MA, USA: Edward Elgar.

Foss, N. (1993), 'Theories of the firm: competence and strategy perspectives', *Journal of Evolutionary Economics*, **3** (2), 127–44.

Foss, N. and J. Christensen (2001), 'A market process approach to corporate coherence', *Managerial and Decision Economics*, **22** (4–5), 213–26.

Fransman, M. (2002), *Telecoms in the Internet Age: From Boom to Bust to . . .*, Oxford: Oxford University Press.

Gompers, P. (1995), 'Optimal investment, monitoring, and the staging of venture capital', *Journal of Finance*, **50** (5), 1461–90.

Gompers, P. (1996), 'Grandstanding in the venture capital industry', *Journal of Financial Economics*, **42** (1), 133–56.

Gompers, P. and J. Lerner (2001), 'The venture capital revolution', *Journal of Economic Perspectives*, **15** (2), 145–68.

Gort, M. and S. Klepper (1982), 'Time paths in the diffusion of product innovations', *Economic Journal*, **92** (367), 630–53.

Hart, O. and J. Moore (1988), 'Incomplete contracts and renegotiation', *Econometrica*, **56** (4), 755–86.

Jensen, M. and W. Meckling (1976), 'Theory of the firm: managerial behaviour agency costs and ownership structure', *Journal of Financial Economics*, **3** (4), 305–60.

Kaplan, S. and P. Stroemberg (2003), 'Financial contracting theory meets the real world: an empirical analysis of venture capital contracts', *Review of Economic Studies*, **70** (243), 281–315.

Kaplan, S. and P. Stroemberg (2004), 'Characteristics, contracts, and actions: evidence from venture capitalist analyses', *Journal of Finance*, **59** (5), 2177–210.

Klein, P. and S. Klein (2002), 'Do entrepreneurs make predictable mistakes? Evidence from corporate divestitures', in N. Foss and P. Klein (eds), *Entrepreneurship and the Firm: Austrian Perspectives on Economic Organization*, Cheltenham, UK and Northampton, MA, USA: Edward Elgar, pp. 173–92.

Klepper, S. (1997), 'Industry life cycles', *Industrial and Corporate Change*, **6** (1), 119–43.

Krafft, J. (2006), 'What do we know about industrial dynamics? Introduction to the special issue', *Revue de l'OFCE*, June, 15–19.

Krafft, J. and J.L. Ravix (2005), 'The governance of innovative firms: an evolutionary perspective', *Economics of Innovation and New Technology*, **14** (3), 125–48.

Krafft, J. and J.L. Ravix (2007), 'The firm and its governance over the industry life-cycle', *Corporate Ownership and Control*, **5** (1), 233–42.

Krafft, J. and J.L. Ravix (2008), 'Corporate governance and the governance of knowledge: rethinking the relationship in terms of corporate coherence', *Economics of Innovation and New Technology*, **17** (1–2), 79–96.

Lazonick, W. and M. O'Sullivan (eds) (2002), *Corporate Governance and Sustainable Prosperity*, New York: Palgrave.

Malerba, F. and L. Orsenigo (1996), 'The dynamics of evolution of industry', *Industrial and Corporate Change*, **5** (1), 51–87.

O'Sullivan, M. (2000), 'The innovative enterprise and corporate governance', *Cambridge Journal of Economics*, **24** (4), 393–416.

Penrose, E. (1959), *The Theory of the Growth of the Firm*, London: Basil Blackwell.

Piscitello, L. (2004), 'Corporate diversification, coherence and economic perfor-
mance', *Industrial and Corporate Change*, **13** (5), 757–87.
Rajan, R. and L. Zingales (1998), 'Power in a theory of the firm', *Quarterly Journal
of Economics*, **113** (2), 387–432.
Ravix, J.L. (2008), 'Nature and governance of the firm: in search of an integrated
perspective', *International Review of Applied Economics*, **22** (4), 463–78.
Schleifer, A. and R. Vishny (1997), 'A survey on corporate governance', *Journal of
Finance*, **52** (2), 737–83.
Teece, D. and G. Pisano (1994), 'The dynamic capabilities of firms: an introduc-
tion', *Industrial and Corporate Change*, **3** (3), 537–56.
Teece, D., G. Pisano and A. Shuen (1997), 'Dynamic capabilities and strategic man-
agement', *Strategic Management Journal*, **18** (7), 509–33.
Zingales, L. (2000), 'In search for new foundations', *Journal of Finance*, **55** (4),
1623–53.

4. Types of complementarity, combinative organization forms and structural heterogeneity: beyond discrete structural alternatives

Anna Grandori and Santi Furnari

'If any approach to defining organizational forms can be regarded as standard, it is one that regards forms as particular *clusters of features*. The example par excellence is Weber's specification of rational-legal bureaucracy in terms of the nature of authority . . ., procedures . . ., and the employment relation of the official . . .' (Polos *et al.* 2002, p. 87).

4.1 INTRODUCTION

In spite of the broad consensus on the above concept, originating in the sociology of organization, apparently there has been much less effort and consensus on a systematic definition of which are the fundamental 'features' of organization, and according to which laws they are supposed to cluster. In the first section this chapter offers a critical re-reading of the notions of organization forms in organization theory and organization economics aimed at singling out what has been established and what stands up to scrutiny on those two important issues.[1] In the second section, building on these elements and on earlier works by the present authors (Grandori 1997, 1999; Grandori and Furnari 2008), the chapter provides a typology of organizational 'features', a theory of how they are expected to combine inspired by an analogy with chemistry, and a formalized operationalization of the main propositions through an innovative application of Boolean algebra.

4.2   LIMITS OF THE 'DISCRETE STRUCTURAL ALTERNATIVES' VIEW OF ORGANIZATION FORMS

A view of organization forms as discrete clusters of features or attributes has been dominant in the major traditions of study concerned with organization internal structure and external networks. Organization theory has characterized organization forms as, for example, unitary-functional versus divisional forms, mechanistic versus organic forms, adhocratic versus bureaucratic and so on. Organizational features have been typically conceived as devices for partitioning and coordinating activities, including the Weberian features of specialization and distinct responsibility, legal authority and formal procedures, enriched by a variety of 'team-like' and mutual adjustment devices (Thompson 1967; Mintzberg 1979). Organizational economics has enlarged the notion of organization and governance forms to include the division of labour and the modes of coordination between firms, and has envisaged 'discrete structural alternatives' such as markets, hierarchies and hybrids (Williamson 1991). The Weberian features of authority and rule-like governance have been accompanied by price/incentive and exit mechanisms as they are central for defining market governance forms, as well as by the informal coordination mechanisms of teams and culture, employed for defining clan forms (Ouchi 1980).

As to the laws of combination among the above mentioned features, classical organization theory argued that each coordination mechanism is to be found in an organized system, under conditions of effectiveness, conditional on the presence (or the presence at some specified intensity) of some contingency variable, such as uncertainty, strategies, technology, type of interdependence and system size (Lawrence and Larsch 1967; Thompson 1967; Pugh *et al.* 1969; Van de Ven *et al.* 1976). As a corollary, in this approach, features/mechanisms of different kind can cluster as they are cumulatively employed in the same system to govern activities and transactions with different characteristics (for example, more or less uncertain and interdependent activities).

Organizational economics has more explicitly characterized organization forms as bundles of attributes, supposed to be similar to each other within a form, and 'different in kind' across forms: 'alternative modes of governance (markets, hybrids, firms, bureaus) differ in kind – which is to say in discrete structural ways' (Williamson 2004, p. 285). The author maintains that, as a corollary, features/mechanisms of different kinds cannot cluster under conditions of effectiveness (the so-called 'impossibility of selective intervention') (*Ibid.*, p. 287): 'selective intervention breaks down because the internally consistent syndromes of incentive, control, and contract law attributes that define markets and hierarchies differ'. Each internally consistent 'syndrome of attributes' is presumed to be superior in the governance of transactions with different characteristics (for example, more or less uncertain and more or less specific transactions).

There are various limitations in these interpretations of the notion of discrete structural alternatives. The term was originally used by Simon (as Williamson stresses) who pointed out that organizational choices (like all social choices) are not based on judgements focused 'on how variables are equated at margin' but 'focused on qualitative and structural questions, typically, on the choice among a small number of discrete institutional alternatives' (Simon 1978, p. 6). Those choices among qualitatively different structural devices has been interpreted in organizational economics as choices among real, full 'institutions', such as 'the market' and 'the firm'. However, and this is the key difference between the approach taken here and that of organizational economics, qualitative differences, and related choices, can be referred to features or mechanisms themselves, not about packages or clusters of features, that is, organization form. Actually, Simon's own examples of 'structural questions' (*Ibid.*) tend to be referred to single governance mechanisms or practices. In his words: 'Not "how much flood insurance will a man buy" but "what are the structural conditions that make buying insurance rational or attractive?" Not "at what levels will wages be fixed" but when will work be performed under an employment contract rather than a sale contract?' Nothing is really said on how these qualitatively different structural elements may or may not combine into more complex, multi-feature, organization forms. Hence, the proposition that qualitatively different elements cannot cluster together is not really a corollary of Simon's thesis. Nor does that proposition seem to have a clear empirical basis: quite the contrary, organizational solutions that combine devices as different in kind as incentives, communities, rules and authority seem to be more the rule than the exception in successful modern economic organization.

Finally, what constitutes similarity and difference 'in kind' has not been clearly defined. While it is clear that a qualitative comparative analysis is different from a quantitative marginal analysis (Simon's concern), it is not clear when a structural element is 'different in kind' from another element (Williamson's concern).

- In the organization theory tradition, the clustering of features is considered as a result of one-to-one correspondences between each feature and a context. There has been little modelling, and especially theoretical modelling, of the interaction effects of the application of various organizational mechanisms, that is, whether the employment

     of, say, programmes, at some intensity, interacts positively or nega-
     tively with, say, the use of teamwork, and at which intensity level.
- In both organization theory and organizational economics it is
  supposed that there is 'one best way of organizing under any given
  circumstance' (defined in terms of the independent contextual variables), that is, possible equifinalities among forms are neglected.

The two last limitations have been to some extent overcome by more
recent configurational views of discrete structural alternatives – the
'configurational' approach in organization studies and the 'complementarity-based' approach in organizational economics – especially because they
have considered the interaction effects among features.

The configurational approach has defined an organization form as 'Any
multidimensional constellation of conceptually distinct characteristics that
commonly occur together' (Meyer *et al*. 1993), as 'tightly interdependent
and mutually supportive elements' assuming that 'what is crucial is that a
relatively small number of these configurations or types encompass a large
fraction of the population of organizations' (Miller and Friesen 1984, p. 1).
Research in this perspective has looked at the actual, observed combinations among wide arrays of organizational devices (actually devices of all
sorts: from formal rules and policies in budgetary processes or in personnel management, to task forces and committees, to environmental scanning
procedures, to central staff units, to the use of equity and so on) and correlated these combinations with indicators of performance. Typically,
configurational approaches posited 'higher effectiveness for organizations
that resemble one of the ideal types defined in the theory. The increased
effectiveness is attributed to the internal consistency among the patterns of
relevant contextual, structural and strategic factors' (Doty *et al*., 1993,
p. 1196).

The complementarity-based approach in organizational economics has
been pointing in a similar direction. Organizational attributes are defined
as 'complementary' if doing (more of) any one of them increases the
returns to doing (more of) the others (Milgrom and Roberts 1995).
Organizational 'features' or 'attributes' have been conceived as 'practices'
of any sort: in empirical studies large sets of practices have been considered, such as teamwork and incentive pay, flexible job assignment and
knowledge management (Laursen and Mahnke 2001; Ichniowski *et al*.
1997); or process and project organization, horizontal integration, delayering, outsourcing and alliances (Whittington *et al*. 1999); and the observed
combinations among them have been correlated with performance.

These approaches have addressed some of the problems of the earlier
notion of organizational and governance form as discrete structural alter-

natives, but have opened up new problems as well. Most notably, on the positive side, interactions among organizational attributes are considered and are at centre stage. Second, the notion of complementarity is wider than that of consistency by 'similarity in kind', as complementarities can also stem, in principle, from differences among the clustering features. Third, equifinality is admitted, that is, the possibility that more than one configuration is effective under any given circumstance (Gresov and Drazin 1997). However, the following problems remain or have emerged (Grandori and Furnari 2008):

- The lists of features or practices considered have been very extensive and different according to the organization problem considered. Field-specific operationalization is certainly fine, but is there any underlying common logic? Content lists are infinite and prediction is impossible if some general properties of elements, predicting the likelihood of different types of links or combinations, are not formulated.
- Combinative laws have been rather post hoc: whatever elements are observed to be combined in practice and correlated to performance are said to be 'complementary' (that is, any combination of elements found under positive performance is defined as an 'internally consistent' configuration); hence the explanatory law is inferred from the very pattern it should explain. No theory of combination is provided that would make it possible to predict and explain effective combinations, let alone to design new ones.
- Configurational researchers have been using correlational methods that obscure the possible equifinality and non-linear relationship among organizational attributes. In other terms, the methods applied can be deemed not well suited to support configurational enquiry (Fiss 2007).
- Forms are defined using each and all the features that appear in the initial list of elements. This does not allow to 'polish the list', to detect which 'features' are more or less relevant in affecting performance outcomes, which differences make a difference.

4.3 ORGANIZATION FORMS AS CHEMICAL FORMULAS

On the basis of the above discussion, it can be concluded that the two basic ingredients for defining organization forms as 'clusters of features' – that is, a general notion of organizational 'features' or components; and general laws of combinations among them – have not been satisfactorily defined thus far. They deserve further and different attacks.

The approach illustrated here does represent a rather different attack to those problems. It is different because it shifts the unit of analysis from the 'attributes' of a whole entity to its constitutive 'elements'. Differences and similarities may become much clearer if analysed at the level of the elementary building blocks of organization, rather than as 'attributes' of an entity or organism. It is the difference that passes between classic zoology (observing and classifying animals into different species because they have different 'attributes' (height and weight, blood temperature, hair or skin, legs or wings) or evolutionary biology (how these attributes have been selected over history) and chemistry or genetics; specifying the basic elements of which all matter is composed and how they combine to generate different organic and inorganic forms of life). The present contribution starts from what may constitute a basic analysis of the latter type, namely, a 'chemistry of organization'.

4.3.1   A Table of Organizational Elements

Some basic qualitative distinctions among features can be defined by using the classical, stylized and generally agreed upon characterization of an organization form as a set of modes of 'division' and of 'connection' among parts of a system (Mintzberg 1979; Marturana and Varela 1980). These 'modes' can be said to be qualitatively different if:

- The system is partitioned into units or is undifferentiated.
- Units are connected through partner-specific communication (either directly or through brokering hubs), or through impersonal, generally available information (such as prices or rules and norms).
- Decisions are taken in an ad hoc way or in a programmed, rule-guided way.
- Decision rights are evenly or unevenly distributed among units (to all of them in a full democracy or, at the other extreme, to one party only in a fully centralized system).

These fundamental properties can be used to define classes of organizational elements (analogous to a 'Table of elements' in natural chemistry) that can be said to be different in kind as the nature of the nodes and links is different (analogously, we believe, to the grouping of natural elements into gases, metals and non-metals according to their atomic structure).

Four general classes of elements, in economic organization, can be defined as different in kind according to the above general properties (Fiske

1992; Miller 1992; Grandori 1999),[2] and are adopted as a starting 'table of elements' for a 'chemistry of organization' (Grandori and Furnari 2008):

- 'Market' elements, whereby differentiated parts of a system are connected by value-based exchange devices (such as incentives, prices and exit); a converse of non-value-based 'associational' devices (such as voice and loyalty).
- 'Bureaucratic' elements (including all kinds of depersonalized rules and planned differentiation among units); a converse of elements of 'informality'.
- 'Democratic' elements, devices through which each part's preference are 'represented' (for example, through vote, voice rights or residual decision rights); a converse of elements of 'centralization'.
- 'Communitarian elements', aligning knowledge and preference through identity and community building, and knowledge sharing; a converse of elements of 'differentiation'.

Table 4.1 (Grandori and Furnari 2008) shows the four fundamental types of organizational elements, the single elements identifiable within each of the four types and a set of contemporary relevant organizational practices predominantly containing each type of element, along with the references to the studies that have discussed the use of these elements. This table is not exhaustive, but not even the Table of elements in natural chemistry was so (many new elements have been identified since its formulation). The important step is to specify elements in terms of general structure and properties – so that new elements can be discovered and so that the composition of any 'dirty' and noisy, more or less complex, observable practice (for example, 'MBO', to quote one that typically includes multiple elements) can be understood. A fortiori, the 'description' of a whole organization and governance 'form' would no longer be expressed as an array of features and practices, but as a compact chemical 'formula', specifying its 'composition' in terms of elements of community, democracy, bureaucracy and market (see examples that follow). This language is general enough to describe the organization and governance forms of systems of economic action at various levels: from the micro-system of work to entire firms, to the organization of industries and networks.

4.3.2 Doses of an Element

In addition to classes of elements, 'states' or 'values' or 'numbers' of elements should be defined in order to formulate meaningful combinatory laws. How can one say that a particular element, for example, 'all to all

Table 4.1 Organizational elements and practices

Types of organizational elements	Single elements	Practices predominantly embodying the element	References
Market-like elements	Prices and incentives	• Pay for performance (individual) • Pay for performance (team and firm-based)	Von Hayek 1945 Hirschman 1970 Williamson 1975, 1991
	Exit	• Outsourcing • Internal labor mobility	Zenger and Hesterly 1997
Bureaucratic elements	Formal rules	• Formal procedures and programmes • Articulation of formal structure (no authority implied)	Gouldner 1954 Blau and Scott 1962 Pugh *et al.* 1969
	Hierarchy		
Communitarian elements	Knowledge sharing	• Knowledge sharing techniques • Project-based self-organization • Teaming	Hofstede 1980 Ouchi 1980
	Preference sharing (objectives alignment)	• Community building practices • Competence- and/or preference based job design-	Kogut and Zander 1996
Democratic elements	Weighting of organizational members preferences	• Empowerment • Responsibility centers	Gouldner 1954 Lammers and Széll 1989 Blair 1995
	Diffusion of decision rights	• Diffusion of decision and reward rights to units	Harrison and Freeman 2004

direct mutual adjustment' or 'teaming', can or cannot combine with others? What is needed are doses of the element, for example, low versus high doses of teaming, as well as some indication of the doses of other elements it can be combined with for generating different substances. In other words, an analogue of the number of atoms of an element entering a chemical formula is required. Through the analogy, it also clearly appears that complementarities can arise among elements employed at any dose. Low values are as interesting as high values. Indeed, there is nothing interesting or valuable in employing 'more of an element'.

In other terms, refining and generalizing Milgrom and Roberts's (1995) notion, rather than definining complementarity only in reference to marginal increases in the application of elements ('more of' X), we define complementarity as referred to any variation in the intensity of application of an element. It may well be that 'more of X' is complementary with 'less of Y' or with an intermediate dose of Y. Hence, we will analyse complementarity among elements in a state, or at a dose: *two elements are complementary, in certain doses, if the returns of applying them in these doses are higher than in other combinations of doses.*

Which levels of an element may be considered low, medium or high depends on the type of system analysed and the context – even the 'normal' level of iron in blood may vary across climates, races and ages. Hence, in our organizational chemistry it seems sensible to define these levels in empirical and relative terms, rather than in absolute terms. Here, whatever the sample of systems considered, we have so far defined 'high' and 'low' in reference to some average or normal value (Grandori and Furnari 2008).

4.3.3 Types of Complementarities and Combinatory Laws

Two goods are complementary if the demand for one increases the demand for the other, because the value of their joint use is higher than the value of their disjoint use (for example, pasta and tomatoes or shoes and bag of the same style). In fact, Milgrom and Roberts's (1995) seminal contribution defines complementarity in an unbounded set as $V(x',x'') > V(x') + V(x'')$, where x' and x'' are any two organizational devices.

We accept this definition, but a further question needs to be answered before a complementarity based explanation of organization forms can be given: what is the origin of the surplus value of the 'joint application' of two organizational devices, that is, where does complementarity come from? In addition, when, precisely, can an application of organizational devices be said to be 'joint'?

Answering these questions leads to a distinction among different possible sources of complementarity. Looking at the gastronomy and fashion examples mentioned above, one may notice that complementarity stems from different sources in the two cases. A pair of shoes and a bag of the same style are complementary because they share similar features but they deploy these features in different parts of a system. Pasta and tomato sauce, on the other hand, have different attributes and their contributions to a good dish are inseparable (that is, the quality of the dish is basically due to interaction effects). Using the notion of 'difference in kind' among organizational elements developed above, it is possible to distinguish two types of organizational complementarities according to whether the elements applied together are different or similar. In addition, though, it should be clarified what 'applied together' means. As the above examples highlight, here too there are at least two ways: the application is to the same system but in different parts, or it is to the very same part (the same activity, transaction, resource and so on). Using the phrase 'application domain' to designate the 'part' of a system to which an element is applied, we have: (a) 'symbiotic' complementarity if surplus value is generated by different elements applied to the same application domain; (b) 'pooled' complementarity if surplus value is generated by similar elements applied to different application domains.

Both types of complementarity involve interaction effects (by definition of complementarity), in the sense that the value of the (symbiotic or pooled) sum is greater than the sum of the values of the parts. The case of symbiotic complementarity is obvious. A puzzle could be a good example of pooled interaction: puzzle pieces are all similar, the value of any single piece alone is almost zero, only the pooling of all parts has a positive value (see an image). As examples of pooled complementarity among organizational practices, one may cite the use of incentives in line and staff units, or the involvement in community building of all units and not merely of some units. Examples of symbiotic complementarities among organizational practices are found when, say, pay for performance, teamwork and formal standardized procedures of performance evaluation are applied to the same people or units.

It will be shown that the distinction is useful as these two types of complementarity have different implications for the laws of combination of organizational elements. In addition, the double distinction between similarity-/difference-based complementarity, and of same/different application domain, implies that there are another two possible combinations that do not generate complementarity: (c) elements that are similar in kind and have the same application domain are substitutes, that is, their combinations are redundant; (d) elements that are dissimilar and have different application domains are independent (neither substitutable nor complementary).

The four types of relationships among two generic types of organizational elements are summarized in Table 4.2.

Table 4.2   Types of relationships among organizational elements

		Application domain (transaction, activity, resource) to which the two generic elements are applied	
		Same domain	Different domain
Difference in kind between two generic types	Same kind	Substituability	Pooled complementarity
of organizational elements	Different kind	Symbiotic complementarity	Independence (neither substitutability nor complementarity)

4.3.4   Evaluation Functions and Multifunctionality

In order to be substantively more precise in specifying which kind of differences may generate complementarity, an evaluation function must be defined. What is a 'good outcome' with respect to which a combination of elements may be evaluated? We propose to use distinct functions rather than one overall performance function (as it has been typically been done in the assessment of discrete structural alternatives), for several reasons:

- The relationship between the overall performance of a system and its organizational configuration is too 'noisy'.
- The performance of economic systems is usually measured financially, which is a useful yardstick for some purposes, but it is not a good indicator of the utility or value generated by its organization, as no monetary single indicator is a good indicator of the value of complex goods in general, in particular where multiple beneficiaries and complex trade-offs are involved (Sen 1999). Hence, it is preferable to use a portfolio of functions, as is typically done in design theory in other fields, such as architecture (Boland and Collopy 2004; March 1976).
- Operationalizing results into qualitatively different consequences allows detection of counter-intuitive combinations between configurations and consequences. For example, it is entirely conceivable to have highly communitarian, identity based combinations generating brilliant economic results (and perhaps too oppressive over-socialization), and highly market-like, incentive driven systems, generating very poor economic results (but perhaps an exciting sports-like social atmosphere).

Among the qualitatively different, relevant parameters against which an organizational combination may be evaluated, at least three seem to be important beyond any reasonable doubt: efficiency, effectiveness and equity (Grandori 1999). Then, in the laws presented below, all these three types of outcomes will be considered. It is worth pointing out that these outcomes received also an initial test in the empirical study (Grandori and Furnari 2008) mentioned below (the effectiveness parameter used in the study has been innovation).

Here it can be further noticed that elements may be more or less specialized with respect to particular outcomes. Some elements are more 'generalist' and multifunctional, while others are more 'specialist' and mono-functional. Possible consequences of the different degree of multi-functionality of elements for combinatory laws are:

- More generalist elements should more frequently be useful components in organizational formulas, that is, in formulas that are effective at producing different types of results, while specialized elements should be useful in the production of only one type of result.
- More generalist elements may be more 'stable', that is, less in need of combination with other elements, and be substitutable by other generalist elements or by a combination of many specialist elements. By contrast, specialist elements should be more 'unstable', that is, they need complements in order to deliver good outcomes, and more precisely they need complements of a different kind.

4.3.5 Expressing Organizational Formulas through Boolean Comparative Analysis

In an earlier paper (Grandori and Furnari 2008), we used Boolean Comparative Analysis (Ragin 1987, 2000) to formalize organization forms as chemical formulas and test a set of basic combinatory laws. Below, we briefly introduce the language of Boolean Comparative Analysis (BCA hereafter), illustrating only the technical features of this methodology that are strictly necessary to understand the subsequent formalization of the combinatory laws.[3]

Let us hypothesize that the adoption of one market-like element (say, monetary incentives) will be per se sufficient to produce a level of firm efficiency above the industry average. Labelling the causal condition 'presence of one dose of market' as M_1 and the outcome 'presence of efficiency above the average' as $E_{>A}$, this hypothesis can be translated into the following Boolean algebra statement:

$$M_1 \rightarrow E_{>A}$$

where, according to standard Boolean algebra notation, $\rightarrow$ denotes the logical implication operator and capital letters indicate the presence of a causal condition.[4]

The typical objective of BCA is to determine the simultaneous presence and absence of causal conditions under which a certain outcome is present. To this end, cases are formalized as combinations of elements through the use of Boolean algebra operators 'AND' ('*') and 'OR' ('+'). These operators allow to specify the relations between more than one causal condition: suppose, for example, that the adoption of highly powered incentives is not sufficient per se to foster firm efficiency without the application of one bureaucratic element (say, an adequate monitoring system). This hypothesis can be formalized into the following Boolean statement:

$$M_1{}^* B_1 \rightarrow E_{>A}$$

where '*' denotes the logical Boolean operator 'AND'. The above statement reads as 'M_1 AND B_1 imply $E_{>A}$': the occurrence of outcome $E_{>A}$ requires the presence of one element of both B and M, that is, B and M in one dose are strictly complementary in the achievement of that outcome. The Boolean operator 'AND' therefore represents relations of complementarity.

Let us now suppose that there are two other complementary elements of a different type that can also produce the same outcome $E_{>A}$: for example C_1 and D_1, representing, respectively, a community-like element (say, teamwork) and an element of democratic governance (say, the distribution of representation rights). The Boolean expression will be:

$$M_1{}^* B_1 + C_1{}^* D_1 \rightarrow E_{>A}$$

where '+' denotes the logical operator 'OR'. The above statement could be read as 'M_1 AND B_1 OR C_1 AND D_1 imply above average E': if any of the two combinations is present, the outcome will occur. Hence the Boolean operator 'OR' represents relations of substitutability (equifinality). Using these operators, BCA employs logical minimization algorithms and probabilistic tests in order to identify the *necessary* and *sufficient* combinations of elements to achieve given outcomes (Ragin 1987, 2000).

In using Boolean algebra language to formalize the hypothesized combinatory laws presented below, we generalize the notations used in the example above. Specifically, we agree to indicate types of elements in capital letters (M = market-like; B = bureaucratic; C = communitarian; D = democratic) and the number of doses (or atoms) for each type of element with a small sub-script at the bottom of the letters, as in chemical formulas. Thus, the generic organizational formula can be written in the form $M_m B_b C_c D_d$.

The empirical study presented in Grandori and Furnari (2008) proposes a way of operationalizing and measuring the notion of 'one dose' or 'one atom' of an element. In that study a dose of an element is measured as the number of practices (see Table 4.1) employed beyond the average level. In some of the laws, a notion of 'maximum' level of application is also used. One way to operationalize this general notion of maximum is to consider the maximum average intensity of application across all the four elements in systems of a certain type in a certain context, as is done in the above men-tioned empirical study (where this value is found to be 4).

The three organizational outcomes considered here will be indicated with capital letters (E = efficiency; I = innovation; F = fairness). The sub-script '$_{>A}$' at the bottom of these letters indicates that the specific organi-zational outcome is achieved at a 'high level', operationalized as above average (of course, other thresholds may be used for operationalizing 'high' performance).

4.3.6 Combination Laws

Combination laws can be expressed as conditions that organizational for-mulas should respect. The first four laws (conditions I to IV) have been for-mulated and received an empirical test in Grandori and Furnari (2008); they are expressed in a more formalized manner here (this is useful for developing the more complex laws of structural heterogeneity presented here). The character of the first four conditions is that of universal laws to which any high performing organizational formula should obey (this obvi-ously does not mean that only one high performing formula exists). The laws of structural heterogeneity (conditions V to XII) are a distinctive con-tribution of the present chapter (only the initial conditions V and VI were conjectured in our former study).

It is extremely likely that in any system, even very simple ones, there are activities of different kinds, and that elements of different kinds are supe-rior in order to regulate these activities (Grandori and Soda 2006). In addi-tion, it is extremely likely that any system, even a small system, that tries to coordinate everything using only one kind of element, no matter which (say plans or incentives) is not viable (Stark 2007). Finally, it is conjectured that, at least at low doses, the four elements entail positive symbiotic comple-mentarities (Grandori and Furnari 2008).

Hence: *The presence of (at least one dose of) elements of different kind is a necessary condition for an organizational formula achieving high perfor-*

mance of any sort ('Law of organizational core variety'). Thus, a testable, formalized proposition is the following:

Condition I

$$M_{\geq 1} * B_{\geq 1} * C_{\geq 1} * D_{\geq 1} \rightarrow E_{>A}$$
$$M_{\geq 1} * B_{\geq 1} * C_{\geq 1} * D_{\geq 1} \rightarrow I_{>A}$$
$$M_{\geq 1} * B_{\geq 1} * C_{\geq 1} * D_{\geq 1} \rightarrow F_{>A}$$

Our discussion of the effects of similarity among mechanisms leads to the observation that mechanisms which are similar in kind are complementary above all if they are used in different parts of the system, that is, they can bring about pooled complementarity, not symbiotic complementarity. If similar elements are employed at increasing doses in the same domain, marginal benefits should decrease.

Hence: *There are decreasing marginal returns, and, beyond some point, negative returns, to increases in the intensity of the same kind of element in the same application domain ('Law of decreasing marginal returns to organizational homogeneity').*

In other words, a necessary condition for high performance is that each and every element is not applied over and above a certain value that we thus define as 'maximum'. Hence, a sufficient condition for low performance is the following:

Condition II

$$X_{\geq max} \rightarrow Y_{<A}$$

where X indicates a generic type of element (M, B, C, D) and Y a generic type of outcome (E, I, F).

People's energy, cognitive capacity and behavioural flexibility is limited; hence, individuals are unlikely to be able to attend and respond simultaneously to: strong incentives; strong demands for identification; intense requirements of conformity to rules and the use of procedures; the right and duty to exert one's best judgement; the need to be, at one and the same time, organizational citizens who are highly entrepreneurial, highly solidaristic, highly compliant, actively and critically participating to the life of the organization. In addition, practices are costly, and choice among alternative investments in different practices may become an issue as the total amount of investment increases.

Hence: *There are decreasing marginal returns, and, beyond some point, negative returns, to increases in the intensity of all kinds of elements in the same application domain ('Law of decreasing marginal returns to organizational variety').*

Formalized testable propositions deriving from the law are those expressed by the following condition:

Condition III

$$M_{\geq max} * B_{\geq max} * C_{\geq max} * D_{\geq max} \rightarrow E_{<A}$$
$$M_{\geq max} * B_{\geq max} * C_{\geq max} * D_{\geq max} \rightarrow I_{<A}$$
$$M_{\geq max} * B_{\geq max} * C_{\geq max} * D_{\geq max} \rightarrow F_{<A}$$

If only this condition III were valid (the simultaneous application of elements in high doses predicts low performance) but not condition II (the application of a single element in a high dose predicts low performance), it would mean that there are negative complementarities, beyond some level, among elements that differ in kind, and not among elements that are similar in kind.

Through an empirical investigation on the combinatory laws expressed above in a sample of 75 large Italian firms, Grandori and Furnari (2008) found strong evidence supporting the hypothesized relationships among similar/different organizational elements: 89 per cent of highly efficient firms and 93 per cent of highly innovative firms respect the combinatory rule 'all different types of organizational elements should be adopted in the firm, with values comprised between a lower and an upper bound' (operationalized as 1 and 3 in the study). In other words, any high performing formula is internally varied, at least at a base level, and the law of decreasing marginal returns applies to each single type of element: that is, the prime origin of the upper bounds are decreasing or negative returns to one-sidedness and homogeneity, not the negative interactions among elements of different kinds. Testing for the necessity and sufficiency of these findings, the authors found respect of the laws to be a statistically significant, necessary and sufficient condition for high efficiency and a significant necessary condition for high innovation.[5]

4.3.7   Introducing Types of Outcomes

In Grandori and Furnari (2008) we also advanced the hypothesis that *the optimal intensity of each element in an organizational formula (within the lower and upper bounds specified by the former laws) is contingent on the type of performance outcome generated ('Law of structural heterogeneity').*

As to efficiency and innovation, we hypothesized that bureaucratic elements are more specialized in the achievement of internal efficiency of a system, while market, communitarian and democratic elements are more specialized in the achievement of innovation. The hypothesis tested was that highly efficient organizational formulas are enriched in bureaucracy, while highly innovative organizational formulas are enriched in one or

more of the other elements. Hence, constraining all the doses of elements (m, b, c, d) to be > 1 due to the first law of organizational core variety:
Condition IV

$$B_b * M_m * C_c * D_d \rightarrow E_{>A} \text{ if } b > m * c * d$$

Condition V

$$B_b * M_m * C_c * D_d \rightarrow I_{>A} \text{ if } m + c + d > b$$

Fairness outcomes were not considered in our earlier study. Here, we hypothesize that they should be generated by *formulas enriched both in bureaucracy and communitarian or democratic elements*, as the former elements are specialized in generating transparency and depersonalization, while the latter in reducing or resolving conflict. Hence:
Condition VI

$$B_b * M_m * C_c * D_d \rightarrow F_{>A} \text{ if } b * (c + d) > m$$

At this juncture, it should be noticed that there are many formulas that satisfy these conditions, that is, formulas that are equifinal in generating high innovation or high efficiency or high fairness. Here, we are going to further refine the laws of structural heterogeneity by introducing further discriminating contingencies (non-organizational variables in varying states).

4.3.8 Introducing Contingencies

The portfolio of equifinal formulas can be restricted if further conditions are added. They can be represented by some contingencies to be met by the formulas. One parsimonious way of doing so is to summarize those contingencies in terms of the nature of tasks and interdependencies to be governed (as done in all research traditions we are drawing on). In particular, the different elements of organizing are known to be specialized to the level of uncertainty of tasks and inter-task relations.

Bureaucratic elements are good in generating static efficiency in stable tasks, hence the proposition that formulas enriched in bureaucracy generate high efficiency contained in our former study is likely to be valid only for static efficiency. A combination of bureaucratic mechanisms with market elements (especially through outsourcing and externalization of activities) is known to be good in generating dynamic efficiency in variable tasks (Mariotti and Cainarca 1986).

Hence, denoting uncertainty as U, qualifying it as either low ($_L$) or high

$(_H)$ and constraining all the doses of elements (m, b, c, d) to be > 1 due to the first law of organizational core variety, the law of structural heterogeneity for static and dynamic efficiency can be expressed as follows:

Condition VII

$$U_L * B_b * M_m * C_c * D_d \rightarrow E_{>A} \text{ if } b > m * c * d$$

Condition VIII

$$U_H * B_b * M_m * C_c * D_d \rightarrow E_{>A} \text{ if } m * b > c * d$$

If the effective organization of innovation is considered, a distinction can also be made between innovation in known tasks and techniques versus innovation in settings where tasks and techniques have to be discovered altogether. Taking into account both classical works (Burns and Stalker 1961) and recent empirical works shedding some light on the 'routinization of innovation' and innovation in mature industries (Kilduff and Sawyer 2003; Brusoni 2005), it can be hypothesized that in mature, known settings the organization of innovation can be more modular, while in highly dynamic and innovative settings it needs to be more integrated. Hence, organizational formulas for *innovation in less uncertain action fields could be richer in market and/or bureaucratic elements (both infuse modularity into a system), while in more uncertain action fields organizational formulas should be richer in community and/or democracy (both infuse integration).*

Condition IX

$$U_L * B_b * M_m * C_c * D_d \rightarrow I_{>A} \text{ if } (m + b) > c * d + (m * b) > c * d$$

Condition X

$$U_H * B_b * M_m * C_c * D_d \rightarrow I_{>A} \text{ if } (c + d) > m * b$$

A new prediction generated by the conditions so far specified is that the set of formulas for high innovation under low uncertainty has an intersection with the set of formulas for high efficiency under high uncertainty (the intersection, that is, the multifunctional formula, being the market and bureaucracy enriched formulas).

Fairness in stable and known activities is also likely to be best achieved through different mechanisms than in uncertain conditions. While transparency and equal opportunities and treatment may generally associate fairness outcomes with some elements of bureaucracy, the level of uncertainty may discriminate between community and democracy as complements: communitarian elements are possibly sufficient in stable setting, while democratic mechanisms and organizational justice provisions should be more robust under uncertain conditions (Miller 1992; Grandori forthcoming). Hence, *organizational formulas for fairness can be hypothesized to be richer in bureaucracy and community in stable settings, and richer in bureaucracy and democracy in dynamic and uncertain settings.*

Condition XI

$$U_L * B_b * M_m * C_c * D_d \rightarrow F_{>A} \text{ if } c * b > m * d$$

Condition XII

$$U_H * B_b * M_m * C_c * D_d \rightarrow F_{>A} \text{ if } d * b > m * c$$

The organizational formulas generated by the above set of conditions are summarized in Table 4.3, which shows all the equifinal formulas written in extended form, assuming that the maximum number of each element is 4 (as found in our recent empirical study in the Italian context). Hence, Table 4.3 gives an immediate, substantive picture of the type and number of contingent formulas resulting from the analysis (equifinal formulas are in bold and underlined in the same way).

4.4   CONCLUSIONS

This work has revisited and revitalized the notion of organization forms as clusters of attributes, providing a systematic classification of attributes as 'organizational elements' – in analogy with natural elements in chemistry – and outlined a series of laws of combinations on how elements can combine into organizational formulas. Some notable features of the conjectured (and partially tested) combination laws are worth noticing:

- They include both universal and contingency laws (that is, specify which 'features' are generally necessary in order to have a high performing organization and which are necessary only under particular circumstances).
- They admit equifinality and predict structural heterogeneity (for example, it is argued that more than one 'cluster of features' can achieve high performance under the same circumstances, and it is specified which ones).

Among the substantive conclusions, it is worthwhile to highlight that:

Table 4.3   Equifinal organizational formulas (by function and contingency)

	EFFICIENCY	INNOVATION	FAIRNESS
LOW UNCERTAINTY	*Formulas enriched in B* $M_1*B_2*C_1*D_1 + M_1*B_3*C_1*D_1 +$ $M_2*B_3*C_2*D_2 + M_1*B_3*C_2*D_2 +$ $\mathbf{M_1*B_3*C_2*D_1} + M_2*B_3*C_1*D_1 +$ $M_2*B_3*C_1*D_2 + \mathbf{M_1*B_3*C_1*D_2} +$ $\rightarrow E_{>A}$	*Formulas enriched in B and M* $M_2*B_2*C_1*D_1 + M_3*B_3*C_1*D_1 +$ $M_3*B_3*C_2*D_2 + M_3*B_3*C_1*D_2 +$ $M_3*B_3*C_2*D_1 + M_3*B_2*C_1*D_1 +$ $\mathbf{M_2*B_3*C_1*D_1}$ $\rightarrow I_{>A}$	*Formulas enriched in B and C* $M_1*B_2*C_2*D_1 + M_1*B_3*C_3*D_1 +$ $M_2*B_3*C_3*D_2 + M_1*B_3*C_3*D_2 +$ $M_2*B_3*C_3*D_1 + \mathbf{M_1*B_3*C_2*D_1} +$ $M_1*B_2*C_3*D_1$ $\rightarrow F_{>A}$
HIGH UNCERTAINTY	*Formulas enriched in B and M* $M_2*B_2*C_1*D_1 + M_3*B_3*C_1*D_1 +$ $M_3*B_3*C_2*D_2 + M_3*B_3*C_1*D_2 +$ $M_3*B_3*C_2*D_1 + M_3*B_2*C_1*D_1 +$ $\mathbf{M_2*B_3*C_1*D_1}$ $\rightarrow E_{>A}$	*Formulas enriched in C or D* $M_1*B_1*C_1*D_2 + M_1*B_1*C_1*D_3 +$ $M_2*B_1*C_1*D_3 + M_2*B_2*C_1*D_3 +$ $M_2*B_2*C_2*D_3 + M_2*B_1*C_2*D_3 +$ $M_1*B_2*C_2*D_3 + \mathbf{M_1*B_2*C_1*D_3}$ $M_1*B_1*C_3*D_1 + M_1*B_1*C_3*D_1 +$ $M_2*B_1*C_3*D_1 + M_2*B_2*C_3*D_1 +$ $M_2*B_2*C_3*D_2 + M_2*B_1*C_3*D_2 +$ $M_1*B_2*C_3*D_2 + M_1*B_2*C_3*D_1$ $\rightarrow I_{>A}$	*Formulas enriched in B and D* $M_1*B_2*C_1*D_2 + M_1*B_3*C_1*D_3 +$ $M_2*B_3*C_2*D_3 + M_1*B_3*C_2*D_3 +$ $M_2*B_3*C_1*D_3 + \mathbf{M_1*B_3*C_1*D_2} +$ $\mathbf{M_1*B_2*C_1*D_3}$ $\rightarrow F_{>A}$

- Bureaucratic elements are highly multifunctional especially under low uncertainty.
- Democratic elements are multifunctional under high uncertainty, especially in the achievement of innovation and fairness.
- Market elements are more specialized elements, especially with regard to innovation and uncertainty.
- In stable settings either efficiency and innovation or fairness and efficiency can be achieved with the same formula (enriched in bureaucracy and either market or community).
- There is no formula in common between efficiency and innovation in dynamic settings or between fairness and innovation in stable settings. This result indicates an area of trade-off for designers, giving an idea of the outcomes that are more difficult to achieve simultaneously in the two settings.
- There are many ways of being innovative in highly uncertain settings (the set of equifunctional formulas is particularly wide). This is an interesting result, which provides a solution for a phenomenon that is currently considered a 'puzzle': how is it possible, and is it 'right' or 'wrong', that diverse organizational arrangements, in particular highly communitarian and highly market-rich arrangements, are observable in the governance of knowledge-intensive activities (Foss 2007)?

The results also have implications for organization redesign and change. Some changes, in terms of meeting different contingencies or of achieving different mixes of outcomes, require changes to more elements, while others may imply changing just one element. For instance, only one additional D element is required in order to find several formulas able to achieve all three objective functions in uncertain settings. This is a significant refinement with respect to the usual application of the notion of complementarity to organizational change. We suggest that the idea that the wider the set of practices that are changed together, the better (due to the presence of interactions among practices) is too rough and resource wasting, and derives from not knowing where complementarities lie. The organizational chemistry framework illustrated here should help in making hypotheses on what elements are complementary, in what doses and under what circumstances; hence, in enhancing our capacity of selective intervention and ad hoc organization design, including a diagnosis of what elements may be kept invariant while others change.

NOTES

1. Recent and relevant contributions in organizational sociology concerned with organiza-
    tion forms, such as the just quoted article by Polos *et al.* or neo-institutionalism, are not
    considered. The reason is that in those approaches the definition of organizational fea-
    tures and the patterns of their clustering are seen as conforming to the expectations of ref-
    erence groups and of the dispensers of legitimacy. Hence those approaches do not offer
    inputs for specifying elements and combinatory laws in a micro-analytic and design-
    oriented way.
2. These contributions are the only ones to our knowledge that conceive these types of
    elements as classes of mechanisms to be combined in order to explain or construct any
    organizational system, rather than as full institutions, that is, as 'discrete structural
    alternatives' themselves, for example, 'the market', 'the firm' and so on (as they are in
    apparently similar typologies, such as those by Williamson, Lindblom or Etzioni).
    Fiske's 'fundamental elements of sociality' are 'market pricing', 'authority ranking',
    'equality matching' and 'communal sharing'; Grandori and Miller contribute to identi-
    fying single elements within each class, such as pricing, exit, voting, teaming, negotia-
    tion, authority and agency, rules and procedures, norms and culture and property
    rights.
3. The concepts and procedures employed in BCA are illustrated in greater detail in Ragin
    (1987, 2000) and on the website www.fsqca.com. Two methodological papers (Fiss 2007,
    Furnari 2007) address specifically the motivations underlying the use of BCA in organi-
    zation design studies.
4. In standard BCA notations, lower case letters indicate the absence of a causal condition.
    Lower case notations will not be used in this chapter for the sake of simplicity.
5. No statistically significant sufficient condition was found for innovation. This is an inter-
    esting asymmetry in the predictability of the outcomes of organizational formulas: as
    innovation is uncertain by definition, organization can set necessary conditions but not
    guarantee the outcome.

REFERENCES

Blair, M. (1995), *Ownership and control: Rethinking corporate governance for the
    21st Century,* Washington DC: Broolings Institute.
Blau, P.M and B.R. Scott (1962), *Formal organizations: A comparative approach,*
    San Francisco: Chandler.
Boland, R.J. and F. Collopy (2004), *Managing as Designing,* Stanford, CA: Stanford
    University Press.
Brusoni, S. (2005), 'The limits to specialization: problem solving and coordination
    in modular networks', *Organization Studies,* **26** (12), 1885–907.
Burns, T. and G.M. Stalker (1961), *The Management of Innovation,* London,
    Tavistock Publications.
Doty, H.D., W.H. Glick and G.P. Huber (1993), 'Fit, equifinality, and organiza-
    tional effectiveness: a test of two configurational theories', *Academy of
    Management Journal,* **36** (6), 1196–250.
Fiske, A.P. (1992), 'The four elementary forms of sociality: framework for a unified
    theory of social relations', *Psychological Review,* **99,** 689–723.
Fiss, P.C. (2007), 'A set-theoretic approach to organizational configurations',
    Academy of Management Review, **32** (4), 1180–98.
Foss, N.J. (2007), 'The emerging knowledge governance approach: challenges and
    characteristics', *Organization,* **14** (1), 29–52.

Furnari, S. (2007), 'Modeling multidimensional fit through Boolean algebra: new methods for combinative organization design', in Luigi E. Golzio and Tommaso M. Fabbri (eds), *'Relazioni di Lavoro e Forme Organizzative: Nuovi Modelli Progettuali'*, Rome, Italy: Carrocci, pp. 19–38.

Grandori, A. (1997), 'Governance structures, coordination mechanisms and cognitive models', *Journal of Management and Governance*, **1** (1), 29–47.

Grandori, A. (1999), *Organizzazione e Comportamento Economico,* Bologna, Italy: Il Mulino; English edn (2001), *Organization and Economic Behavior,* London: Routledge.

Grandori, A. (forthcoming), 'Poliarchic governance and the growth of knowledge', in Nicolai J. Foss and S. Michailova (eds), *Knowledge Governance*, Oxford, UK: Oxford University Press.

Grandori, A. and G. Soda (2006), 'A relational approach to organization design', *Industry and Innovation*, **13** (2), 151–72.

Grandori, A. and S. Furnari (2008), 'A chemistry of organization: combinatory analysis and design', *Organization Studies,* **29** (2), 315–41.

Gresov, C. and R. Drazin (1997), 'Equifinality: functional equivalence in organization design', *Academy of Management Review,* **22** (2), 403–28.

Gouldner, A.W. (1954), *Patterns of Industrial Bureaucracy*, New York: The Free Press.

Harrison, J.S. and E.R. Freeman (2004), 'Democracy in and around organizations', *Academy of Management Executive,* **18** (3), 49–53.

Hirschman, A.O. (1970), *Exit, Voice and Loyalty: Responses to Decline in Firms, Organizations and States*, Cambridge, MA: Harvard University Press.

Hofstede, G. (1980), *Culture's Consequences: International Differences in Work-Related Values,* London: Sage Publications.

Ichniowski, C., S. Kathryn and G. Prennushi (1997), 'The effects of human resource management practices on productivity: a study of steel finishing lines', *American Economic Review,* **87** (3), 291–313.

Kilduff, M. and S. Sawyer (2003), *Economizing on Bounded Rationality: Networking Through the Machine in Extreme High Reliability Software Production,* Copenhagen: EGOS Colloquium.

Kogut, B. and U. Zander (1996), 'What firms do? Coordination, identity and learning', *Organization Science,* **7** (5), 502–18.

Lammers, C. and G. Széll (1989), *Organizational Democracy: Taking Stock. International Handbook of Participation in Organizations,* vol. I, Oxford, UK: Oxford University Press

Laursen, K. and V. Mahnke (2001), 'Knowledge strategies, firm types and complementarity in human resource practices', *Journal of Management and Governance,* **5** (1), 1–22.

Lawrence, P. and J. Lorsch (1967), *Organization and environment*, Boston: Harvard Business School Press.

Marturana, H.R. and F.J. Varela (1980), *Autopoiesis and Cognition: The Realization of the Living,* London: Springer.

March, L. (ed.) (1976), *The Architecture of Form*, Cambridge, UK: Cambridge University Press.

Mariotti, S. and G. Cainarca (1986), 'The evolution of transaction governance in the textile-clothing industry', *Journal of Economic Behavior and Organization,* **7**, 351–74.

Meyer, A.D., A.S. Tsui and C.R. Hinings (1993), 'Configurational approaches to organizational analysis', *Academy of Management Journal,* **36** (6), 1175–95.

Milgrom, P. and J. Roberts (1995), 'Complementarities and fit: strategy, structure and organizational change in manufacturing', *Journal of Accounting and Economics,* **19**, 179–208.

Miller, G.J. (1992), *Managerial Dilemmas. The Political Economy of Hierarchy,* Cambridge, UK: Cambridge University Press.

Miller, D. and P.H. Friesen (1984), *Organizations: A Quantum View*, Englewood Cliffs, NJ: Prentice Hall.

Mintzberg, H. (1979), *The Structuring of Organizations*, Englewood Cliffs, NJ: Prentice Hall.

Ouchi, W.G. (1980), 'Markets, bureaucracies and clans', *Administrative Science Quarterly,* **25**, 129–41.

Polos L., M.T. Hannan and G.R. Carroll (2002), 'Foundations of a theory of social forms', *Industrial and Corporate Change,* **11** (1), 85–116.

Pugh, D.S., D.J. Hickson, R.C. Hinings and C. Turner (1969) 'An empirical taxonomy of structures of work organizations', *Administrative Science Quarterly,* **14**, 115–26.

Ragin, C.C. (1987), *The Comparative Method: Moving Beyond Qualitative and Quantitative Strategies,* Berkeley, CA: University of California Press.

Ragin, C.C. (2000), *Fuzzy-Set Social Science,* Chicago, IL: University of Chicago Press.

Sen, A. (1999), *Commodities and Capabilities,* Oxford, UK: Oxford University Press.

Simon, H.A. (1978), 'Rationality as process and as product of thought', *American Economic Review,* **68** (2), 1–16.

Stark, D. (2007), 'Entrepreneurship as the exploitation of uncertainty', paper presented at the Workshop on Uncertainty: Economic Action with Partial Knowledge of the World, Center on Organizational Innovation, Columbia Business School, NYC, 7–8 September.

Thompson, J.D. (1967), *Organizations in Action*, New York: McGraw-Hill.

Van de Ven, A.H., A.L. Delbecq and R. Koenig (1976), 'Determinants of coordination modes within organization', *American Sociology Review,* **41**, 322–38.

Von Hayek, F. (1945), 'The use of knowledge in society', *American Economic Review,* **35,** 519–30.

Whittington, R., A. Pettigrew, S. Peck, E. Fenton and M. Conyon (1999), 'Change and complementarities in the new competitive landscape: a European panel study, 1992–1996', *Organization Science,* **10** (5), 583–600.

Williamson, O.E. (1975), *Markets and Hierarchies: Analysis and Antitrust Implications,* New York: The Free Press.

Williamson, O.E. (1991), 'Comparative economic organizations: the analysis of discrete structural alternatives', *Administrative Science Quarterly,* **36**, 269–96.

Williamson, O.E. (2004), 'Herbert Simon and organization theory: lessons for the theory of the firm', in Mie Augier and James G. March (eds), *Models of a Man*, Cambridge, MA: MIT Press, pp. 279–97.

Zenger, T.R. and W.S. Hesterly (1997), 'The disaggregation of corporations: selective intervention, high powered incentives and molecular units', *Organization Science,* **8** (3), 209–22.

5. Oliver Williamson and the logic of hybrid organizations

Claude Ménard[1]

> 'Whereas I was earlier of the view that transactions of the middle kind were very difficult to organize and hence were unstable, [. . .], I am now persuaded that transactions in the middle range are much more common'. (Williamson 1985, p. 83)[2]

5.1 INTRODUCTION

The literature about modes of organization that process transactions out of the usual market relationships but without integrating has expanded very rapidly over the last decade.[3] Although exploratory papers on inter-firm agreements and, more generally, on 'non-standard contracting' were published in the 1980s, the actual take-off in the analysis of these 'intermediate forms' dates from the 1990s. Transaction cost economics has played a leading role in these developments. The publication of *The Economic Institutions of Capitalism* by Williamson in 1985, followed by his paper on 'Comparative economic organization' in 1991 are landmarks that have influenced analysts far beyond economics, reaching managerial sciences, sociology and so on.

However, the exponential growth of publications pertaining to these arrangements has not necessarily clarified the topic. As noted by Oliver and Ebers (1998, p. 549), '. . . [the] increase in the number of studies has contributed to a rather messy situation marked by a cacophony of heterogeneous concepts, theories, and research results'. The vocabulary itself is not stabilized when the literature abounds with such terms as hybrids, clusters, networks, symbiotic arrangements, supply chain systems, administered channels and so on. In this 'cacophony' Williamson represents an exception: he has developed a concept, 'hybrids', that he has rooted in transaction cost economics, thus proposing a coherent approach to a relatively well-delineated topic. At the same time his analysis has considerably evolved, from the general considerations regarding these 'unstable' arrangements of the mid 1970s to the refined analysis of this mode of organization as a class of its own in the 1990s. During this process, a rigorous representation of hybrid organizations has progressively emerged.

This chapter examines this evolution in order to exhibit what I consider some of its main results. Section 2 traces the emergence of the concept of 'hybrid organizations'. Section 3 develops the properties characterizing these arrangements and differentiating them from markets as well as from hierarchies. Section 4 concludes with a glance at some unsolved problems and possible extensions. The underlying thesis of the chapter is that over 20 years of publications Williamson has provided powerful tools for understanding the nature and role of a major 'institutional structure of production' (Coase 1991).

5.2   THE EMERGENCE OF A THEORETICAL ENTITY

A review of the status of 'hybrid organizations' in the three books published by Williamson in 1975, 1985 and 1996 provides a very instructive approximation of the evolution of his conception of these forms. Comparing *The Mechanisms of Governance* to *The Economic Institutions of Capitalism* and to *Markets and Hierarchies* probably overemphasizes the discretionary changes in Williamson's approach, since these books are based on papers spread over years and partially rewritten in order to produce a coherent set. On the other hand, the comparison has its advantages since it brings out the progressive shaping and refinement of the analytical framework developed by the author.[4]

5.2.1   1975

Markets and Hierarchies is unambiguously built around the dichotomy suggested by its title. What motivated Williamson at the time was to provide a convincing explanation for the trade-off between these two polar cases, from which the now famous 'make or buy' problem derives. The book goes even further in explicitly identifying organizations with (integrated) firms, thus relegating alternative arrangements to the background. As stated on page 8: 'I furthermore regard organizational form – by which I mean the hierarchical structure of the firm, the way in which internal economic activities are decomposed into operating parts subject to internal contracts – to be distinctly interesting and warranting separate attention'; and, later (Williamson 1975, p. 109): 'The "relevant" contracts, for the purpose of this book, are those which cluster around these modes', namely, markets and hierarchies. Therefore the book shows no apparent interest in arrangements falling in-between and even considers these forms as unstable and of limited interest. However, a closer examination of some passages exhibits the emergence of questions explored years later.

A major contribution of *Markets and Hierarchies* is the innovative role devolved to contracts in organizing transactions, thus placing the combination of these two concepts, contracts and transactions, at the forefront of economic analysis. Chapter 6, and particularly its first section, on 'interfirm exchange', provides an important building block in that respect, where, in order to qualify his analysis of vertical integration, Williamson emphasizes the incompleteness of contracts and the significance of informal relations and sanctions that accompany business relationships. After a relatively long quotation from Richardson (1972, p. 387), who had insisted on the continuum of arrangements, from commodity markets to clusters, groups and alliances, Williamson concludes: 'I nevertheless urge that focusing on the significant differences between normal sales [that is, markets] and hierarchical relations is useful' . . . and that it is through the exploration of these polar cases that the properties of 'intermediate forms of contracting' or 'ambiguous categories' could be assessed (Williamson 1975, p. 109).

On the one hand, this statement confirms the methodological choice made by the author to focus on polar cases; on the other hand, it acknowledges indirectly the existence of forms not fully captured by these cases. The emphasis in the same section on the positive role of incomplete contracts in the development of inter-firm activities reinforces this opening. Similar indications are found in Chapter 3: by contrasting peer group associations with hierarchies, Chapter 3 suggests the existence of alternative forms for organizing cooperative activities. However, it is Chapter 12, on oligopoly, and particularly its second section on 'Oligopoly regarded as a problem of contracting' (*Ibid.*, p. 238 *seq.*) that in my view provides the most explicit elements which later papers would develop and systematize. In his discussion of the difficulties encountered by oligopolies in their contracting activities, that is, in their quest for bi- or multilateral agreements, Williamson emphasizes three problems that were to increasingly mobilize his attention in the future and which are particularly significant for inter-firm agreements, namely, coordination, gains provided by joint agreements and enforcement.

5.2.2   1985

However, it is really *The Economic Institutions of Capitalism* that represents a landmark in the conceptual construction of the hybrid as an entity of its own. It is in this book that the idea of an intermediate form of organization, between markets and hierarchies, is fully acknowledged, and that properties of these arrangements began to be explored.

Besides the opening quotation of this chapter, several other passages make room for hybrid organizations. The first sentence of Chapter 1 reads as follows: 'Firms, markets, and relational contracting are important economic institutions' (Williamson 1985, p. 15). Now this quotation remains ambiguous when put in its context. On the one hand, it reads as a clear affirmation that these 'economic institutions' are three different arrangements. On the other hand, the same chapter also refers to relational contracting as the contract law of firms (and, ambiguously again, of bilateral governance).[5] It is actually in Chapter 3, on 'The governance of contractual relations', based on a paper initially published in 1979, which has become one of the most often quoted of Williamson's papers, that the concept of hybrid organizations receives its first rigorous content, if not its full name. The existence of these arrangements as distinct from markets as well as hierarchies is clearly asserted, and explained by reference to two attributes of transactions, uncertainty and the presence of specific assets. Since then, it has become firmly embedded in the theoretical framework that Williamson was developing to make the transaction cost approach operational. Building on Macneil (1974, 1978), a constant reference thereafter, this chapter initially emphasizes the role of uncertainty in explaining these forms that do not yet have a stable name. When uncertainty is such that comprehensive contingent claims contracting 'is apt to be prohibitively costly if not impossible', thus discarding markets as a solution, transactions submitted to such constraints may still be possible either by removing them from the market and internalizing them in a firm or by devising 'a different contracting relation that preserves trading but provides for additional governance'. This last solution relies on a specific contract law, the 'neoclassical contracting law' in Macneil's terminology (Williamson 1985, p. 70).

A few pages later, another attribute of transactions, that is, the specificity of assets involved, is introduced in order to better characterize this variety of arrangements, which are now developed under the heading of 'trilateral governance'. This 'intermediate institutional form' (*Ibid.*, p. 75) would be particularly appropriate for dealing with mixed or highly specific transactions. The discussion remains somewhat ambiguous. 'Trilateral governance' relates to 'neoclassical contracting', mainly characterized by incompleteness in order to provide flexibility to adjust and by third-party assistance in order to solve disputes. It borders on bilateral governance, with which it shares properties regarding the degree of specificity of assets involved; however, it is distinct with respect to its contractual form since bilateral governance relies on 'relational contracting', which also characterizes the unified governance of integrated firms (see Figure 3.2 in *Ibid.*, p. 79).[6] The main point, however, is the conclusion that 'an intermediate institutional form is evidently needed' (p. 75).

Therefore, the concept of organizational forms between markets and hierarchies and with characteristics of their own definitely emerges in *The Economic Institutions of Capitalism*. However, the concept still suffers from a lack of precise characterization that the absence of an easily identifiable label signals. It took several years before Williamson could devise a satisfactory formulation.

5.2.3   1996

The Mechanisms of Governance, published in 1996, synthesizes these developments and provides new insights for a better understanding of the nature and forms of these intermediate arrangements. Although there are elements throughout the book, the main contribution with respect to hybrids is Chapter 4, based on the influential paper on 'Comparative economic organization: the analysis of discrete structural alternatives' initially published in Williamson (1991b). It proposes a concept and identifies dimensions characterizing this class of arrangements.

An important aspect of this chapter is the unambiguous affirmation that 'the hybrid form of organization' represents a well-defined class among the 'discrete structural alternatives' for organizing transactions in a market economy. It acknowledges the long neglect of 'intermediate or hybrid forms' (Williamson 1996, p. 93). Although some fluctuations in the analysis and in the vocabulary persist, the theoretical relevance of the concept is now clearly asserted.

One source of fluctuations in the book, and in more recent papers, concerns the exact partition of the set of modes of organization. Chapter 4 focuses on three classes: markets, hierarchies and hybrids. However, Chapter 3, based on a text published in 1989, identifies four different arrangements, adding 'bureaus' to the previous subsets,[7] while a paper published in 2000 introduces 'regulation' as another component. In my opinion these hesitations in establishing well-defined classes of arrangements reflect the difficulty of identifying the different structures underlying the organization of transactions in a complex market economy. It expresses the fact that the theory needs developments and refinements, without hampering its content.

Another related hesitation concerns the terminology. Although the label 'hybrid' tends to prevail, other expressions show up here and there. Reminiscent of the previous periods, hybrid arrangements are also identified as 'non-standard forms' (*Ibid.*, Prologue, p. 3) or 'non-standard contracting' (Chapter 3, p. 75), expressions that give Williamson an opportunity to emphasize the importance of protective safeguards (for example, section 3.2, pp. 62 *seq.*). However, the main competitor of the term 'hybrid' is the notion that these forms are 'intermediate' (see particularly pp. 104 and 107). The advantage of this last expression is to ground the idea solidly in transaction cost economics, while terms such as 'clusters', 'networks', or 'chain systems' proposed by different authors are purely descriptive. Indeed, the qualification of 'hybrids' as intermediate forms establishes that their existence find an explanation in the same variables identified in the theory of markets and hierarchies, namely the characteristics of the transactions they organize. Hybrids develop as a mode of organization adequate for dealing with 'middle range' uncertainty and 'non-trivial' dependence related to the presence of specific assets. What differentiates hybrids from markets is that (i) they adapt better to 'consequential disturbances' through the development of 'elastic contracting mechanisms' (p. 96), without sacrificing some of the powerful incentives provided by autonomy of ownership among partners; and (ii) they provide efficient tools for managing the risks of opportunism generated by moderate bilateral dependency due to specific investments, without falling into the bureaucratic harassment of integration. However, using the expression 'intermediate' for designating hybrids also has disadvantages. The main drawback is that it tends to dissolve the idea of arrangements of their own, with fully specific properties. Ambiguities resulting from this uncertain terminology show up in some illustrations chosen. For example, franchising is indicated as a relevant case, but reciprocal trading and public utility regulation are also listed as hybrids (for example, Chapter 4, section 1.2).[8] In more recent papers regulation is considered a specific mode of organization (Williamson 2000).

Notwithstanding these difficulties and hesitations, the key point remains the unambiguous evolution from *Markets and Hierarchies* to *The Mechanisms of Governance*, with the emergence of 'hybrids' as a concept in its own right, designating a specific modality for organizing transactions of certain types in market economies. As clearly stated in 1996 ([1991b]), '[T]he hybrid form of organization is not a loose amalgam of market and hierarchy but possesses its own disciplined rationale' (Williamson 1996, p. 119). But what are exactly the characteristics of hybrids?

5.3   FUNDAMENTAL PROPERTIES OF HYBRIDS

Williamson's approach to hybrid arrangements is deeply embedded in his general approach to organizations, which is to understand how 'governance structures' are crafted in order to 'economize on bounded rationality while simultaneously safeguarding the transactions in question against the hazard of opportunism' (*Ibid.*, Chapter 7, p. 174 [1988b]). This provides a unified theoretical framework for analysing the variety of arrangements, giving transaction cost economics a major advantage in the field of organization theory in which most explanations are ad hoc and/or essentially descriptive.[9] On the other hand, as acknowledged by Williamson in a passage about the relative neglect of hybrid forms in transaction cost economics, '. . . the abstract attributes that characterize alternative modes of governance have remained obscure' (p. 94).[10] Several papers from the late 1980s and early 1990s have contributed to the identification of these attributes. What follows is a section on systematizing these ideas and their application to hybrid organizations.

5.3.1 Existence

Hybrid organizations develop when significant resources specific to the relationship among partners or dedicated to their trading activities are shared while ownership remains distinct. It is this combination of maintained autonomy in making decisions while mutual dependence develops to a nontrivial degree that characterizes hybrids and generates the need for a different mode of governance. Therefore the existence of hybrids depends upon the same attributes that explain the other organizational arrangements, that is, the degree of specificity of investments made in the relationship and the uncertainty associated to contractual hazards.

Although the specificity of assets occupies a central position in his explanation of the trade-off among governance structures, Williamson pays little attention to the role and characteristics of this variable in identifying the properties of hybrids. Of course, the presence of investments creating a significant dependence among partners is constantly reaffirmed as the source of contractual agreements proper to hybrids. As already stated in 1985, an 'intermediate institutional form is needed' when 'occasional transactions of the mixed and highly specific kinds' must be organized (Williamson 1985, p. 74). The intriguing point in 1985 has less to do with the importance of the degree of asset specificity required than with the emphasis on the occasional character of the transactions at stake as the explanation of why intermediate forms are preferred to bilateral or unified governance, which would be too costly for monitoring infrequent transactions. This passage may be reminiscent of the previous propensity to consider hybrids as unstable forms, an idea that other passages of 1985 criticized and that would later disappear. An extensive footnote in Williamson (1988a) fixed the different tone that predominates thereafter regarding hybrids. It stresses that: 'Hybrid forms of contracts – those for which private ordering safeguards have been crafted – are often able to cope effectively with intermediate degrees of asset specificity.'[11] The Williamson

(1991b) paper formalizes this in a model that explicitly identifies hybrids as the form suited to an intermediate degree of asset specificity.

The other dimension that explains the existence of hybrids is the presence of 'consequential' or 'semi-strong' disturbances. The role of uncertainties as a rationale for the development of non-standard contracting was already considered in 1975 (Williamson 1975, Chapter 3), in the discussion of the nature of peer group associations. Pooling resources represents at least three advantages for facing uncertainty: (i) it buffers the effects of unanticipated contingencies; (ii) it mitigates adverse selection through ex ante screening of partners; (iii) it mitigates moral hazard through ex post monitoring. Similar arguments are applied to hybrid forms in 1996 (Williamson 1996, Chapter 4 [1991b]), in relation to their capacity to produce rents. Indeed, hybrids develop because 'associational gains' are expected. A main purpose and effect of non-standard organizational forms is that they economize on transaction costs, thus generating a comparative advantage (*Ibid.*, p. 3). But this advantage also exposes them to the risk of free riding from partners who remain autonomous, with three main sources of potential opportunism. One is the possibility of a deliberately induced breach of contract. A second one is the uncertain valuation of specific investments which increases the risk of 'expropriation'. A third is the incompleteness of contracts, with inadequate adaptation clauses for dealing with unforeseen contingencies.

The combination of asset specificity and consequential disturbances thus explains the existence of hybrids, although the formal model places emphasis on the former variable, considered as the ultimate determinant. In fact, without specific investments, uncertainty would not significantly challenge hybrids: rather, this form would then lose its main justification. Properties of hybrids result from this combination of specific investments and consequential disturbances. Hybrids are not simply rent seekers, as often argued. They are specific governance structures chosen for the efficient organization of transactions sharing these attributes.[12] They are distinctive in three respects: (i) they obey a specific contract law; (ii) they rely more on autonomy for adapting than hierarchies and they require more cooperation than markets; (iii) they benefit from more intense incentives than hierarchies but less than markets since they require more control. I now turn to an exploration of these properties.

5.3.2   A Distinctive Contract Law

'Hybrid modes of contracting are supported by neoclassical contracts' (Williamson 1996, p. 96 [1991b]). Following Macneil (1974, 1978), Williamson has developed a typology of contracts that matches his classification of governance structures. Classical contracts are well adapted to markets; neoclassical contracts fit hybrids; and hierarchies, operating as 'their own court of appeal', rely on 'forbearance law' (Williamson 1985, Chapter 3 [1979]; 1996, Chapter 4 [1991b]).[13]

Two main features characterize neoclassical contracts. First, they tend to be of the long-term type, with their main focus on governance clauses intended to constrain opportunism, for example, hostages or take-or-pay procurement clauses (Williamson 1996, pp. 93–4). Second, they embed an important role for third-party assistance in resolving disputes and evaluating performances.[14] Neoclassical contracts favour arbitration rather than litigation, with arbitrators taking advantage of their specific knowledge to mitigate conflicts and maintain the continuity of the contractual relationship (*Ibid.*, Chapter 5, section 3). Continuity matters because specific assets are needed for generating rents. Safeguards are central in a mode of organization in which private ordering continuously confronts contractual hazards (2005, p. 43).

However, this also means that contracts tend to be complex and costly. The costs of establishing detailed and relatively complete contracts to deal with these hazards while maintaining continuity become rapidly prohibitive. These costs result from potential maladaptation due to the intertemporal character of hybrids (continuity matters); from haggling costs incurred by efforts to correct ex post misalignments, particularly with regard to sharing rents; from set up and running costs associated with the specificity of assets involved; and from the bonding costs of effecting secure commitments (Williamson 1985, p. 21, 1996, p. 176 [1988b]). In order to keep these costs under control and to maintain flexibility, neoclassical contracts usually provide only a framework, contrasting with the relatively complete contracts that typically organize transactions on markets. As a result, ex post governance structures prevail over ex ante incentives, a point that substantially differentiates transaction costs from agency theory (Williamson 1988b, p. 589; see also Williamson 1996, p. 10).

Additional safeguards are needed that cannot easily be embedded in contracts. Forms of governance develop for enforcing and monitoring agreements, complementing contracts. The central feature of these arrangements, 'the identification, explication, and mitigation of contractual hazards' (Williamson 1996, p. 3), makes the choice of a mode of governance for dealing with these hazards a crucial one (*Ibid.*, p. 104). 'Private ordering through ex-post governance is therefore where the main action resides' (p. 10). Part of the ordering operates through contractual mechanisms, mainly through (i) clauses penalizing contract violators; (ii) credible commitments; and (iii) some extra protective safeguards. Violators can be penalized by hostage clauses and the realignment of incentives (hence the importance of haggling in hybrids). 'Reciprocal exposures' is an important constraint on opportunism in that respect (*Ibid.*, Chapter 5 [1983]). It also has a positive effect in embedding credible commitment. Williamson often quotes the case of franchising to illustrate his point, with an emphasis on the double side moral hazard (*Ibid.*, Chapter 7, section 5; already in 1983, 1989 and so on). In order to deal with the opportunism of franchisees, the franchisor may use hostage clauses to deter franchisees from exploiting demand externalities (this was the argument developed by Klein and Leffler (1981)). But franchisees also have incentives to behave efficiently and to put pressure on the franchisor. If the owner did not create an efficient structure, they may have an incentive to become owners and to 'create an agent to police quality or otherwise devise penalties that deter quality deterioration' (Williamson 1996, p. 181). However, credible commitment remains a limited tool. Reputation is a case in point: reputation models assume that exchanges take place between autonomous partners, thus neglecting the significant dependence among partners in a hybrid arrangement (*Ibid.*, Chapter 6, p. 157). Hence the search for extra protective safeguards (*Ibid.*, Chapter 3) such as clauses to realign incentives, private ordering supplanting court ordering, and the implementation of complex trading networks to guarantee continuity and facilitate adaptation.

To summarize, the contract law of hybrids is 'more elastic than [the classical contract law of markets] but more legalistic than [the forbearance contract law of hierarchies]' (*Ibid.*, p. 104). Neoclassical contracts are highly adjustable frameworks that require complementary supports to fill gaps, correct errors and treat omissions (Williamson 1993).

5.3.3   Adaptation Mode

As already mentioned, continuity of the relationship is a central feature of hybrid organizations because it can generate added value by encouraging specific investments. However, the combination of locked-in investments, which provides a potential terrain for opportunism, and of the bounded rationality of parties confronted with consequential uncertainties, challenges this continuity. There are a considerable number of situations in which 'comprehensive contingent claims contracting is infeasible and organizational structures which support adaptive, sequential decision making have merit' (Williamson 1987, p. 618), which is why neoclassical contracts develop. However, the legal feature supporting these contracts does not suffice to explain the implementation and continuity over time of cooperation among partners: 'there is more to governance than contract law' (Williamson 1996, p. 101 [1991b]). References to contracts as mere frameworks come from Llewellyn, according to whom a contract between two parties 'almost never accurately indicates real working relations, but . . . affords a rough indication around which such relations vary, an occasional guide in case of doubt, and a norm of ultimate appeal when the relations cease in fact to work' (Llewellyn 1931, p. 737).

This explains the emphasis on ex post adaptation. Although adaptation is relevant for all contractual arrangements, it plays a particularly critical role in hybrids since this arrangement preserves ownership autonomy while simultaneously requiring durable relationships. On the one hand, autonomy may generate efficiency, allowing one party to adapt rapidly to consequential disturbances without consulting the other partners (Williamson 1996, p. 104 [1991b]). On the other hand, hybrids involve interdependence, so that adaptation requires mutual consent in order to maintain cohesion and continuity in the relationship. But collective decision making takes time. A consequence is that adaptation in hybrids fails when confronted with frequent and significant disturbances. 'An increase in market and hierarchy and a decrease in hybrid will thus be associated with an (above threshold) increase in the frequency of disturbance' (*Ibid.*, p. 116 [1991b]). Squeezed between these opposite forces, hybrids require special adaptive mechanisms 'to effect realignment and restore efficiency when beset by unanticipated disturbances' (*Ibid.*, p. 96).

What are these mechanisms? Williamson does not develop this aspect in detail, and it is also largely ignored in most of the literature on hybrids, clusters, networks and so on (Ménard 2004). However, three important and complementary devices are identified and analysed in several papers (particularly Williamson 1996, Chapter 7 [1988b], Chapter 3 [1989] and Chapter 4 [1991b], and 1990). One is the existence of contractual clauses allowing space for non-contractual modes of adaptation, enabling parties to deal with unanticipated disturbances in order to maintain the relationship. Williamson cites the example of the 32-year agreement between the Nevada Power Company and the Northwest Trading Company, which defined a tolerance zone for absorbing external shocks and required information disclosure when substantial adaptation was needed (Williamson 1996, p. 96). References to agreements between rail freight companies and road carriers are also relevant (Palay 1984, 1985). A second mechanism is arbitration, that is, the recourse to private arbitrators rather than to courts and litigation for solving conflicts. The emphasis here is on the learning process associated with arbitration.[15] A third mechanism is the implementation of specific forms of private 'government' for monitoring hybrid arrangements. The main illustration is given by an extensive quotation from Gerlach (1987) and its commentary in Williamson (1990, p. 7). The example is that of Japanese enterprise groups which have developed two complementary modes of coordination, an internal government[16] and informal meetings that 'provide a forum for interaction among group firms' (Gerlach 1987, p. 128). This also comes close to the lesson drawn from Palay (1984, 1985) on the role of managers monitoring intermediation in bilateral agreements and, more generally, on the role of complex trading networks developed to guarantee continuity and facilitate adaptation through reciprocity, collective decision making and combined ownership of some assets (Williamson 1996, p. 62 [1989]).

The existence of an 'administrative apparatus' (*Ibid.*, p. 104 [1991b]) that reduces the autonomy of decisions among partners in order to coordinate more efficiently and to resolve disputes is probably the furthest Williamson has gone in identifying a specific form of 'governance' for hybrids that goes beyond contracts. The need for such 'machinery' partially originates from the difficulties of finding rules for sharing rents in hybrids. Adaptation mechanisms interact with incentives.

5.3.4   Incentives

One main problem that hybrids face, which may explain the initial skepticism of Williamson regarding their viability in the long run, is to reach an agreement and establish clear rules about how to share joint gains. Incentives remain more powerful in hybrids than in hierarchies, thanks to the distinct property rights maintained among partners; however, parties also have more constraints and less initiative than on markets, due to their non-trivial interdependence. 'As compared with the market, the hybrid sacrifices incentives in favor of superior coordination among the parts. As compared with the hierarchy, the hybrid sacrifices cooperativeness in favor of greater incentive intensity' (*Ibid.*, p. 107 [1991b]).

The fundamental reason why partners select this mode of arrangement is of course that they expect rents from their joint actions. A central question then arises: how will parties share this rent? What distribution rule should be adopted that can preserve the comparative advantage of a hybrid arrangement while mitigating risks of opportunistic strategies? The answer is not trivial for at least two reasons. One has to do with the very nature of neoclassical contracts, that is, their incompleteness, which makes ex ante a comprehensive statement about the distribution of gains usually unfeasible.[17] A second reason relates to the risks entailed by specific investments and the difficulty of implementing adequate safeguards. Operating in an uncertain environment and depending to a significant degree on decisions made by partners at risk of behaving opportunistically, hybrids develop mechanisms to realign incentives (for example, severance payments, penalties for premature termination). However, these are limited responses (*Ibid.* [1989], p. 62), and 'Concerns for "equity" intrude' (*Ibid.* [1991b], p. 104).

Cooperation may help solve these problems, but we know little about cooperative rules.

Indeed, beside the general statement that hybrids benefit from better incentives than hierarchies although weaker than those provided by markets, few passages deal with the specific characteristics of these incentives and how they are shared. Three complementary factors may explain this relative neglect. (i) Transaction cost economics offers a differentiated product: while agency theory focuses almost exclusively on incentives, transaction cost theory emphasizes modes of organization as 'mechanisms of governance'. (ii) The fundamental assumption that contracts are incomplete directs the attention to a different perspective: 'all of the relevant contracting action cannot be concentrated in the *ex-ante* incentive alignment but some spills over into *ex-post* governance' (*Ibid.*, p. 236; emphasis in original). Therefore, giving priority to the analysis of ex post non-contractible conditions makes sense for a general theory of organization. (iii) This research strategy is reinforced by the quasi-absence of empirical studies on hybrids at the time Williamson developed his theory.[18] The difficulty in collecting data about rent sharing remains a key issue in studying incentives in hybrids. Digging into the details of how partners do business together continues to encounter strong resistance.

5.4 CONCLUSION

Williamson has made a substantial contribution to the conceptualization and analysis of modes of organization that are neither markets nor hierarchies. With over 40 years of research and publication, he has progressively exhibited the importance of these 'non-standard' arrangements in market economies, and he has convinced a large number of theoreticians in economics and managerial sciences of that importance. But he has also gone further, identifying major dimensions of hybrids that theory must take into consideration. I have tentatively systematized some of these dimensions in this chapter: the existence of specific contract laws governing hybrids, the presence of modes of adaptation that involve non-contractual mechanisms, and the complex nature and role of incentives in a structure in which autonomous holders of property rights develop interdependent activities.

Another important contribution by Williamson lies in the identification of unsolved problems, opening the door to more extensive research. With respect to hybrids, I would summarize these problems under three main headings. The first set of problems has to do with the nature and characteristics of the mechanisms of governance implemented in hybrids. As early as 1975, in his chapter on peer groups,[19] Williamson delineated some difficulties of coordination raised by agreements among autonomous partners, particularly (i) the complex devices and significant costs imposed by collective decision making; (ii) the information problem resulting from unequal distribution of capabilities among partners; and (iii) the risk of opportunistic behaviour between parties who remain autonomous decision makers in the last resort, this risk existing ex ante with non-disclosure or disguise of what one can really contribute and ex post with the temptation for each partner to take advantage of bounded rationality and incomplete contracts to absorb rents generated by the agreement. These difficulties raise the question of the mechanisms to implement for governing hybrid relationships and of their costs in comparison to other modes of governance.[20] The second set of unsolved problems has to do with innovation and changes. Williamson has repeatedly acknowledged how little we know and how much we need to know about forces that can explain the emergence of new types of arrangements among hybrids as well as forces that can constrain these forms (for example, bureaucratization or weak entrepreneurial incentives). A third set of problems that he identified and which are beginning to be explored more systematically concerns the complex interactions between the institutional environment and the modes of governance operating within the rules it defines. Although the problem was already present in earlier works (for example, Williamson 1975, Chapter 2), it is in his paper in 1991 (Williamson 1996, Chapter 4 [1991b]) and in the model introduced in 1993 (*Ibid.*, Chapter 9) that more precise indications for further developments are suggested. Three possible changes in the institutional environment ('shifting parameters') deserve particular attention: (i) changes in property rights that may increase or decrease the risk of expropriation by partners, thus altering the attractiveness of hybrid arrangements; (ii) changes in contract law, since improvements may lower the costs of hybrid contracting; and (iii) changes in the rules of the game that affect agents' behaviour, for example, rules of transparency that may improve reputation effects, reducing risks of opportunism and increasing the comparative advantages of hybrid arrangements. Williamson not only identified these possible interactions between the environment and the embedded modes of governance, but he also provided tools for analysing them.

   Beyond specific contributions, what makes this analysis of modes of governance that are neither markets nor hierarchies particularly attractive to theoreticians of organizations is the provision of a unified framework: hybrids submit to the same forces and can be explained by the same characteristics allowing an understanding of markets, hierarchies and the trade-off between them. This unifying theory, transaction cost economics, has been nicely and succinctly summarized as follows: Once acknowledged '. . .

[that] all complex contracts are unavoidably incomplete (because of bounded rationality), [that] contract as promise is fraught with hazards (because of opportunism), and that the object of economic organization is that of adaptation, then the object of economic organization reduces to the following: adapt to disturbances (of both autonomous and bilateral kinds) in ways that economize on bounded rationality while simultaneously safeguarding the transactions in question against the hazards of opportunism' (*Ibid.*, p. 162). If parsimony is a virtue of good theorizing, transaction cost economics is indeed a virtuous approach to organizations.

NOTES

1. I would like to thank Oliver Williamson for his comments on a first draft of this chapter. I also benefited from extensive discussions with Robert Gibbons on the issues developed here. The usual disclaimer obviously applies.
2. Also: 'Thus although the earlier literature, mine included (1975), worked out of a binary firm or market framework, later work has disclosed the need to make prominent provision for the intermediate (hybrid) contracting theory' (Williamson 1988a, fn. 5, p. 110 in 1991a).
3. For a detailed examination, see Ménard (2004).
4. Let me emphasize this point here. Referring almost exclusively to these three books does not reflect the details of the evolution of Williamson regarding the issues at stake. However, many papers previously published were 'adapted' for the purpose of the book in which they were included. Since this chapter does not intend to trace the details of the evolution of the author but rather explores the content of his contributions to the analysis of hybrid organizations, I refer to the most recent versions, that is, the books. However, I indicate the initial date of publication in brackets when the date matters or because of its significance for the interpretation I propose.
5. Another and somehow similar ambiguity is the distinction between intra-firm, inter-firm and hybrid modes of contracting (Williamson 1990, p. 8).
6. The discussion on the trilateral governance is very short (less than one page) compared to that on bilateral governance (over two pages).
7. The same partition (markets, hierarchies, hybrids and bureaus) is proposed in 1999.
8. The underlying idea is that regulatory agencies operate as mediators between public utility firms and their customers (Williamson 1996, p. 96).
9. In a companion paper (Ménard 2004) I suggested calling these explanations configurations rather than theories, following Oliver and Ebers (1998) on this subject.
10. Initially published as Williamson (1991b). For convenience I refer to pages in *The Mechanisms of Governance* (Chapter 4).
11. Fn. 5, p.110 of the book from 1991a in which this paper is included.
12. Note that beside the case of franchising, repeatedly developed, few examples are provided. References are made mostly to bilateral agreements, particularly to Palay (1984, 1985) and to Joskow (1985, 1987) and, in 1990, to Japanese organizations as enterprise groups. There are also short references to joint ventures and alliances.
13. 'Relational contract' has disappeared from the picture, and from the index, in 1996.
14. In 1985 (Williamson 1985, Chapter 3) third parties are compared to architects, operating as relatively independent experts between general contractors and customers.
15. This is substantiated by an extensive quote from Fuller (1963, pp. 11–12), in which the author insists on the access of arbitrators to 'quick methods of education not open to the courts', for example, frequent interruptions and questions, open arguments among parties, help of informed persons on both sides.

16. '. . . high level executive councils which symbolically identify group members and the boundaries of the social unit' (Gerlach 1987, p. 128).
17. This argument was already developed in 1975 regarding non-standard contracting practices (for example, Williamson 1975, p. 239).
18. One must add that group incentives remain a largely underdeveloped topic in economic theory generally speaking.
19. Williamson 1975, Chapter 3, particularly section 2. There are also premonitory indications in Chapter 7 on the limits to vertical integration.
20. Elaboration on this problem can be found in (Williamson 1996, Chapters 4 and 6).

REFERENCES

Coase, R.H. (1991), 'The institutional structure of production', Alfred Nobel Memorial Prize Lecture in Economic Sciences, Nobel Foundation, 12 pages; Repr. in *American Economic Review* (1992), **82** (4), 713–19.

Fuller, L.L. (1963), 'Collective bargaining and the arbitrator', *Wisconsin Law Review,* January, 3–46.

Gerlach, M. (1987), 'Business alliances and the strategy of the Japanese firms', *California Management Review*, **30** (Fall), 126–42.

Joskow, P. (1985), 'Vertical integration and long-term contracts: the case of coal-burning electric generating plants', *Journal of Law, Economics, and Organization*, **1** (1), 33–80.

Joskow, P. (1987), 'Contract duration and relationship-specific investment: empirical evidence from the coal market', *American Economic Review*, **77** (May), 168–85.

Klein, B. and K. Leffler (1981), 'The role of market forces in assuring contractual performance', *Journal of Political Economy*, **89**, 615–41.

Llewellyn, K. (1931), 'What price contract? An essay in perspective', *Yale Law Journal*, **40** (May), 704–51.

Macneil, I.R. (1974), 'The many futures of contracts', *Southern California Law Review*, **47** (May), 691–816.

Macneil, I.R. (1978), 'Contracts: adjustments of a Long term economic relation under classical, neoclassical, and relational contract law', *Northwestern University Law Review*, **72**, 854–906.

Ménard, C. (2004), 'The economics of hybrid organizations', *Journal of Institutional and Theoretical Economics*, **160** (3), 345–76.

Oliver, A.L. and M. Ebers (1998), 'Networking network studies: an analysis of conceptual configurations in the study of inter-organizational relationships', *Organization Studies*, **19** (4), 549–83.

Palay, T.M. (1984), 'Comparative institutional economics: the governance of the rail freight contract', *Journal of Legal Studies*, **13** (June), 265–88.

Palay, T.M. (1985), 'Avoiding regulatory constraints: contracting safeguards and the role of informal agreements', *Journal of Law, Economics, and Organization*, **1** (1), 155–75.

Richardson, G.B. (1972), 'The organization of industry', *Economic Journal*, **82**, 383–96.

Williamson, O.E. (1975), *Markets and Hierarchies: Analysis and Antitrust Implications*, New York: The Free Press.

Williamson, O.E. (1979), 'Transaction cost economics: the governance of contractual relations', *Journal of Law and Economics*, **22** (2), 3–61.

Williamson, O.E. (1985), *The Economic Institutions of Capitalism*, New York: The Free Press and Macmillan.

Williamson, O.E. (1987), 'Transaction-cost economics: the comparative contracting perspective', *Journal of Economic Behavior and Organization*, **8** (4), 617–25.

Williamson, O.E. (1988a), 'The logic of economic organization', *Journal of Law, Economics and Organization*, **4** (1), 65–93.

Williamson, O.E. (1988b), 'Corporate finance and corporate governance', *Journal of Finance*, **43** (3), 567–91.

Williamson, O.E. (1989), 'Transaction cost economics', in R. Schmalensee and R. Willig (eds), *Handbook of Industrial Organization*, vol. 1, Amsterdam: North Holland, pp. 136–82.

Williamson, O.E. (1990), 'The firm as a nexus of treaties: an introduction', in M. Aoki, B. Gustafsson and O.E. Williamson (eds), *The Firm as a Nexus of Treaties*, London: Sage Publications, pp. 1–25.

Williamson, O.E. and S. Winter (eds) (1991a), 'Introduction', in *The Nature of the Firm*, New York: Oxford University Press, pp. 3–17.

Williamson, O.E. (1991b), 'Comparative economic organization: the analysis of discrete structural alternatives', *Administrative Science Quarterly*, **36** (2), 269–96.

Williamson, O.E. (1993), 'Transaction cost economics and organization theory', *Industrial and Corporate Change*, **2** (2), 107–56.

Williamson, O.E. (1996), *The Mechanisms of Governance*, Oxford, UK: Oxford University Press.

Williamson, O.E. (2000), 'The new institutional economics: taking stock/looking ahead', *Journal of Economic Literature*, **37** (3), 595–613, initially published in *Newsletter of the International Society for New Institutional Economics*, **2** (2), Fall 1999.

Williamson, O.E. (2005), 'Transaction cost economics', in C. Menard and M. Shirley (eds), *Handbook of New Institutional Economics*, Dordrecht, Berlin and New York: Springer, pp. 41–65.

6. Organization of firms, knowing communities and limits of networks in a knowledge-intensive context

Patrick Cohendet and Patrick Llerena

6.1 INTRODUCTION

This contribution addresses the issues of organization and competitiveness of firms in a knowledge-intensive context. A knowledge-intensive context refers to an industrial context where the competitive pressure requires the integration of different bodies of specialized knowledge and the production of an ever increasing diversity. These conditions are met in some traditional sectors, such as automobile or aeronautics, but also in creative industries, such as film making, video games or fashion companies.

The main challenge which arises in this context is the emergence of new organizational forms, allowing for both diversity creation and economic efficiency. Networks of firms seem to be an overwhelmingly accepted organizational solution. They allow the combination of a variety of competences and access to specialized and demand-specific knowledge. However networks have limits and have some impact on the view and role of firms. The main purpose of this chapter is precisely to clarify the nature of those limits and their origins. We shall, in fact, argue that the viability of a variety-based industrial organization cannot rely on 'simple' networks of firms, but mainly should instead rely on the existence of more complex, interactive networks, associating formal structures, such as firms, and informal structures, such as elementary sources of specialized knowledge: the knowing communities. These latter are the loci of the creation of new specialized knowledge and a means to take into account the fixed costs associated with the building of a shared specialized body of knowledge.

However, taking into account the 'knowing communities' also implies the need for a relevant theory of the firm, which is able to consider simultaneously a transaction perspective of the firm and its related division of labour, and a knowledge perspective with the related structure of knowledge creation and distribution. From our point of view, the dual theory of the firm developed elsewhere by the authors (Cohendet and Llerena 2005) is an appropriate one, as we shall show in the last section of the chapter.

6.2 VIABILITY OF THE NEW PRODUCTION REGIME: THE LIMITS OF THE INFORMATION-INTENSIVE PRODUCTION SYSTEM, SPECIALIZATION AND THE ROLE OF COMMUNITIES

According to Ehud Zuscovitch (1998), economic development relies on increasing specialization that crosses a new threshold of complexity due to the tremendous potential of product variety made possible by the rapid dissemination of information technologies. This Information Intensive Production System (IIPS) regime differs from the preceding regime based on increasing returns from the production of standardized commodities. In IIPS the challenge is to deal with increasing variety while maintaining economic efficiency: this is the role of networks.

The role of networks, according to this view, is explained by the fact that the differentiation of goods calls for the differentiation of skills, something that it is very difficult for firms to address. In the mass production regime specialization remained in the private (and, if possible, secret) domain of firms. This was possible because variety was limited. But in IIPS even specialization must be shared. A highly specialized skill can only be maintained if competence is shared among many users. Partnership becomes the condition for viability. Cooperation enables partners to develop skills in a mutually beneficial way: each party specializes and agrees to share learning according to some specific types of agreements. This is why the network as a social process may be thought of as a new industrial organization, and implies the following characteristics:

- A network is a new form of industrial structure that tackles the fundamental challenge of simultaneously increasing variety and efficiency. However, if partner-contingent specialization increases mutual benefits and ultimately joint profits, at the same time it increases individual risk: it must therefore include a risk reducing device. The network offers a major risk sharing mechanism through the progressive building of trust. Trust is then considered as a tacit agreement in which, rather than seeking out the best opportunity at every instant, each agent takes a longer perspective of the transaction, as long as their traditional partner does not go beyond some mutually accepted norms.

- A network can be considered as an extension of the domain of competences of firms. The firm's belonging to networks appears in the form of goodwill (see also Kogut 2000) and is an essential asset that becomes part of its portfolio of competences. Networks are mechanisms devised to avoid transaction costs in the building of knowledge,[1] and also to reinforce the importance of trust between participants. For a given firm, the network delineates those firms with which the interactions are regulated by the rules of building and reinforcing knowledge, and those firms (which do not participate in the network) with which the interactions are essentially regulated by transaction costs.

- A network offers the possibility of internalizing externalities. In technological partnerships spillovers are mastered to a large degree by reciprocity arrangements and partners do find that the benefits of sharing and sometimes even diffusing knowledge overcome the welfare or profits losses.[2] The network is a mechanism for which the weak appropriation hypothesis of the traditional model does not apply. When product variety is limited, any leakage of information may entail serious losses simply because the total output is affected. Under increasing variety, increased differentiation drives the system towards multiple micro-markets where imitation is much more difficult.

- A network offers a flexible organizational solution for joint specialization, provides some protection for property rights of intangible assets and, more importantly, alleviates the capital accumulation constraint on the division of labour and growth. This organizational solution is capable of dealing with learning and differentiation when information intensity increases. The network renders specialization essentially a social process and creates the same separation between specialization and ownership as did the limited liability feature in the case of capital mobilization.

- A network is at the centre of the relationship between specialization and surplus creation under IIPS. Under its various forms, differentiation generates an extremely high potential for cross-fertilisation: skills combination may stimulate creativity and productivity. In a Schumpeterian perspective it continuously stimulates new combinations. In short, the network is an arena where both creation and allocation of resources are at play simultaneously. New solutions elaborated in networks are permanently 'surimposed' on former structures.

However, while emphasizing the advantages of networks as the key mechanism of the IIPS regime, the viability of such a regime based on networks is questioned. Sustainable differentiation or the ability of the industrial structure to manage large product variety is a major concern. In order to advance the analysis of the relationship between networks, differentiation and surplus creation, the principles of interactivity must be thoroughly understood.

In the next section we propose to tackle this question of the viability of IIPS by exploring the micro dimension of IIPS at the intra-firm level.[3] At this intra-firm level we propose to highlight the functioning of knowing communities as the active units of specialization, and to consider the implication for a relevant theory of the firm.

6.3 NETWORKS AND THE LIMITS OF SPECIALIZATION

As a new form of industrial structure that tackles the fundamental challenge of simultaneously increasing variety and efficiency, networks of firms have limits. In a context where pressure for ever larger variety is expressed by the economic environment there is a need for an increasing proliferation of specialized and distinct firms to be integrated by network structures. The building of a sufficient level of trust within the network may succeed in diminishing the transaction costs between partners or at least may keep them at a reasonable level, but it cannot prevent the growing constraint of a different source of costs: the fixed (sunk costs) associated with the building of knowledge. Within a given firm the ability to integrate an increasingly diverse number of specialized bodies of knowledge is not infinite. First, because ever growing absorptive capabilities (which are far from being a free good) are required for understanding external knowledge; second, because the ability to design cognitive platforms of integration is required for shaping external knowledge into a form suitable for further exploitation by the firm; and, third, because in this system the firm is compelled to specialize ever further in its domain of specialized knowledge. This requires the building of an infrastructure of knowledge (models, grammar, codes and so on) that generates increasing sunk costs with the growing risk that these costs may no longer be compensated by the advantages of networks.

Moreover, a natural tendency of these networks of firms is to exert pressure on firms and drive them to become super specialized units in a given domain of knowledge. In our view this is not the vocation of firms (in the last instance the natural consequence of this phenomenon is the dissolution of firms into markets). Firms are not machines for producing an ever more advanced type of specialized knowledge: they are places of coordination of different bodies of knowledge that assure efficient organization of an existing division of work, and matrices where the delicate integration of dispersed forms of knowledge is permanently elaborated and refined.

The risk is thus high that the development of networks will face a limit, as firms risk being overwhelmed when dealing with knowledge that becomes too complex. To some extent, such a situation is comparable with the risk of overflow of information that leads firms to abandon the functional forms of organization for the multidivisional form in order to cope more efficiently with information. This problem was solved by a division of work between the hierarchy in charge of strategic decision making and the divisions in charge of operational decisions. However, here in the IIPS system, firms have to cope with a far more severe problem of complexity – dealing with an overflow of knowledge – which cannot be solved by a simple reorganization of internal structures of firms: it implies revisiting both the intra and inter dimensions of interactions among specialized units of knowledge.

Our position is that this risk of a knowledge overflow calls for a different form of collaborative organization to cope with variety and efficiency. We argue in the following that this form cannot rely on a simple network of firms, but on more complex networks associating firms and that elementary source of specialized knowledge, the knowing communities. The reasons for considering knowing communities are at least twofold: first, they are the natural loci where specialized knowledge is being formed (the elementary active units of specialization); second, they take over in their functioning the fixed costs associated with the building of a specialized aspect of knowledge.

6.4   KNOWING COMMUNITIES AS ACTIVE UNITS OF SPECIALIZATION

A knowing community can be defined as a gathering of individuals who accept to exchange ideas voluntarily and on a regular basis concerning a common interest or objective in a given field of knowledge. Through this regular exchange, common cognitive platforms and common social norms are built that assure the cohesion of the community and guide the newcomers' behaviour. The critical role of knowing communities in the building of useful knowledge for society has recently been popularized by successful examples, such as the Linux open source community or the role of the community of 'reps' at Xerox.[4] These examples underline the role of communities as modes of economic coordination that 'economize' on hierarchy to produce useful knowledge.

As the knowledge-based economy expands, knowing communities play an increasing role, because they can take over some significant parts of the 'sunk costs' of the process of generation or accumulation of specialized parcels of knowledge.[5] These costs correspond, for instance, to the progressive construction of languages and models of action and interpretation that are required for the implementation of new knowledge, which cannot be covered through the classical signals of hierarchies (or markets). This setting is likely to compensate for some organizational limitations (learning failures) that firms are facing when confronted with the need to continuously innovate and produce new knowledge.

Knowing communities can be found in traditional work divisions and departments, but they also cut across functional divisions, spill over into after-work or project-based teams, and straddle networks of cross-corporate and professional ties.

> For example, within firms, classical communities include functional groups of employees who share a particular specialization corresponding to the classical division of labour (e.g. marketing or accounting). They also include teams of employees with heterogeneous skills and qualifications, often coordinated by team leaders and put together to achieve a particular goal in a given period of time.

Knowing communities can be of different natures in the way they deal with knowledge: some may focus on the accumulation and exploitation of a given field of knowledge (communities of practice), others on the exploration of a new field of knowledge (epistemic communities).

As underlined by Boland and Tenkasi (1995, p. 351), knowledge-intensive firms can be viewed as organizations composed of multiple communities with highly specialized technologies, expertise and knowledge domains:

> Organizations are characterised by a process of distributed cognition in which multiple communities of specialised knowledge workers, each dealing with a part of overall organizational problem, interact to create the patterns of sense making and behaviour displayed by the organization as a whole. Organizations are necessarily characterised by distributed cognition because their critically important processes and the diversity of environments and technologies to be dealt with are too complex for one person to understand in its entirety. Communities develop unique social and cognitive repertoires which guide their interpretation of the world.

As Wenger (1998, p. 137) noted, a community drawing on interaction and participation to act, interpret and innovate, acts 'as a locally negotiated regime of competence'. Therefore, communities are suppliers of sense and collective beliefs for agents, and play a central role of coordination in the firm.

6.5   KNOWING COMMUNITIES AS CONTRIBUTING TO THE FIRM'S ABSORPTIVE CAPABILITIES

If knowing communities in firms could thus be seen as elementary units of specialized knowledge, they also provide another potential advantage to firms: they strongly contribute to equipping firms with absorptive capabilities. Knowing communities are never bound within the limits of organizations. They permanently interact in their specialized domains of knowledge with the outside world by collecting new ideas and benchmarking the best conditions of practice. They nurture the organization by continuously bringing new units of specialized knowledge which have just been tested and validated in the outside world. The different communities in the organization could thus be seen as a set of diverse sources of absorptive capabilities that potentially allow firms to benefit from a diversity of knowledge. As Cohen and Levinthal (1990) remarked:

> Diversity of knowledge plays an important role: in a setting in which there is uncertainty about the knowledge domains from which potentially useful innovation may emerge, a diverse background provides a more robust basis for learning because it increases the prospect that incoming information will relate to what is already known. In addition to strengthening assimilative power, knowledge diversity also facilitates the innovative process by enabling the individual to make novel associations and linkages.

However, as Cohen and Levinthal (1990) also emphasized:

> Absorptive capabilities refer not only to the acquisition or assimilation of information by the organization, but also to the organization's ability to exploit it. Therefore, an organization's absorptive capacity does not simply depend on the organization's direct interface with the external environment. It also depends on transfers of knowledge across and within subunits that may be quite removed from the original point of entry. To understand the sources of a firm's absorptive capacity, we focus on the structure of communication between the external environment and the organization as well as among the subunits of the organization, and also the character and distribution of expertise within the organization.

This remark leads to the crucial issue of both the interactions between a community and the hierarchical structures of the firm, and the interactions between knowing communities.

In fact, we need a relevant theory of the firm, able to combine a transaction view in terms of activities and of division of labour, on the one side, and a knowledge-based or a competence-based view, in terms of division of knowledge, on the other.

6.6 THE PROPOSED ALTERNATIVE PERSPECTIVE: THE THEORY OF THE DUAL STRUCTURE OF THE FIRM

If the common view nowadays is that transactions and competences are complements, the nature and intensity of the interaction between transactions and competences differ radically according to the theoretical approaches on the firm. Behind this debate, there is a very fundamental issue dealing with the relationships between the division of labour and the division of knowledge.

Keith Pavitt (1998, 2002) already emphasized the importance of these distinctions in the growing knowledge-intensive economy. The starting point of Pavitt's analysis of the relationship between the division of labour and the division of knowledge is the large multidivisional firm, with established R&D activities and 'a product range that has grown out of a common, but evolving technological competence'. These firms are considered by Pavitt as the largest single source of the new technological knowledge on which innovation depends.

From these premises, following Nelson (1994), Pavitt distinguished two complementary elements in firm-specific knowledge:

1. A 'body of understanding', based on competences in specific technological fields, 'and reflected in the qualification of corporate technical personnel, and in the fields they patent and publish' (Pavitt 1998, p. 436).
2. A 'body of practice', related to the design, production and use of a specific product model, which is generally obtained through the combination of experience, experimentation and interactions among different parts of the organization. A body of practice 'consists largely of organizational knowledge that links a body of understanding with a commercially successful (or more broadly useful) artefact' (*Ibid.*).

The distinction between bodies of understanding (technologies) and bodies of practice (products) helps clarify the notion of 'diversity', which is confused in the evolutionary theory of the firm. As Pavitt emphasized, large firms are generally active in a range of technologies broader than the products they make. He showed that for the individual firm, technological diversity provides the basis for manufacturing and improving its products, and that for the economy as a whole, greater diversity amongst firms in their mixes of specialized technological knowledge enables them to explore and exploit a fuller range of products markets. The distinction between technological diversity and product diversity is well expressed in the following:

> At any given time, advances in some fields of technology open major opportunities for major performance in material, components, and subsystems (e.g. Economies of scale in continuous processes, economies of miniaturization in information processing). The directions of these improvements are easily recognized, even if they require the commitment of substantial resources for their achievement, e.g. Moore's Law in the semiconductors. Thus experimentation and diversity do not take place between different technologies. On the contrary, rich and well-known directions of improvements in underlying technologies create opportunities for diversity and experimentation in product configurations. Technological opportunities create product diversity. There is no convincing evidence that technological diversity created product opportunities. (*Ibid.*, p. 441)

Pavitt's developments on the notion of diversity offer some convincing arguments that help understand the limits of evolutionary analysts who place too much emphasis on firm-specific technological competences, and who are thus led, for instance, to set major technological improvements (technological discontinuities) at the heart of the theory of the innovative firm. Pavitt also added a number of insightful comments, such as the fact that firms rarely fail because of an inability to master a new field of technology, but because they do not succeed in matching the firm's system of coordination and control against the nature of the available technological opportunities. In his interpretation competition is not based on technological diversity, but on diversity and experimentation in products. The main problem concerns coordination and control. However, in these developments, Pavitt implicitly assumes:

1. With regard to technological developments or product developments, the production of new knowledge is done 'in-house' by firms. As regards improvements in a given technology, this is achieved through activities performed within the firm. The division of knowledge is shaped by the division of work. Only those who do have the possibility to know more.
2. The initial situation is basically one where firms have a given body of understanding (an existing level of technological diversity) and their bodies of practice will adapt to find the 'right tuning' to the existing bodies of understanding.

We extend Pavitt's vision on the nature of the innovative firm by questioning the idea that the division of work 'comes first'. Pavitt himself, in a co-authored paper with Brusoni *et al.* (2002), when asking 'why do firms know more than they do?', suggested such a perspective. But they considered mainly situations of large firms in cases of modular platforms. In a knowledge-based economy we argue that the very essence of the meaning of the knowledge-based economy is that the division of knowledge comes 'first'.

In short:

- The traditional theories that view the firm as a processor of information consider that transactions come first and firms may then manage to accumulate competences. This order of priority respects the classical vision of the predominance of the division of labour. In the classical Smithean vision the division of labour (the way firms decide which activities to undertake) drives the division of knowledge, which may result from learning-by-doing processes. This is, for instance, what Williamson clearly had in mind when he advocated that there is room in the traditional vision of the firm to implement some of the characteristics of knowledge (Williamson 1999). Room may exist, but it is very limited. The transactional criteria come first and shape the nature of activities that a given firm will undertake, and the activities that will be undertaken by the rest of the industry. And once the division of labour has operated, then the accumulation of knowledge through (passive) learning-by-doing processes may take place a posteriori as a by-product of the division of labour.
- The approaches that view the firm as a processor of knowledge address the idea that the division of knowledge comes first: firms decide in which specific fields of knowledge they will build their competitive advantages. Then, once this cognitive decision is taken, they can determine the activities to be undertaken in order to sustain the fields of knowledge they have chosen. The division of knowledge (which distributes interpretative capabilities among actors) drives the division of labour (which distributes activities among those actors).

Our view is that when the economic environment is stable, the traditional view is acceptable: the division of labour can first operate by determining the activities to be carried out by each firm. Then, from this division of labour firms can accumulate specialized knowledge ex post. But as the environment becomes more uncertain, and as firms need to increase their ability to innovate in order to cope with changing environments, they have to create new knowledge 'from the inside out' to redefine both problems and solutions. They cannot rely on a pre-existing division of labour. The cognitive processes tend to come first, and drive the division of labour.

From our standpoint the core statement of the competence theory of the firm is the following: the firm should be seen *in primis* as a processor of knowledge. In this cognitive perspective the focus of attention is the key limiting factor. To be more precise, the cognitive steps to be followed by the firm are the following:

1. The firm will first focus its limited attention on its core competences. Within this set of core competences the firm functions as a knowledge processor that gives full priority to the creation of resources. Such a focus means that the activities belonging to the 'core' of the firm are not considered as tradable on the market: they are 'disconnected' from any 'make or buy' trade-off as suggested by transaction cost theory. However, the scope of the set of core competences is limited; focusing on core competences is by definition very costly. This requires specific sunk costs, forging and managing cooperation with institutions that have complementary forms of knowledge, accessing and absorbing the most recent scientific results related to core competences and so on. For a given firm, in terms of the exchange of knowledge, this zone is characterized by 'partners' or 'quasi integrated' suppliers, who produce high value components or systems that are highly strategic. These could be wholly owned suppliers or partly owned suppliers in which the firm holds an equity stake and typically transfers personnel to work on a part-time or full-time basis. The suppliers participate in long-term strategic plans, capital investments and capacity planning, and personnel transfers. The formal duration of the typical contract is long term, and most contracts are renewed automatically. Suppliers also tend to contribute to building the firm's knowledge base, and benefit from the absorptive capacities accumulated by the firm. But it is also important for the firm to enhance the absorptive capacities of the suppliers themselves. The firm provides assistance to suppliers, not only in the areas of quality, cost reduction, factory layout and inventory management, but also in terms of increasing technological competences and research facilities. What is essentially transferred in this zone are creative ideas through multiple functional interfaces (manufacturing to manufacturing, engineering to engineering and so on). This requires permanent capabilities for benchmarking within the group of partners, a substantial investment in inter-firm knowledge shared routines and regular socialization activities. In contrast, the relationship with competitors in this zone is highly unstable and conflicting, and generally leads to acquisitions or mergers.

2. In decreasing order of attention, next comes the domain of non-core competences. This is the domain of activities in which the firm 'knows' well what to do, but does not necessarily invest significantly in the systematic production of new knowledge to place it at the leading edge of competition. To render its knowledge effective, the firm mainly has to function within networks and diverse types of alliances where it can access the complementary forms of knowledge required to make its own knowledge valuable. What is at stake in this zone is the mutual exchange of complementary forms of knowledge. Networks offer precisely such an opportunity. Thus a given economic agent is differentiated from another through their specific body of tacit knowledge. By means of networks, agents can organize an efficient circulation of codified knowledge aided by a structure that renders different segments of agent-specific tacit knowledge compatible. Agents accept to specialize in a given area of tacit knowledge, because they are confident that the other agents will increase their specialization in complementary forms. This reduces the risks of overspecialization, but relies centrally on building mutual trust and reciprocity in the production of knowledge. The fact of taking into account the degree of trust raises an important issue, which has to do with the choice between specialization and cooperation in the production of knowledge.[6] Trust is relevant for the reliability of other specialized producers of complementary knowledge.[7] In such a perspective one should not be overly concerned about excessive uncontrolled spillovers and risks of excessive imitation, precisely because of significant transaction costs. Imitating is very costly, and loose cooperation in informal networks allowing a certain control of the diffusion of spillovers among agents can be an efficient form of collaboration. One of the key determinants of innovative networks is the constant trade-off by agents between, on the one hand, delimiting property rights and, on the other hand, terminating rights of access to complementary forms of knowledge.

3. Finally, away from the domain of attention on competences, one finds the peripheral activities. Once the set of activities that belong to the core and non-core competences has been chosen, the other activities that do not belong to the domain of competences are managed under traditional methods which may rely on the transaction cost approach. These activities are necessary to support the domain of competences and they generally correspond to the larger number of activities and employment positions in the firm. By definition, these activities do not require a strong commitment in terms of knowledge. The firm merely needs to 'be informed' of the best practices of external firms

and organizations that can offer equivalent support services, and if it appears that these activities are too costly to be run within the firm compared to market mechanisms (according to transaction costs criteria), they will be outsourced. This is a zone of 'quasi market' relations, where the degree of supplier-buyer interdependence is generally low. Products are standardized and require few interactions with other inputs. Contracts are arm's-length, the duration of which depends on the classical transactional parameters. For a given firm, in terms of supplier management practices, this zone requires minimal assistance to suppliers together with single functional interfaces (sales to purchasing, for instance), and the practice of price benchmarking. In terms of technology transfer, what is at stake in this zone is the exchange of an artefact, rather than innovative ideas or new tacit knowledge.

Such a ranking of activities was suggested by Langlois and Foss (1996), when they argued that beyond core competences, firms rank their activities according to an index of growing distance. Moving gradually away from the core, one enters a domain which is increasingly regulated by the classical need to process information. A rendering along the lines of the modern economics of organization may be as follows: as firms move further and further away from their core businesses, they are faced with increasing adverse selection and moral hazard, since management becomes less and less able to monitor employees efficiently or to evaluate their human capital. Agency costs rise correspondingly, producing the net profitability disadvantage associated with further integration (for a similar story, see Aghion and Tirole 1995).[8]

One of the main consequences of this 'lexicographic' choice (first focusing on competences, then managing the periphery) is in terms of governance structures. The ranking of activities seems to suggest the need for the firm to define at least two distinct governance priorities:

1. A structure to manage competences in order to align dispersed knowledge and expectations. Within this 'core' structure some contractual schemes may naturally be implemented (for example, stock options or specific rewards for inventors within the organization), but these are not essential when compared with the priority given to the stimulation of collective learning processes.
2. A structure conceived along the transaction costs criterion to manage the periphery. Within this second structure of governance classical contractual schemes are dominant to ensure the information processing that is central to the functioning of the periphery.

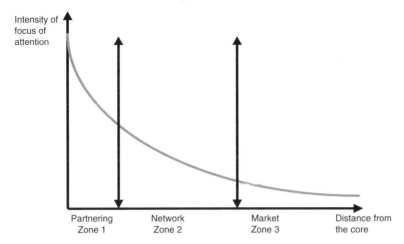

Source: Amesse and Coherdet (2001).

Figure 6.1 *Ranking of activities of the firm (distance from 'core competence')*

Figure 6.1 illustrates the above ranking of knowledge activities within the firm. The first zone (Zone 1) is the core itself. The second zone (Zone 2) is one where the firm holds significant pieces of knowledge, but needs to access complementary forms of knowledge held by other firms to be able to develop and use the knowledge efficiently. This zone is characterized by 'networks'. The third zone (Zone 3) is the peripheral zone, where the firm does not hold any specific advantage in terms of knowledge.

As a consequence, the dual theory of the firm offers a theoretical framework that combines the two opposed perspectives: that based on activity and that based on knowledge-based ones. As shown, the lexicographic order integrates a rationale for the existence and role of complex network interactions involving firms and knowing communities.

6.7 CONCLUSION

We started by questioning the viability of a knowledge-intensive and variety-based production system: our end result concerns two related analytical needs:

1. To consider 'knowing communities' as active elementary units of specialization, crucial to the building of specialized knowledge, bearing the related sunk costs and contributing to the firm's absorptive capacities.

2. To reconsider the theory of the firm in order to be able to combine an activity-based perspective, rationalizing the networks of firms as a relevant organization for the industry, with a knowledge-based perspective, allowing for knowledge creation and the existence of knowing communities.

In our view these are necessary conditions for the variety-based production depending on networks to be viable. We have argued that networks reduced to the sole interaction of hierarchical structures such as firms cannot be viable, since they will unavoidably face the limits of ever increasing specialization and the ever increasing sunk costs which are associated with building such new knowledge firms. Rather, the theory of the firm has to analyse more complex, interactive networks, associating formal structures, such as firms, and informal structures, such as elementary sources of specialized knowledge. As Brown and Duguid (1991, p. 54) underlined, a vision of this nature may lead to a new conception of the firm: 'as a collective of communities, not simply of individuals, in which enacting experiments are legitimate, separate community perspectives can be amplified by inter-changes among communities. Out of this friction of competing ideas can come the sort of improvisational sparks necessary for igniting organizational innovation.'

NOTES

1. Cohendet and Llerena (2005) have repeatedly argued that in their domain of competences firms do not follow the transactional criterion. Moreover, this criterion is somewhat disconnected in these strategic areas for knowledge building. In contrast, the transactional criterion fully functions in the domain of periphery of the firm.
2. By including priority-to-members mechanisms, networks necessarily introduce inefficiencies and welfare losses. However, this can be justified if these costs are offset by efficiency gains in the form of enhanced capacity to differentiate skills and products, and hence to contribute to economic growth.
3. See Zusvovitch (1998); Willinger and Zuscovitch (1998).
4. One of the most widely cited studies of knowing communities was carried out by Orr (1990) concerning the activities of a team of photocopier reps at Xerox. According to Orr, the job of a rep is best described as a continuous improvisation taking place in a network of relationships between clients, machines and other reps. Reps work autonomously. They intervene on Xerox clients' business premises where they have to repair a machine, by themselves most of the time. Together, they form a community of practice, which provides mutual help and the collective problem solving of unusual breakdowns. When they talk about machines, technicians actually build up a common identity while exchanging the expertise each of them gained from various experiences. They create a stock of operational competences in sharp contrast with handbooks and user guides that are promoted by the hierarchy. This regularly updated repertoire is transmitted through oral culture. It allows reps to cope with managerial evolutions that downplay their role by increasingly relying on work methods disconnected from the reality of workers and machines.

The highly technical work of reps appears as a socially distributed resource, stored and disseminated above all by informal conversations. Moreover, through their ability to maintain constant interactions with other communities (engineers, designers and so on) in the organization, reps are at the origin of many creative ideas at Xerox.

5. See, for instance, Cowan and Foray (1997).
6. As argued by Zuscovitch (1998, p. 256): 'Trust is a tacit agreement in which rather than systematically seeking out the best opportunity at every instant, each agent takes a longer perspective to the transactions, as long as his traditional partner does not go beyond some mutually accepted norm. Sharing the risks of specialization is an aspect of co-operation that manifests an important trust mechanism in network functioning. Specialization is a risky business. One may sacrifice the "horizontal" ability to satisfy various demands in order to gain "vertical" efficiency in an effort to increase profitability. Any specializing firm accepts this risk, network or not. A risk-sharing mechanism is essential because, while aggregate profits for participating firms may indeed be superior to the situation where firms are less specialized, the distribution of profits may be very hazardous. To make specialization worthwhile, the dichotomous (win-lose) individual outcome must be smoothed somehow by a cooperative principle of risk sharing.'
7. The institutionalization of incentives for validation (peer refereeing, for instance) in epistemic communities may vary widely. The choice for an agent to specialize in one domain of knowledge (and to bear the sunk costs) in cooperation with other agents that accept to specialize in complementary types of knowledge is an important line of research to understand the management of knowledge by organizations.
8. The above representation is essentially static. It corresponds to the actual ranking of activities within the firm at a given moment in time. However, the dynamic functioning of activities could be interpreted along the lines of the evolutionary theory of the firm (Cohendet, *et al.* 2000). Through the combined mechanisms of selection and variation in the body of existing routines, there always arises the possibility of transforming a set of secondary routines situated in the periphery into a new competence. Naturally, the reverse mechanism is also possible. For instance, routines that belong at a given moment in time to the core domain could be 'declassified' to the competence of the peripheral domain over time if they happened not to be successful. It must be emphasized that in the selection process that operates on routines, in addition to the classical external competitive environment, the attention of the firm operates as an internal element of selection.

REFERENCES

Aghion, P. and J. Tirole (1995), 'Some implications of growth for organizational form and ownership structure', *European Economic Review, Papers and Proceedings,* **39**, 440–55.

Amesse, F. and P. Cohendet (2001), 'Technology transfer revisited from the perspective of the knowledge-based economy', *Research Policy*, **30** (9), 1459–78.

Amin, A. and P. Cohendet (2004), *Architectures of Knowledge: Firms, Capabilities and Communities*, Oxford, UK: Oxford University Press.

Boland, R.J. and R.V. Tenkasi (1995), 'Perspective making and perspective taking in communities of knowing', *Organization Science*, **6** (4), 350–72.

Brown, J.S. and P. Duguid (1991), 'Organizational learning and communities of practice: toward a unified view of working, learning and innovation', *Organization Science*, **2** (1), 40–57.

Cohen, W.M. and D.A. Levinthal (1990), 'Absorptive-capacity – a new perspective on learning and innovation', *Administrative Science Quarterly*, **35** (1), 128–52.

Cohendet, P. and P. Llerena (2005), 'A dual theory of the firm between transaction and competences: conceptual analysis and empirical considerations', *Revue d'Economie Industrielle*, **110** (2ème trim), 175–98.

Cohendet, P., P. Llerena and L. Marengo (2000), 'Is there a pilot in the evolutionary firm?', in N. Foss and V. Mahnke (eds), *Competence, Governance and Entrepreneurship. Advances in Economic Strategy Research*, Oxford, UK: Oxford University Press, pp. 95–115.

Cowan, R. and D. Foray (1997), 'The economics of codification and the diffusion of knowledge', *Industrial and Corporate Change*, **6** (3), 594–622.

Kogut, B. (2000), 'The network as knowledge: generative rules and the emergence of structure', *Strategic Management Journal*, **21** (special issue), 405–25.

Langlois, R. and N. Foss (1996), 'Capabilities and governance: the rebirth of production in the theory of economic organization', *Kyklos*, **52** (2), 201–18.

Nelson, R. (1991), 'How do firms differ, and how does it matter?', *Strategic Management Journal*, **12** (Winter), 61–74.

Orr, J. (1990), 'Talking about machines: an ethnography of a modern job', Ph.D. thesis, Cornell University, Ithaca, New York: Cornell University Press.

Pavitt, K. (1998), 'Technologies, products and organization in the innovating firm: what Adam Smith Tells us and Joseph Schumpeter doesn't', *Industrial and Corporate Change*, **7** (3), 433–52.

Pavitt, K. (2002), 'Innovation routines in the business firm: what corporate tasks should they be accomplishing?', *Industrial and Corporate Change*, **11** (1), 117–33.

Wenger, E. (1998), *Communities of Practice: Learning, Meaning and Identity*, Cambridge, UK: Cambridge University Press.

Williamson, O.E. (1999), 'Strategy research: governance and competence perspectives', *Strategic Management Journal*, **20** (12), 1087–108.

Willinger, M. and E. Zuscovitch (1988), 'Towards the economics of information-intensive production systems', in G. Dosi, C. Freeman, R. Nelson and L. Soete (eds), *Technical Change and Economic Theory*, London: Frances Pinter, pp. 239–55.

Zuscovitch, E. (1998), 'Networks, specialization and trust, in P. Cohendet, P. Llerena, H. Stahn and G. Umbhauer (eds), *The Economics of Networks*, Berlin: Springer Verlag, pp. 243–64.

PART II

APPLIED ANALYSES

7. Short-term gain, long-term pain? Implications of outsourcing for organizational innovation and productivity

Andreas Reinstaller and Paul Windrum

7.1 INTRODUCTION

This chapter examines the relationship between new internet-based ICTs, organizational innovation and outsourcing. We consider the range of routines that are being outsourced, and discuss the latest empirical findings regarding the potential benefits and costs of outsourcing activities. These suggest that outsourcing may have advantages in the short run but have negative long-run implications for competitive performance. We argue that a key issue is the impact of outsourcing on a firm's capacity to engage in organizational innovation.

In order to examine this issue, we develop a model of organizational innovation. In this model, the goal of managers is to identify an organizational architecture that more effectively integrates all the administrative routines and productive activities of the firm. As part of the process of innovation, managers can choose to carry out an activity in-house or to outsource that activity. Key factors influencing this decision are the relative information costs of organizing activities internally, and the information costs associated with setting up and maintaining interfaces with external suppliers. Herein lies the importance of new ICT. The introduction of new ICTs can alter the relative costs of internal and external administration. This captures an important stylized fact about knowledge-intensive business services (KIBS), such as business consultants, financial services and ICT services: the rapid expansion of KIBS over the last decade is strongly connected with the introduction and diffusion of internet-based networking ICTs.

The chapter is organized as follows. Section 2 reviews recent empirical studies in order to identify a set of potential benefits and potential disadvantages associated with the outsourcing of routines. Recent empirical literature has highlighted differences in short and long-run benefits and costs. In the short run, outsourcing enables firms to reduce the wage bill (by substituting their own labour with cheaper labour hired by the servicing firm). Additionally, savings are made by the fact that the outsourced activities no longer need to be administered internally. However, there are long-term costs. Increased costs of logistics, in order to integrate the business service provider effectively with the remaining internal activities of the firm, mean management and administrative functions are not reduced overall. More importantly, there is empirical evidence to suggest that outsourcing can be detrimental to the innovative capacity of a firm and, hence, has a negative impact on its long-run productivity growth.

Section 3 introduces the key concepts of organizational architecture and organizational innovation. It then outlines the core theoretical approach that is used to conceptualize organizational innovation. This is based on a modular theory of the firm, which is founded on the twin principles of increasing specialization and the modularization of complex organizational structures. Increasing the modularity of an organizational structure leads to improvements in efficiency through specialization. It also enables a firm to realize system economies that push ahead the productivity frontier. At the core of the theoretical framework is a transmission mechanism between ICT adoption, organizational innovation and outsourcing. This transmission mechanism makes it possible to analyse the conditions under which the adoption of new ICT leads to organizational innovation, de-verticalization and outsourcing. Using this theoretical framework we can critically discuss the long-run implications of outsourcing on productivity. Section 4 describes the simulation model that is used to investigate this long-run phenomenon. It specifies the alternative strategies for organizational innovation available to the firm, the way in which learning is modelled, and the decision rules for ICT adoption and the outsourcing of activities. Section 5 discusses the outputs generated by the simulation model. The results make clear the manner in which the outsourcing of activities restricts the long-term opportunities for organizational innovation, leading to lower productivity growth. Section 6 pulls together the overall findings, and points to interesting directions for further research.

7.2   POTENTIAL ADVANTAGES AND POTENTIAL COSTS OF OUTSOURCING

The 1990s saw a dramatic rise in the number of specialized business service firms. The sheer range of activities being outsourced is highlighted by

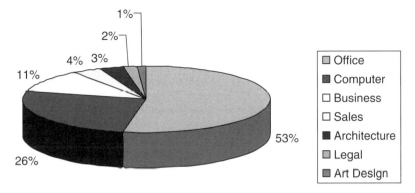

Source: McCarthy (2002).

Figure 7.1 *Variety of activities being outsourced*

McCarthy's 2002 study of outsourcing by US firms. Activities not only include basic back-office activities, such as payrolls, but they also include advanced, back-office activities, such as legal services, and client-facing front-office activities in sales and marketing. The share of activities being outsourced by the firms in this study is presented in Figure 7.1.

While acknowledgement of the role played by business services in economic development is not new (see, for example, Greenfield 1966), empirical studies of their impact are new. For example, Windrum and Tomlinson (1999) tested the contribution to services and manufacturing sectors of knowledge-intensive business services (KIBS), such as business consultants, financial services and ICT services. Using input-output data from 1970 to 1990, they examined Germany, Japan, the Netherlands and the UK. KIBS were found to have a positive impact on both service and manufacturing sectors in all four countries over the 20-year period. Similar findings have been identified in studies by Drejer (2001), Peneder *et al.* (2003) and Tomlinson (2003). So, while the use of business services is not new, there has been a significant growth in the level of outsourcing.

A number of studies have sought to identify the key drivers for outsourcing. One of the best known is in the Morgan Chambers study of FTSE 100 firms (Morgan Chambers 2001). In addition, there is The Outsourcing Institute's study of outsourcing in Japan (Outsourcing Institute 2005). Taken together, these studies provide a consistent picture, presented in Table 7.1. The top three ranked drivers are the same in each study: reduction of operating costs, improving the focus of the business through a reorganization of the activities that are conducted in-house and those that are externally sourced, and access to skills and technologies that

Table 7.1   Drivers of outsourcing by rank

Morgan Chambers study	Outsourcing Institute study
Cost saving	Reduce and control operating costs
Focus on core business	Improve company focus
Access to skills and technology	Gain access to world-class capabilities
Risk management	Free internal resources for other purposes
Quality service improvement	Resources are not available internally
Change enabler	Accelerate re-engineering benefits
Business development	Function is difficult to manage/out of control
Other	Make capital funds available
	Share risks
	Cash infusion

are not held in-house. In each survey these three drivers together account for more than 60 per cent of all responses.

The same three drivers have been highlighted in the literature on KIBS. First, KIBS provide their clients with high quality information on new business opportunities, new trends in the marketplace and the business potential of new technologies, such as new ICTs. Second, through the outsourcing of specific inputs to KIBS, clients can improve productivity and competitive performance as existing in-house inputs are substituted for higher quality, externally sourced inputs. Third, KIBS are exemplars of novel business models. They provide a concrete illustration of new business models and, through their ongoing relationship, introduce clients to these new ways of working and new technologies. Antonelli (1998), for example, highlights the role of KIBS on the diffusion of new ICTs. KIBS are leading advocates of new, internet-based technologies because these technologies enable them to more effectively interface with clients and, as a consequence, to more effectively intermediate experience, information and knowledge across clients. In this way, KIBS have become key intermediaries, improving the efficiency and speed of learning within innovation networks.

There exists a set of potential disadvantages associated with outsourcing. These can have negative long-run implications for organization innovation and, hence, long-run productivity growth. An empirical study based on a large-scale survey of medium and large-size Swedish manufacturing and service firms has been conducted by Bengtsson and von Hartman (2005).[1] They found that companies' evaluations of the direct effects of outsourcing, for example, cost reduction through the reduction of direct personnel, were fulfilled. However, management and administrative functions were not reduced. Indeed, firms reported a strongly negative impact of outsourcing on logistics, for example, manufacturing lead times, delivery times and accuracy. They also reported negative impacts on quality and adaptation to customer demands. The findings indicate that outsourcing is accompanied by more complex logistics, increasing the internal administrative overhead. Bengtsson and von Hartman report that these logistics problems were more common amongst companies that outsource to low-cost countries.

These findings are supported in other research. First, it is observed that the contract needs to be monitored and measured carefully. This can prove expensive, and increasingly expensive, if skills in the client firm are lost over time (Domberger 1998). Second, governance inseparability between client and supplier means that considerable investment in interpersonal and administrative relations between firms is necessary in order to support the new division of labour (Steinmueller 2003, Miozzo and Grimshaw 2005). Third, poorly delivered services will negatively affect a client's production or, where end-user services are delivered, a client's brand and reputation (Hinks and Hanson 2001). Fourth, the security of sensitive information needs to be considered, with an increased risk of disclosure of the clients' sensitive internal information (Mylott 1995). Fifth, there are well documented cases of knowledge and information, acquired by the service provider, being shared with a client's competitors. Clients believed that services and information would be proprietary, while the service providers saw the transactions as the basis for further business within the same sector.

However, it is not just low-skilled activities that are being outsourced. Complex production and advanced R&D are also being outsourced. The inseparability of ICT from production means that suppliers are not turn-key, i.e. they cannot be easily substituted (Miozzo and Grimshaw 2005). Prencipe (1997) highlights the dangers of outsourcing activities based on simple notions of core and non-core competences. The outsourcing of what today appear to be non-core competences can seriously impair the development of new (core) technological competences in the future. Separation of development and production hampers innovation. Brusoni *et al.* (2001) emphasize the importance of retaining control over R&D, and the ability to coordinate the R&D, design and manufacturing activities of suppliers.

A particularly important finding has been made by Gianelle and Tattara's (Chapter 10 in this book) extensive empirical study of the impact of outsourcing by textile, clothing and footwear manufacturers in the Veneto region of Italy.[2] They find that, in the vast majority of cases, there is a one-off reduction in cost as Italian labour is substituted by cheaper foreign labour. The machinery and the production techniques that are used remain unchanged. Thus, machines previously used in the Veneto area were merely shipped abroad to be used by the new providers. Gianelle and Tattara observe that the reorganization of production may bring about management innovations (product modularization, export of knowledge and so on) in the future, but that these have not happened to date. Only when this occurs will there be further improvements in productivity.

To summarize, a growing body of empirical research suggests that short-run gains may be more than offset in the longer term, leading to lower long-run productivity growth. In order to explore these issues we formulate a theoretical framework that contains a specific transmission mechanism between ICT adoption, organizational innovation and outsourcing. The framework explains why outsourcing can negatively impact organizational innovation and productivity in the long run. Specifically, outsourcing reduces the total set of modular elements that can be experimented with in the future. With fewer components under their control, managers are unable to experiment with all possible organizational combinations. The danger is that this puts the discovery of more efficient organizational architectures out of reach. Hence, the firm can become locked in to a suboptimal architecture. In this event an outsourcing firm will achieve lower productivity growth than a firm that did not engage in outsourcing because the latter is free to explore the entire space of organizational architectures. This argument is developed in the following sections of the chapter.

7.3   ORGANIZATIONAL INNOVATION AND OUTSOURCING

The goal of organizational change is the identification of an organizational architecture that more effectively integrates all the administrative activities of the firm. An organizational architecture is a hierarchical structure that solves two key problems. The first is the 'fundamental coordination problem'; namely, how to most effectively organize the value-adding activities and information flows of the firm in order to maximize profit. In addition, managers need to resolve the 'agency problem': to realize and enforce coordination and control in production, both internally and across the boundary of the firm.

Organizational innovation involves the search for new organizational architectures that alter the organizational structure of the firm, and change the boundary between the firm and markets (verticalization/de-verticalization). As described above, it is a search process that is conducted within a complex search space containing many dimensions, and in which the dimensions are related to one another in highly non-linear ways. Dealing with this organizational complexity requires managers to engage in ongoing strategic experimentation and learning. It is this ongoing problem-solving activity that drives organizational change and innovation over time.

Our analysis is based on a modular theory of the firm, developed in recent work by Langlois and Robertson (1995), Baldwin and Clark (1997), Langlois (2002, 2003) and Marengo and Dosi (2005). The theory brings together Adam Smith's principles of specialization and the division of labour (Smith 1776), and Herbert Simon's discussion of complexity and the near-decomposability of complex problems (Simon 1996, 2002), and provides a useful means of discussing organizational change and innovation. We will use this theory to identify the set of conditions under which modularization is associated with outsourcing to specialist KIBS, and to consider the impact of new ICTs on the decision to outsource.

Simon (1996, 2002) provides an important insight into problem-solving activity in general. He provides us with an idea of how problem-solving activity occurs in complex systems. Simon suggested that complex problems can be made more manageable by breaking them down into a set of constituent parts, or 'modular components'. In this way, the number of distinct elements in a system is reduced by grouping them into a smaller number of sub-systems. The great advantage of modularization is that improvements can be made to one sub-component of the system without the need to change all other parts of the system (as would be the case if there were no modularization). There is a cost, however. This is associated with the establishment and maintenance of organizational interfaces between sub-components. Such interfaces enable a sub-component to function compatibly with all sub-components. This ensures the organizational structure as a whole functions in an integrated way, while maintaining a high degree of independence for each sub-component.

Smith's principle of specialization through the division of labour is a way of dealing with this problem-solving activity. Smith's classic example is the pin factory. A range of complex value-adding processes are broken down and divided into a finer set of specialized functions. This specialization raises the efficiency of production. While Smith's example is of specialization in the organization of production, the principle holds equally for specialization in the organization of administration (our current focus). Firms engage in continual, ongoing experimentation in all aspects of the organization, not just production. This includes decisions about what to produce, the inputs that are required, what should be produced in-house or bought in markets, the geographical location of production, sales and so on, the appropriate organization structure of the firm, and the information and communication requirements of the organization. Placing Smith's discussion within Simon's framework of decomposable complex problems, the problem that faces managers is how to decompose a set of interrelated, value-adding activities into a set of modular sub-systems and, second, how to coordinate these sub-systems. Through successful modularization, a complex system is transformed into a nearly decomposable one.

To this theory we add the concept of 'system economies' introduced by Nightingale *et al.* (2003). In our interpretation system economies are mostly due to improvement in the control of a given set of productive activities and, hence, operate at the meta level. Managers seek to improve productivity by reorganizing the way in which the firm's value-adding activities interact. This productivity improvement is gained through the design of a more effective organizational architecture. Organizational innovation, the process through which new designs are arrived at, involves either splitting the administrative tasks into more organizational modules or, alternatively, the integrating of organizational modules to increase control of the modular elements and their interaction. A superior organizational design improves the coordination and control of goods, traffic, materials, funds, services and information that flows through the complex supply, production and distribution activities of the firm. In this way, better organizational architectures (i.e. more effective modularization schemas) increase the productive utilization of the firm's installed productive capacity.

Organizational innovation begets further organizational innovation over time. Managers gain a more specific view of the different activities of the firm, and see the potential creative opportunities that arise by breaking down 'departmental silos' and creating novel synergies between activities (i.e. new organizational combinations). For example, creating stronger interactions between the sales and production departments may lead to new product opportunities being realized. These, in turn, may lead to economies of scope and, if able to develop new markets, economies of scale. This picks up on the point made by Baldwin and Clark (1997) that the more modular the organizational architecture, the greater the likelihood of stimulating new inventions, i.e. innovation in products/services, distribution and the other key value-adding activities of the firm.

We suggest that the extent of organization specialization ultimately depends on a number of demand and supply side factors. On the demand side, it will depend on the extent of the market (i.e. increases in population and income), and the degree of competition (the elasticity of demand) (Young 1928). On the supply side, it is affected by the availability of ICTs that enable activities to be subdivided and coordinated, and which enable managers to deal with the agency problem. To do this, managers must be able to generate information on the parts of the organization for which they are directly responsible, and to interact with one another in order to exchange information about different parts of the organization. Together, the demand and supply side factors determine the extent to which activities can be effectively modularized and technical hierarchies established.

A number of issues can be discussed within this theoretical framework. To start with, it clarifies the relationship between new ICTs and more effective administrative control, leading to system economies. The application of new, improved ICTs enables further modularization of the organization to occur by lowering the cost of managing and controlling information, leading to increased system economies.[3] It was Chandler (1962, 1977) who first claimed that technology directly affects organizational structure. His observation goes to the heart of our discussion. New ICTs alter the set of feasible technological opportunities in production and the division of labour (the fundamental coordination problem), and the opportunities for effective coordination and control within and across the boundary of the firm (the agency problem). These alter the relative efficacy of holding activities in-house and outsourcing. Depending on the particular vintage of ICTs, technological opportunities and cost reductions may stimulate verticalization or de-verticalization.

Internet-based ICTs significantly reduce external coordinational costs. This opens up new opportunities for outsourcing within new, experimental organizational architectures. Over the last decade, a new generation of 'networking' ICTs (built on open web and internet protocols) have provided the means for a radical reorganization of supply chains, opening up previously inconceivable levels of interaction between companies. This includes new opportunities for outsourcing to specialist KIBS providers. The networked corporation has emerged as a consequence of inter-firm networking activities along the supply chain. There is a flattening of the hierarchy of the firm, a tendency towards vertical disintegration and for individual business units to become smaller in size.

It is important to note that the relationship between new ICTs and outsourcing is not simple. Different types and vintages of ICTs have different impacts on internal and external communication costs. Internet technologies, for example, lower the cost of internal administration (through applications such as intranets) as well as reducing the administration cost of external interaction. Others reduce internal costs only. The ICTs discussed by Chandler – i.e. calculators, typewriters, Hollerith electric tabulating machines and book-keeping machines – were limited in their application to internal administrative activities (Reinstaller and Hölzl 2004). Chandler (1977) and Yates (2000) discuss the way in which these technologies were essential for the emergence of the modern hierarchical organization from the 1860s to the 1930s. Large corporations were the key purchasers of these new technologies, and these technologies in turn further enhanced their ability to grow in size, with a tendency towards vertical integration and the greater centralization of activities by bringing activities in-house, increasing the hierarchy within the firm.

A second issue that is central to this chapter is the implication of outsourcing for long-run firm performance. On the one hand, as discussed, internet-based technologies reduce the cost of setting up organizational and information interactions with KIBS. This makes it possible to outsource activities that can be delivered more cheaply by the external supplier. At the same time, outsourcing reduces the internal administration overheads of the firm. However, there are limits to the benefits of modularization. To start with, while internal administration overheads are reduced, external administration overheads rise because an effective interface with an external provider needs to be set up and maintained. The net benefit, in terms of administrative overheads, depends on whether the cost of the external interface is greater or less than the cost of the internal interface. This is the non-separability effect discussed by Steinmueller (2003) and Miozzo and Grimshaw (2005). They suggest that governance structures that oversee interface interactions between client and supplier represent large, sunk investments. Consequently, suppliers are not easily substituted.

A potentially important downside is the impact of outsourcing on the client's long-run potential for organizational innovation and, hence, on its long-run productivity growth. To understand this, let us apply the transmission mechanism just discussed. If new, internet-based ICTs significantly reduce external administration costs compared to internal administration costs, there is a stimulus for outsourcing. However, by outsourcing, the set of internal activities under the direct management of the firm is reduced. This reduces the set of modular elements with which managers can experiment and innovate to create new, more efficient organizational architectures. In the long-run this can lead to a lower productivity growth of the client firm. Prencipe (1997) and Brusoni *et al.* (2001), for example, stress the need to retain control over R&D, not just for the activity itself, but because it is important to maintain control of the coordination of R&D, design and manufacturing activities.

7.4   THE MODEL: ORGANIZATIONAL INNOVATION, INFORMATION TECHNOLOGIES AND OUTSOURCING

In this section we develop a simulation model that captures some of the core ideas of organizational modularity, and discuss how ICTs and the outsourcing of business services can affect the long-run performance of a firm.

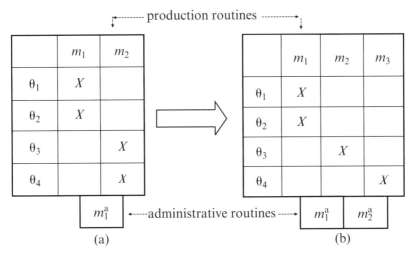

Figure 7.2   Interdependence and modularity in organizational architectures

For this purpose we define the organization as a complex system. The model focuses on the administrative layer within the firm and analyses the influence of innovations in business administration on shop floor productivity. Management seeks to improve this system by searching for better organizational architectures. We also analyse the influence of new ICTs on this choice. As firms are boundedly rational, strategies for organizational innovation are adaptive. The management learns from its past experience of organizational restructuring.[4]

7.4.1   Organizational Architectures

Figure 7.2 shows how we conceptualize an organizational architecture. We assume the administration of a firm delivers services to productive routines that generate a firm's value added. The quality of these services, θ_1 to θ_4 in Figure 7.2, has an impact on the performance of productive routines. These services are produced by organizational routines m_1 and m_2 (Figure 7.2a), which produce a subset of all services. These two routines are linked together through a coordination routine m_1^a. More generally, the organization of a firm consists of a set of n_t organizational modules or routines m_i, grouped by means of n_{t-1} organizational routines m_j^a into an organizational architecture $d_t = \langle m_1, m_2, \ldots, m_{n_t}; m_1^a, m_2^a, \ldots, m_{n_{t-1}}^a \rangle$.[5] Since the division of labour inside the firm can vary over time, n_t carries the time index t. The array $d_t \in D$ corresponds to the particular organizational architecture of the administrative activities that are in use within the firm at time t. It is drawn from of a finite space D of possible organizational architectures, which the management explores over time.

Each of the routines used in an architecture consists of λ_i sub-routines or $m_i = \langle x_h \rangle_{h=1}^{\lambda_i}$; λ_i is allowed to vary across routines. These routines produce a vector θ of k services for the productive routines that are operated by the firm. Together these output characteristics meet well-defined customer needs in the market in which the firm operates. In our model the organization of a firm is therefore defined through the characteristics of an organizational architecture d_t given by n_t organizational modules m_i, and k service characteristics. The number of modules n_t is therefore a measure of the degree of modularity of the organizational architecture.

The sub-routines x_h in each module m_i are strongly related to one another, i.e. the performance of each sub-routine $\phi(x_h)_t$ at time step t affects the performance of all other sub-routines in the module, and its performance is in turn influenced by all other sub-routines $\phi(x_{-h})_t$ in the module. Viewed this way round, it implies that the performance of all sub-routines $\phi(x_{-h})_t$ change if $\phi(x_h)_t$ changes. It also follows that a subset $k_i \subset k$ of output characteristics is directly and indirectly affected by all x_h sub-routines in a module m_i. The overall performance $\phi(m_i)_t$ of a module m_i is therefore the result of negative and positive feedbacks between the sub-routines it contains. These interdependencies reflect a situation that is typical in team production, where the skills and activities of the team members are closely complementary and integrated. As a result, if one member performs under par, the work efficiency of all other members is affected.

If the management wants to improve service θ_3 produced in organizational module m_2, then changing the work profile of the related activity x_h will actually imply that the performance of the sub-routine producing service θ_4 is also affected. In the simulations $\phi(m_i)_t$ will be determined by drawing λ_i values from a uniform distribution with $\phi(x_h)_t \rightarrow \text{Uniform}[0,1]$ and calculating the average over the λ_i sub-routines. The impact of all n service producing administrative routines on firm performance is then given by, $\Phi_t = \frac{1}{n} \sum_{i=1}^{n} \phi(m_i)_t^6$.

In Figure 7.2b the problem of strong complementarity is resolved by splitting routine m_2 into two distinct sub-routines, each focused on producing one service. The coordination problem between the two sub-routines is solved by introducing a coordination mechanism between the two, that is, the modules m_i are linked through organizational and administrative routines m_1^q that act as interfaces between routines and neutralize strong complementarities. As a consequence, hierarchy increases and the coordination overhead increases. This captures Simon's (1996) idea of realizing near-decomposable architectures in order to better control complex

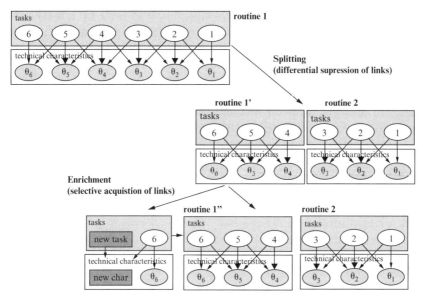

Figure 7.3 *Splitting and enrichment as strategies in organizational redesign*

problems. In this process 'system economies' are realized (see Nightingale *et al.* 2003).

7.4.2 Organizational Learning: Exploitation versus Exploration

Managers are assumed to use a set of strategies S to explore the space of organizational architectures D. The strategy space $S = (s_1, s_2, s_3)$ consists of three strategies, each of which is used with probability μ_j at each time step t. The firm pursues them to improve the administrative services that have an impact on the performance of productive routines used on the shop floor. The first strategy s_1 corresponds to learning by doing. In this case all values for $\phi(x_h)_{t+1}$ are redrawn. If the average over the λ_i sub-routines increases, this will correspond to a performance improvement. The second and the third innovation strategies involve changing the organizational architecture of the firm. This is illustrated in Figure 7.3. The firm may engage in identifying and neutralizing some of the complementarities that bind sub-routines into a module. This may enable it to split a more complex activity into a number of less complex routines and redesign its organization accordingly. This decomposition strategy s_2 is called 'splitting'. It corresponds to the development of a near-decomposable architecture of administrative routines. Finally, it may pay the firm to redesign its production and organization by organizing smaller routines into larger, more complex modules. This is the reverse strategy of decomposition. It involves the selective acquisition of complementarity relationships between previously unrelated routines, say by supporting the development of synergies. This integration strategy s_3 will be termed 'job-enrichment'. In both s_2 and s_3 the organizational architecture is changed, with poorly performing routines replaced by better performing routines.[7] In this case all performance values $\phi(x_h)_{t+1}$ for the elements in the new module(s) are redrawn. If their joint average increases, this will also correspond to a performance improvement.

These strategies are assumed to affect the performance Φ_t of productive routines through system economies, i.e. by allowing for improved control of productive routines, pushing the productivity of a given technology towards its limit.

As discussed earlier, the literature on modularity advances the argument that an increase of the modularity of a system also leads to an improvement in the innovation rate. This is because modularity allows a better understanding of the workings of a system, making it easier to recombine routines, increasing the probability of discovering better ways of doing things. In our case we will assume that, depending on the degree of decomposition of the administration of the firm given by the number of routines n, the likelihood of discovering better ways of organizing the production process will increase if the firm invests in this exploration process. This will push ahead the performance Φ_t of productive routines by a factor $(1 + \varepsilon_t)$, where $\varepsilon_{t+1} = \varepsilon_t(1 + \tau)$. In the simulation parameter τ has a small positive value as does ε_t at $t = 0$. The probability of the firm making an innovation ε_t is determined by a Poisson process with an arrival rate α. Following Silverberg and Verspagen (1994), we assume the firm's investments have first increasing and then decreasing returns. This is captured by a logistic representation of the arrival rate given by

$$\alpha_{t+1} = \frac{\alpha_{min}\alpha_{max}}{\alpha_{min} + (\alpha_{max} - \alpha_{min})^{-(r*n_t)}} \tag{1}$$

Here α_{min} represents a small autonomous probability of making a fortuitous innovation without investing in this type of innovation, and α_{max} corresponds to an asymptotic saturation level of the arrival rate. As can be seen, this process depends on the propensity to invest r and on the degree of decomposition. This captures the innovation potential.

The firms maximizes profits $\Pi_{d_i}(s_t)$. The behaviour of the firm is given by the probability distribution over three alternative strategies. The innovation policy mix $s_t = [\mu_{1,t}s_1 \ \mu_{2,t}s_2 \ \mu_{3,t}s_3]'$, with $\mu_{1,t} + \mu_{2,t} + \mu_{3,t} = 1$, evolves through reinforcement learning given some initial probabilities $\mu_{j,t=0}$. This probability should not be interpreted as conscious randomization. Rather, it indicates (from the perspective of the outside observer) how likely it is that the decision maker will choose each of the three strategies. The reinforcement learning dynamics are those of Arthur (1991), where each of the strategies is allocated strength according to its past contribution to the performance of the firm.

$$\mu_{j,t+1} = \mu_{j,t} + \frac{\Delta\Pi(s_j)_t - \mu_{j,t}\sum_j\Delta\Pi(s_j)_t}{\sum_j\sum_t\Delta\Pi(s_j)_t}, \tag{2}$$

where $\Delta\Pi(s_j)_t = \Pi(s_j)_t - \Pi(s_j)_{t-1}$ indicates the change in the performance improvement between two time steps t and $t - 1$ where strategy s_j was used. Equation 2 reinforces the strategies that performed best in the past, i.e. those that previously maximized profits.

7.4.3 Costs of Production

Let us assume that white-collar routines are not productive in themselves, but improve the utilization and development of the firm's productive resources. More precisely, we assume that the services produced by an administrative activity m_i have an impact on the performance of productive routines, $\phi(m_i)_t$. As mentioned previously, the impact on the unit costs of productive routines by all n modules is given by Φ_t. In order to run simulations, we choose a simple and well-behaved functional form to represent the effect of performance improvements on the unit costs of productive routines – one that captures the central ideas while ensuring unstable outcomes are avoided. We specify this as Equation 3,

$$vc_{d_t} = w_p l_p e^{-(1+\varepsilon_t)\Phi_t}, \tag{3}$$

where w_p is the average wage bill per unit of output paid for productive routines, and l_p is the unit labour requirement.

In the administration of a firm there are two types of routines. The first set of routines produces services for productive routines. The second set of routines coordinate the interaction between these services. Only service producing administrative routines are outsourced since coordination routines typically reflect critical management skills. We will also assume that the number of services a module produces is proportional to its skill intensity, i.e. the more services an activity produces, the higher are the skills required to carry them out. This implies that the average wage paid to these routines is higher than to routines where only a few services are produced. For simplicity we assume that the unit wage cost paid to productive routines for producing one service is the same as carrying out one coordination task.

Information technologies affect coordination costs. We distinguish between the cost of internal coordination and the cost of external coordination. Total administrative overhead costs are then defined by

$$oc_{d_i} = \left(zl_a w\bar{\lambda} + (1 - z) \sum_\ell p_\ell \right) + l_c w(v_{int}e^{-\theta_{int}} + v_{ext}e^{-\theta_{ext}}), \qquad (4)$$

where l_a and l_c are the unit labour requirements for service and coordination routines, w is the going wage rate paid per 'skill unit', $\bar{\lambda}$ is the average number of services produced in each administrative activity, p_ℓ are the prices paid for outsourced routines, v_{int} and v_{ext} are the number of internal and external coordination routines, and θ_{int} and θ_{ext} reflect the impact of the use of ICTs on internal and external coordination costs, respectively. Variable z $(0 \le z \le 1)$ weights the unit costs of production of administrative services produced in-house and those externally produced by their respective share in the total number of services that are produced.

We assume a subcontractor typically has a cost advantage in producing a particular service. If a specific service producing administrative module m_i is outsourced, the unit cost of production of its services by the service firm is then given by

$$cs_\ell = l_{a,\ell} w\lambda_{i,\ell}\gamma_\ell + l_{c,\ell} w(v_{int,\ell}e^{-\theta_{int}} + v_{ext,\ell}e^{-\theta_{ext}}), \qquad (5)$$

where γ now reflects the comparative cost advantage service firm l has in producing the services of administrative activity m_i. In the simulations we will assume that $\gamma \to N(1, \sigma^2)$, i.e. the cost advantage, is normally distributed around a mean of 1 with some variance σ^2. Variables $l_{a,\ell}$ and $l_{c,\ell}$ reflect the relative unit labour requirements for service producing and coordination routines, and $v_{int,\ell}$ and $v_{ext,\ell}$ give the number of internal and external coordination routines the service supplier has to manage. Assuming the supplier has some market power, such that they are able to charge a positive mark-up ξ over costs, the unit price for the services of supplier l to the outsourcing firm is given by

$$p_\ell = (1 + \xi)cs_\ell \qquad (6)$$

Suppose the firm has a certain propensity r to invest part of its revenues into the exploration of innovation potentials due to the modularity of the administration. These costs are then given by

$$rc_t = rp_t q_t, \tag{7}$$

where p_t and q_t are the prices charged and the quantities sold at a time step t.

Profits

If the firm acts in an environment in which monopolistic competition prevails, it will face a downward sloping (inverse) demand given by

$$p_t = \frac{Is}{q_t^{1/\eta}} \tag{8}$$

where p_t is the price the firm is able to charge at time t, Is is the amount of income customers spend on the firm's product, q_t is the firm's output and η, $\eta > 1$, is the price elasticity of demand. Following standard theory, the optimum output and price for a given organizational architecture d_t are given by

$$q_{d_t}^* = \left[\frac{Is(1 - 1/\eta)}{vc_{d_t} + oc_{d_t}} \right]^\eta \tag{9}$$

Therefore, for each organizational architecture d_t, the firm tries to maximize profits

$$\Pi_{d_t}^*(s_t) = Is \left[\frac{Is(1 - 1/\eta)}{vc_{d_t} + oc_{d_t}} \right]^{\eta - 1} - (vc_{d_t} + oc_{d_t}) \left[\frac{Is(1 - 1/\eta)}{vc_{d_t} + oc_{d_t}} \right]^\eta - rc_t - c_t \tag{10}$$

by reducing unit costs of production. In the model the firm does this by pursuing different strategies s_t of organizational innovation. The term c_t reflects fixed capital cost. We assume the firm needs to keep its capital-output ratio constant and therefore invests or disinvests as output changes.

The innovation and outsourcing decision

The decision to adopt an organizational innovation, and the decision to outsource, will depend on the economic profitability of doing so. Therefore the management of the firm will calculate the expected profits $E[\Pi_{d'_{t+1}}(s_t)]$

the new organizational architecture d'_{t+1} is likely to generate, and compares this with the profit generated by the current architecture. Hence, the decision rule to adopt a new organizational architecture d'_{t+1} is given by the following inequalities:

$$\begin{cases} \Pi_{d_t}(s_t) \geq E[\Pi_{d'_{t+1}}(s_t)] & \text{reject innovation} \\ \Pi_{d_t}(s_t) < E[\Pi_{d'_{t+1}}(s_t)] & \text{accept innovation} \end{cases} \quad (11)$$

Depending on the management strategy, a firm may have a certain propensity to pursue outsourcing as a strategy such that, given strategy parameter os, $0 \leq os \leq 1$, it calculates the expected profits of outsourcing these services to other firms, leading to an organizational architecture d''_{t+1} with probability pr_{os}

$$\text{if} \quad pr_{os} > os \begin{cases} E[\Pi_{d''_{t+1}}(s_t)] \leq E[\Pi_{d'_{t+1}}(s_t)] & \text{in-house} \\ E[\Pi_{d''_{t+1}}(s_t)] > E[\Pi_{d'_{t+1}}(s_t)] & \text{outsource} \end{cases} \quad (12)$$

These are the decision rules the firm follows in order to maximize profitability at each moment in time.

7.5   RESULTS

Using the model, we examine four different scenarios. The parameters used to calibrate the model are given in the Appendix. The results of the simulation runs are presented in Figure 7.4. The plots in the top quadrant of Figure 7.4 show the development of productivity in the firm. The bold line represents the mean over 50 runs for each parameter setting, while the thin dashed lines represent the 95 per cent confidence interval of the results of the runs. The plots in the middle of Figure 7.4 show the development of overhead costs over time and, finally, the plots in the bottom quadrant show the depth of hierarchy of the firm's administration structure.

The first two scenarios, presented in the left part of Figure 7.4, juxtapose the impact of ICTs on performance, and the costs of the firm for a given high propensity of managers to choose outsourcing as a strategy. The results for low internal/high external coordination costs are represented by dash-dot-dash lines, while those for equally efficient internal and external communication costs are represented by unbroken lines.

To start with, the results indicate that the probability to outsource is greater the higher is the propensity for managers to outsource and the lower

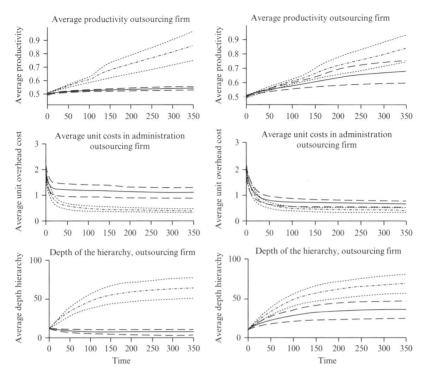

Note: Left: Scenario with high outsourcing propensity by management. Right: Scenario with low outsourcing propensity by management. Dash-dot-dash lines represent runs with low internal communication costs only for a given outsourcing propensity. Unbroken lines represent runs with low internal and external communication costs for a given outsourcing propensity. The bold lines represent means over 50 runs, the thin dashed lines 95 per cent confidence intervals around these means.

Figure 7.4   Simulation runs

are external coordination costs. Second, a firm that engages in outsourcing will suffer higher average unit costs than if it had not engaged in outsourcing. While managers engaging in outsourcing will enjoy a short-run cost cutting benefit at the outset, they unwittingly reduce the long-run innovation potential of the firm because modular sub-systems are no longer under their control. This precludes them from engaging in certain types of organizational innovation (i.e. recombination and splitting strategies) in the future, leading to lower long-term productivity growth and, hence, higher average costs.

It should be noted that managers are learning myopically over time. They do not have information on the payoffs of all possible choices and engage in pure learning-by-doing. That is to say, they can only observe the payoffs associated with their own past choices. Implicitly, we are assuming that managers are unable to observe the pay-offs of other firms, who may choose different strategies. This is a reasonable assumption because, unlike physical products and services which can be obtained and reverse engineered, managers do not have ready access to information on other firms' organizational structures, administrative services and the performance of such organizational structures. The onus is therefore on learning from one's own experience.

Under these circumstances, the managers of the firm perceive there to be cost-cutting potentials if ICTs lead to a fall in external coordination costs. In this case managers proceed to outsource a high number of service routines. As a consequence, the depth of the hierarchy is reduced and in the beginning overhead costs fall as well. Productivity also grows initially. It grows at a much slower rate than if the firms had not outsourced, but of course the firm will not actually 'see' this in practice because it has chosen to pursue the outsourcing trajectory. Unfortunately, as the firm continues along this path, productivity growth continues to fall and can even begin to stagnate as organization innovation opportunities are ever further reduced due to the ongoing outsourcing of organizational modules. The upshot is that managers who focus on the short-run cost-cutting benefits of outsourcing unwittingly reduce the scope for long-run organizational innovation, inhibiting system economies, and thereby reduce long-run productivity growth. This accords with recent empirical findings.

An alternative scenario is that new ICT lowers internal coordination costs. This would support the development of increased modularity in the firm's administration. As the activities become more specialized, it is easier to improve the quality of their service to the productive routines. At the same time, the long-run potential for radical organizational innovations is exploited successfully. The long-run productivity of the firm under this scenario outperforms alternative scenarios where external coordination costs are lowed by new ICTs and firms engage in outsourcing. These results lend support to the thesis that the 'quick-fix' strategy, to outsource in order to reduce costs, endangers the long-run performance and survival of firms.

On the right hand side of Figure 7.4 we present the results for the scenarios where managers' propensity to outsource are low. Again, we consider what happens if ICT reduces external coordination costs and what happens if ICTs reduce internal coordination costs. Once again, the finding is that ICTs which stimulate internal organizational innovation outperform the scenario where ICTs stimulate outsourcing. As before, the reason is that the long-run productivity potential of the firm depends on the degree of decomposition of administrative routines. Therefore firms are always better off in the long run if they keep the service routines in-house and reap all the benefits of organizational innovation. Bear in mind that once routines are outsourced, suppliers in the model charge a constant price and no longer improve the quality of the services they deliver. As a consequence, producing services in-house is the superior (dominant) strategy.

The results mirror the observations of the empirical studies discussed in Section 3. However, it is important to observe that long-run productivity of the runs with low external coordination cost comes close to the long-run productivity levels where external coordination costs are high in the upper end of the confidence interval. This outcome depends on the propensity of the firm to invest in radical organizational innovation. It suggests that if a firm chooses to (moderately) outsource and is inclined to do so by low external coordination costs, it should scale up its investment in radical organizational innovations, which will better exploit the innovation potentials.

7.6 CONCLUSIONS AND DIRECTIONS FOR FURTHER RESEARCH

This chapter has investigated the thesis that outsourcing routines to business services (KIBS) can cut certain types of administrative costs but reduce long-run productivity growth. This is the striking thesis emerging from recent empirical research on the long-term impact of outsourcing on the innovative capability and productivity growth of client firms. The chapter summarized the short- and long-term costs and benefits of outsourcing, and proceeded to place them on a more analytical footing by developing a framework of organizational innovation that integrates decisions to outsource with the introduction of new ICTs that reduce external coordination costs. The framework specified a transmission mechanism between the adoption of new ICTs, alternative strategies for organizational restructuring, system economies and the decision to outsource.

The framework has been implemented in a model of organizational innovation. Simulations conducted on this model enable us to consider the short- and long-run impacts of outsourcing on administration overheads and on long-term productivity growth. The interesting finding is that managers can become locked into a low productivity growth trajectory associated with the outsourcing of routines, if they are myopic and learn through their own actions. They perceive outsourcing to cut overhead costs in the short run (as expected), and so engage in further outsourcing thereafter. This is to the detriment of long-run productivity gains (system economies) generated though organizational innovation. This occurs because the potential for organizational innovation is reduced when modular components are outsourced, placing them beyond the control of the firms' management. The findings accord well with the empirical data, and provide a salutary warning for managers and policy makers on the potential long-term implications of outsourcing.

Looking ahead, there is a need to extend the analysis in future research. The current set of results hinge upon a number of conditions. In our model outsourcing is purely cost driven, and important potential interactions between suppliers and service firms, as well as the exchange of competences, are neglected. Additionally, service suppliers provide a one-off cut in cost. They do not subsequently interact with their customer in order to deliver further quality or cost improvements. This accords with the empirical literature previously discussed but, again, may not be universally true. Some KIBS providers, for example, may provide exceptions to this finding. Hence, we will explore the alternative case in future research, where the interaction between service suppliers and firms stretches to the process of organizational innovation. Another simplification in the current version of the model is that it ignores potential conflicts and resistance to organizational change. These may play an important role in management decisions, and are also likely to have an impact on a firm's long-run productivity. In the current model the development of a near-decomposable administrative hierarchy is a frictionless process with perfectly flexible labour markets. Further research will address this issue.

NOTES

1. The analysis is based on a set of written questionnaires collected from 267 firms. All firms have more than 50 employees and are drawn from the ISIC sectors 28–35: metal goods, machinery, office equipment and computers, other electronics, telecoms, instrumentation and the automotive industry.
2. Their statistical findings are drawn from a panel containing 48 joint stock companies, based in the Veneto area, that are in the clothing and footwear sector. They are mainly medium-size firms that have delocalized important production phases abroad.
3. Brynolfsson and Hitt (2000) studied the impact of large ICT investments over the last decades on productivity. They find that, on their own, costly investments have little impact on productivity. They do, however, have very significant impacts on productivity when they are matched with complementary changes in the organizational design.
4. Issues of agency and control in the firm are addressed in Reinstaller (2007).
5. A routine is the process whereby a vector of inputs is transformed into a vector of outputs through the use of specific knowledge, skills and modes of coordination. See Nelson and Winter (1982, Chapter 5). The terms module and routine are used interchangeably in this chapter. We assume that routines are somewhat self-contained elements of the production process.
6. This representation of organizational designs and their impact on the performance of productive activities corresponds to a generalized NK model (Altenberg 1995).
7. Wagner and Altenberg (1996) have discussed decomposition and integration as potential evolutionary mechanisms of change within genetics.

APPENDIX

Table 7.A1   Parameter values used to calibrate the model

Variable	Range/value
Efficiency of internal and external coordination routines $\{\theta_{int}, \theta_{ext}\}$	Scenario with high external coordination costs $\{0.1, 10\}$ Scenario with external coordination cost same as internal $\{10,10\}$
Outsourcing propensity os	$os = 0.2$, $os = 0.9$
Total number of services F	$F = 100$
Wage bill w	$w = 1$
Performance improvement τ	$N(0.01, 0.0025)$
Supplier cost advantage γ	$N(1, 0.0625)$
Investment propensity r	$N(0.02, 0.0025)$
$\alpha_{min}, \alpha_{max}$	$\alpha_{min} = 0.01$ $\alpha_{max} = 1$
l_p	0.8
l_a	$l_a = \dfrac{F}{F + v_{int} + v_{ext}}(1 - l_p)$
l_c	$l_c = \dfrac{v_{int} + v_{ext}}{F + v_{int} + v_{ext}}(1 - l_p)$
z	$z = \dfrac{F - Nos}{F}$ Nos = number of outsourced services; $\sum_{\ell} \lambda_{i,\ell} = Nos$
$l_{a,\ell}$	$l_{a,\ell} = \dfrac{\lambda_{i,\ell}}{\lambda_{i,\ell} + v_{int,\ell} + v_{ext,\ell}}$
$l_{c,\ell}$	$l_{c,\ell} = \dfrac{v_{int,\ell} + v_{ext,\ell}}{\lambda_{i,\ell} + v_{int,\ell} + v_{ext,\ell}}$
Total consumer income allocated to the firm in each period Is	$Is = 100$
Elasticity of demand η	$\eta = 1.5$
Initial degree of decomposition of the techno-organizational architecture n_0	$n_0 = 5$
Average supplier mark-up	$\xi = .05$
$\mu_{i,0}$, $i = 1, 2, 3$	$\mu_1 = \mu_2 = \mu_3 = 0.3$, at $t = 0$

REFERENCES

Altenberg, L. (1995), 'Genome growth and the evolution of the genotype-pheno-type map', in W. Banzhaf and F.H. Eckman (eds), *Evolution and Biocomputation*, Berlin and Heidelberg: Springer-Verlag, pp. 205–59.

Antonelli, C. (1998), 'Localized technological change, new information technology and the knowledge-based economy: the European evidence', *Journal of Evolutionary Economics*, **8** (2), 177–98.

Arthur, B.W. (1991), 'Designing economic agents that act like human agents: a behavioural approach to bounded rationality, *American Economic Review*, **81**, 353–59.

Baldwin, C.Y. and K.B. Clark (1997), 'Managing in an age of modularity', *Harvard Business Review*, **75** (5), 84–94.

Bengtsson, L. and L. Von Hartman (2005), 'Outsourcing manufacturing and its effect on firm performance', paper presented at CINet, Brighton, 4–6 September.

Brusoni, S., A. Prencipe and K. Pavitt (2001), 'Knowledge specialisation, organisational coupling, and the boundaries of the firm: why do firms know more than they make?', *Administrative Science Quarterly*, **46** (4), 597–621.

Brynolfsson, E. and L.M. Hitt (2000), 'Beyond computation: information technology, organisational transformation, and business performance', *Journal of Economic Perspectives*, **117** (Fall), 339–76.

Chandler, A.D. (1962), *Strategy and Structure*, Cambridge, MA: MIT Press.

Chandler, A.D. (1977), *The Visible Hand: The Managerial Revolution in American Business*, Cambridge, MA: Belknap Harvard University Press.

Domberger, S. (1998), *The Contracting Organization: A Strategic Guide to Outsourcing*, Oxford, UK: Oxford University Press.

Drejer, I. (2001), 'Business services as a production factor', CEBR working paper 2001–7, CEBR, Copenhagen.

Greenfield, H.I. (1966), *Manpower and the Growth of Producer Services*, Columbia, New York: Columbia University Press.

Hinks, J. and H. Hanson (2001), 'In-house or outsourced? Making the decision', in J. Hinks and J. Reuvid (eds), *Strategies for Outsourcing and Facilities Management: Managing Business Support Service*, London: Kogan Page, pp. 41–9.

Langlois, R.N. (2002), 'Modularity in technology and organization', *Journal of Economic Behaviour and Organization*, **49** (1), 19–37.

Langlois, R.N. (2003), 'The vanishing hand: the changing dynamics of industrial capitalism', *Industrial and Corporate Change*, **12** (2), 351–85.

Langlois, R.N. and P.L. Robertson (1995), *Firms, Markets and Economic Change*, London: Routledge.

Marengo, L. and G. Dosi (2005), 'Division of labor, organizational coordination and market mechanisms in collective problem-solving', *Journal of Economic Behavior and Organization*, **58** (2), 303–26.

McCarthy, J.C. (2002), '3.3 million US service jobs go offshore', Techstrategy brief, Forrester Research Inc., November, Cambridge, MA, USA.

Miozzo, M. and D. Grimshaw (2005), 'Modularity and innovation in knowledge-intensive business services: IT outsourcing in Germany and the UK', *Research Policy*, **34** (9), 1419–39.

Morgan Chambers (2001), 'Outsourcing in the FTSE 100', www.cw360.com/outsourcingreport, 30 September 2007.

Mylott III, T.R (1995), *Computer Outsourcing: Managing the Transfer of Information Systems*, Englewood Cliffs, NJ: Prentice Hall.

Nightingale, P., T. Brady, A. Davies and J. Hall (2003), 'Capacity utilisation revisited: software, control and the growth of large technical systems', *Industrial and Corporate Change*, **12** (3), 477–517.

Nelson, R. and S. Winter (1982), *An Evolutionary Theory of Economic Change*, Boston, MA: Belknap Press of Harvard University Press.

Outsourcing Institute (2005), 'New Workplace: outsourcing in Japan', www.outsourcing.com, 30 September 2007.

Peneder, M., S. Kaniovski and S. Dachs (2003), 'What follows tertiarisation?: structural change and the role of knowledge-based services', *Service Industries Journal*, **23** (2), 47–66.

Prencipe, A. (1997), 'Technological competencies and product's evolutionary dynamics: a case study from the aero-engine industry', *Research Policy*, **25** (8), 1261–76.

Reinstaller, A. (2007), 'The division of labor in the firm: agency, near-decomposability and the Babbage principle', *Journal of Institutional Economics*, **3** (3), 293–322.

Reinstaller, A., and W. Hölzl (2004), 'Complementarity constraints and induced innovation: some evidence from the first IT regime', in J. Foster and W. Hölzl (eds), *Applied Evolutionary Economics and Complex Systems*, Cheltenham, UK and Northampton, MA, USA: Edward Elgar, pp. 133–54.

Silverberg, G. and B. Verspagen (1994), 'Collective learning, innovation and growth in a boundedly rational, evolutionary world', *Journal of Evolutionary Economics*, **4** (3), 207–26.

Simon, H.A. (1996), 'The architecture of complexity: hierarchical systems', in H.A. Simon (ed.), *The Sciences of the Artificial*, Cambridge, MA: MIT Press, pp. 183–216.

Simon, H.A. (2002), 'Near decomposability and the speed of evolution', *Industrial and Corporate Change*, **11** (3), 587–99.

Smith, A. (1776), *An Enquiry into the Nature and Causes of the Wealth of Nations*, Oxford, UK: Clarendon Press.

Steinmueller, W.E. (2003), 'The role of technical standards in co-ordinating the division of labour in complex system industries', in A. Principe, A. Davies and M. Hobday (eds), *The Business of Systems Integration*, Oxford, UK: Oxford University Press, pp. 133–52.

Tomlinson, M. (2003), 'A new role for business services in economic growth', in D. Archibugi and B. Lundvall (eds), *The Globalizing Learning Economy*, Oxford, UK: Oxford University Press, pp. 97–107.

Wagner, G.P. and L. Altenberg (1996), 'Perspective: complex adaptations and the evolution of evolvability', *Evolution*, **50** (3), 967–76.

Windrum, P. and M. Tomlinson (1999), 'Knowledge-intensive services and international competitiveness: a four country comparison', *Technology Analysis and Strategic Management*, **11** (3), 391–408.

Yates, J. (2000), 'Business use of information and technology during the industrial age', in A.D. Chandler and J.W. Cortada (eds), *A Nation Transformed by Information*, Oxford, UK: Oxford University Press, pp. 107–36.

Young, A.A. (1928), 'Increasing returns and economic progress', *Economic Journal*, **38** (6), 527–42.

8. The general profile of the outsourcing firm: evidence for a local production system of Emilia Romagna[1]

Massimiliano Mazzanti, Sandro Montresor and Paolo Pini

8.1 INTRODUCTION

Empirical evidence shows that both the volume and the value of intermediate inputs and business production services contracted out by firms, that is, of outsourcing, have risen dramatically in the last two decades (Domberger 1998; Spencer 2005). The determinants and the implications of the 'buy-rather-than-make' decision have thus become a core topic in industrial organization. In particular, the attention of standard approaches has focused on transaction costs (for example, Grossman and Helpman 2002), ownership allocation and efficient investments (for example, Grossman and Hart 1986), formal versus real authority (for example, Aghion and Tirole 1997) and, in general, on the resulting incentive conflicts (Foss 2000).

Outsourcing has also attracted the attention of 'non-standard' approaches, which have focused on production, rather than transactions, by addressing the role of firms' capabilities and competences (for example, Mahnke 2001). Along the same line, the contractual analysis of the vertical scope of the firm refers to 'real time' (for example, Langlois 1992; Argyres and Liebeskind 1999) by pointing to path-dependency and inertia (Cacciatori and Jacobides 2005).

In spite of the inner differences of these two approaches, it has recently been argued that understanding vertical integration and disintegration could benefit from overcoming the 'production-transaction dichotomy' implied by their independent analyses (Langlois and Foss 1999; Montresor 2004). A combined research effort has thus been recommended from both of the parties (for example, Jacobides and Winter 2005; Nooteboom 2004; Williamson 1999).

While sharing this point of view, in this chapter we claim that a further effort of combined analysis is required in order to capture the embedded nature of the outsourcing firm. That is to say, outsourcing decisions are also affected by the network of relationships the firm hosts internally (in particular, in the form of industrial relations) and establishes externally (in particular, with its suppliers), embedded in specific economic and institutional contexts at the regional and sub-regional level (for example, Taymaz and Kilicaslan 2005).

In order to embed the outsourcing firm it is necessary to abandon the standard view of the firm as a 'monolithic' unit of analysis. Rather, the firm is simultaneously embedded in several contexts (Granovetter 1985), four of which emerge from the literature as the most relevant for the outsourcing decision, namely: (i) the organization which governs its transactions and hosts its resources and competences (Section 2.1); (ii) the market of the inputs (labour, in particular) that the firm uses in its production process (Section 2.2); (iii) the market of the industry in which the firm competes with its output (Section 2.3); and (iv) the technological system in which the firm faces and undertakes the innovation process (Section 2.4).

Accordingly, in this chapter we propose a multi-level analysis of the outsourcing firm, by referring to it as: (i) an organizational unit of analysis; (ii) a production unit of analysis; (iii) an industrial unit of analysis; and (iv) an innovation unit of analysis. In this way we aim to identify a more general theoretical profile of the outsourcing firm, which retains the manifold nature of its embeddedness. Such a profile is then empirically investigated by referring to a specific local production system, hosted by the Italian province of Reggio Emilia (in the Emilia-Romagna region).

The structure of the chapter is the following. Section 2 will address the outsourcing arguments that can be drawn from the literature for each of the four levels of analysis investigated, and translate them into 'expected' correlations. Section 3 will sketch the distinguishing features of the local production system of Reggio Emilia and present the dataset of the application and the econometric model through which the identified theoretical correlations are tested. Section 4 will comment on the emerging profile of the Reggio Emilia outsourcing firm. Section 5 offers the concluding remarks.

8.2 FROM THE OUTSOURCING DETERMINANTS TO THE OUTSOURCING FIRM

The theoretical literature on the outsourcing firm is massive. It would be beyond the scope of this chapter to recompile all the contributions in an exhaustive survey, and it would not be strictly functional to this chapter's aim.

Since we seek to identify the features of the outsourcing firm, and not 'one' or 'the' outsourcing theory, we will draw on different bodies of literature on economic variables and mechanisms which appear relevant in linking the firm's outsourcing decision with the four contexts mentioned above.

In this sense, rather than making a 'shopping-list' review of the topic, we intend to organize the literature in order to achieve a more general and appropriate understanding of the outsourcing firm.

8.2.1   The Outsourcing Firm as an 'Organizational' Unit of Analysis

Looking at the outsourcing firm as an 'organizational' unit of analysis means considering the role of the constituencies with which it is identified in organizational economics. Depending on the theoretical approach these may be: transactions, property-rights, contracts, resources, competences and the like. In particular, we focus here on two of the most widely debated organizational approaches, namely transaction cost economics (TCE) and the resource-competence approach (Williamson 1999). In seeking to combine the two, the main outsourcing arguments at this level of analysis can be organized as follows (Table 8.1).

Asset specificity and governance inseparability (Table 8.1: i, ii, iii, iv)
According to standard TCE (for example, Grossman and Helpman 2002) and, although with differences, property-rights theories (for example, Antras and Helpman 2004), outsourcing is an efficient governance mechanism for those transactions which do not create potential hold-up problems among agents. In particular, transactions involving specific assets, which spur rent seeking behaviour by opportunistic agents, would be better managed within the firm's boundaries rather than outside (Williamson 1975). The reverse would hold true for non-specific assets.

By introducing 'history' into TCE, 'governance inseparability' (Argyres and Liebeskind 1999) is shown to be as important as asset specificity: in brief, new contractual arrangements (such as a prospective outsourcing) are interlinked with, and affected by, the existing contractual nexus of the firm, as it has emerged along its history. It has been argued (for example, Mahnke 2001) that governance inseparability is typically, although not exclusively, related to the presence and role of unions in the firm's outsourcing decisions, as a higher union density makes the firm's governance less inseparable. Furthermore, governance inseparability can be expected to be the more relevant, the older the firm, and the 'thicker' the nexus of contracts which constitute its model of governance. These two variables should thus be expected to act as a countervailing force to outsourcing.

Table 8.1 Expected outsourcing correlations: organizational level

Label	Outsourcing variable	Definition	Positions	Relation with outsourcing
i $ASPEC$	asset specificity	$\left[\dfrac{1}{N_j} \cdot LOCREV_j\right] \cdot REV_{ij}$	N_j = n. of firms in branch j; $LOCREV_j$ = local share of branch j's revenues; REV_{ij} = firm i's share of branch j's revenues	–
ii $UNION_i$	union density (governance inseparability)	$\dfrac{UEMP_t}{EMP_t}$	EMP_i = n. of employees; $UEMP_i$ = n. of unionized employees	–
iii $FIRMAGE_i$	firm age (governance inseparability)	$lg(2002 - SETYEAR_i)$	$SETYEAR_i$ = firm i set-up year 2002: latest year of the survey	–
iv $ASPEGOV_t$	asset specificity conditional on governance inseparability	$ASPEGOV1_t = ASPEC_t \cdot UNION_t$; $ASPEGOV2_t = ASPEC_t \cdot UNIOUT_t$	$UNIOUT_i$ = 1 unions either informed or consulted; $UNIOUT_i$ = 0 neither informed nor consulted	+/–
v $INTASS_t$	intangible assets (intensity of)	$\dfrac{\sum_{t=1998}^{2001} \dfrac{INTINV_{it}}{CAPINV_{it}}}{4}$	$INTINV_{it}$ = intangible investments in t; $CAPINV_{it}$ = invested capital in t	–
vi $ORGPLA_t$	organizational placement (interface knowledge)	$\dfrac{NOUTDIV_t}{NOUT_t}$	$NOUTDIV_t$ = n. of out. activities with division; $NOUT_t$ = n. of out. activities	+
vii $ORGHIER_t$	organizational hierarchy (interface knowledge)	$\dfrac{NHIER_t}{NDIV_t}$	$NHIER_t$ = n. of hierar. levels among divisions; $NDIV_t$ = n. of organizational divisions	+/–

Table 8.1 (continued)

Label	Outsourcing variable	Definition	Positions	Relation with outsourcing
viii *PRODDIF$_t$*	product differentiation		$PRODDIF_t = 1$ if both large and small production $PRODDIF_t = 0$ if either one or the other	+
ix *GEODIV$_t$*	geographical diversification	$\dfrac{\sum_g (REV_{ig} - MREV_{ig})^2}{4}$	g = REG, NAT, EU, INT $MREV_{ig}$ = mean of the 4 g	+
x *MKTUNC$_j$*	market uncertainty	$\sqrt{\dfrac{\sum_{t=1998}^{2001}(REV_{jt} - MREV_{jt})^2}{4}}$	REV_{jt} = sector j's revenues in t $MREV_{jt}$ = mean of REV_{jt}	non-signif.
xi *MKTASPE$_t$*	market uncertainty conditional on asset specificity	$MKTUNC_j \cdot ASPEC_t$		−

What is more, governance inseparability might affect the role of specific assets for outsourcing decisions. Indeed, the firm might find it impracticable to externalize even non-specific assets – when conflicting with other governance arrangements already in place – or end up with outsourcing even specific assets – when this is instead a means for their actual implementation. The interaction of asset specificity with governance inseparability would thus have an ambiguous effect on outsourcing.

Intangible assets and interface knowledge (Table 8.1: v, vi, vii)
TCE explanations of outsourcing also claim that tangible assets are less costly to externalize than intangible assets (for example, human capital intensive), as the required information is more verifiable in contracts involving 'implementation' rather than 'technical' transactions (for example, Gonzalez-Diaz *et al.* 2000). However, outsourcing is also affected by other knowledge-related features emerging from a resource-competence approach to the firm (for example, Montresor 2004), in particular, by knowledge on the interfaces among the firm's assets to be outsourced and those remaining within its boundaries (Nellore and Soderquist 2000). As firms' activities and capabilities are easier to separate from each other the more this 'interface knowledge' is explicit (for example, represented by norms and rules), its degree of codification is an important outsourcing factor to be taken into account. For example, the organizational placement of the outsourced activities in the firm, typically in a corresponding division, represents an outsourcing enabler with an expected positive effect on its decision. The hierarchical degree of the firm's organization, on the other hand, represents both a means for codifying interfaces-knowledge through formal authority, but also a spanner for multiple decision-control mechanisms, which might make outsourcing more conflictive: its expected relationship is thus ambiguous.

Interrelationships among transactions (Table 8.1: viii, ix)
Still according to TCE, externalization to the market is recommended when the dissimilarity of the firm's products and the geographical dispersion of its plants become so high as to make their internal monitoring excessively costly (Coase 1937, reprint in 1988, pp. 45–6). The degree of product differentiation and of geographic diversification of the firm could thus be seen as spurring outsourcing; other reasons for outsourcing differentiated and diversified activities put forward in alternative theoretical accounts include the need for developing intensive and extensive communication channels (Kelley and Harrison 1990).

Market uncertainty and asset specificity (Table 8.1: x, xi)
Finally, according to TCE the firm's outsourcing decision is advantageous providing the uncertainty it faces on the market is not so high as to make relational contracts inescapable (Williamson 1975, pp. 23–5). To be sure, still in accordance with TCE, the costs of re-contracting when faced with possible higher uncertainty actually impede outsourcing only if the relevant transaction requires specific investments, being otherwise unpredictable. It is thus the interaction between these two variables that should be expected to make outsourcing disadvantageous.

8.2.2 The Outsourcing Firm as a 'Production' Unit of Analysis

The firm as a 'production' unit of analysis refers to the manner in which it is addressed in standard microeconomics. It is viewed as a 'technical centre', which transforms factors of production into production output by bearing various kinds of costs: labour costs and capital costs, first and above all. In this vein labour microeconomics and industrial relations, focusing on so-called 'market mediated work arrangements' (Bartel *et al.* 2005), have put forward some outsourcing arguments which can be structured as follows (Table 8.2).

Labour costs and skill content of the firm's activities (Table 8.2: i, ii, iii)
Savings on labour costs are usually considered the most important determinant of what is called 'operative outsourcing': the higher the relative wage paid by one firm with respect to its competitors, the greater the opportunity of saving by contracting out to the latter. However, this interpretation assumes the presence of a sort of 'dual labour market', between the outsourcing client and the provider. If a 'developmental' or a network/cluster approach is instead adopted, for which outsourcing is established between 'similar' firms by following a 'strategic' rationale, rather than searching for lower wages (Deavers 1997), labour costs may have no impact and thus can be expected to be non-significant (Taymaz and Kilicaslan 2005).

Naturally, higher wages immediately prompt reflection on the skill intensity of the outsourcing firm's activities, with respect to which two alternative outsourcing patterns can be suggested, still with an ambiguous outcome (*Ibid.*). On the one hand, the client with a relatively more skilled labour force might wish to embark on greater specialization in 'non-production' activities (for example, R&D, engineering) and thus outsource a greater proportion of standard production activities. Conversely, it might be that firms endowed with high skills are less willing to outsource in order not to lose core activities and thus risk impoverishing the organizational

Table 8.2 *Expected outsourcing correlations: production level*

Label	Outsourcing variable	Definition	Positions	Relation with outsourcing
i $RELWAGE_{ij}$	relative wage	$(LABCOST98\_01_{ij} - MLABCOST98\_01_j)/100$	$LABCOST98\_01_{ij}$ = average labour cost (1998–2001) of firm i in sector j $MLABCOST98\_01_j$ = sectoral mean of $LABCOST98\_01_{ij}$	$+$ or non-signif.
ii $SKILL_t$	skill content (of the firm activities)	$\dfrac{QUALEMP_t}{EMP_t}$	EMP_t = n. of firm i's employees $QUALEMP_t$ = n. of firm i's qualified employees	$+/-$
iii $RWSKILL_{ij}$	relative wage conditional on skill content	$RELWAGE_{ij} \cdot SKILL_{ij}$		$+/-$
iv $UNION_t$	union density (cost of labour)	$\dfrac{UEMP_t}{EMP_t}$	EMP_t = n. of firm i's employees $UEMP_t$ = n. of firm i's unionized employees	$+$
v $FIRMUNC_t$	firm uncertainty	$\dfrac{\sqrt{\sum_{t=1998}^{2001}\left(REV_{it} - MREV_{it}\right)^2}}{4}$ $\dfrac{\sqrt{\sum_{t=1998}^{2001}\left(REV_{jt} - MREV_{jt}\right)^2}}{4}$	REV_{tt} = firm i's revenues in t REV_{jt} = sector j's revenue in t $MREV_{tt}$ = mean of REV_{tt} in 1998–2001 $MREV_{jt}$ = mean of REV_{jt} in 1998–2001	$+$

competences on which the firm's success has been built up. In the latter case, once interaction with the skill content has been taken into account, the effect of the cost of labour in terms of outsourcing should be negative. By retaining both cases, the expected sign of this interactive variable is instead ambiguous.

Union density: labour costs and governance inseparability (Table 8.2: iv)
Another popular determinant of a firm's higher wages is the pervasiveness of unions' presence within the firm (that is, union density), which should thus be positively correlated with outsourcing (Abraham and Taylor 1996). On the other hand, we should consider that the unions' bargaining power also increases the firm's 'governance inseparability', and thus its outsourcing constraining effect. Similarly, the outsourcing inducing effect stimulated by the higher cost of unionized labour could offset that of governance inseparability mentioned above with regard to the organizational level. On this aspect, therefore, the two levels clash and the expected sign depends on which of the two prevails.

Firm uncertainty and demand variability (Table 8.2: v)
The costs the firm bears to accommodate the workload in facing an uneven demand for its products and services (for example, Houseman 2001) are as important as the costs of labour, and they also stimulate outsourcing. First of all, smoothing the flow of work through outsourcing could be for the firm less costly than rescheduling peak-demand periods and off-peak periods internally, through flexible work arrangements (Abraham and Taylor 1996, p. 398).

Second, in deciding the proper 'capacity reservation strategy', installing a fixed capacity and obtaining additional capacity by outsourcing might be less costly – in terms of capacity setting costs – than installing a fixed capacity and postponing the unsatisfied capacity demand to future periods (de Kok 2000).

8.2.3   The Outsourcing Firm as an 'Industrial' Unit of Analysis

As an 'industrial' unit of analysis the firm uses outsourcing as a strategic instrument to compete with its rivals in the sector where they operate. 'Make-or-buy' is represented by industrial organization as a crucial trade-off in facing intra-industry competition (Shya and Stenbacka 2003, p. 205), in turn dependent on the nature and order of the firms' moves and, more in general, on the features of the relevant market structure. The most remarkable among them are the following (Table 8.3).[2]

Table 8.3   *Expected outsourcing correlations: industrial level*

Label	Outsourcing variable	Definition	Positions	Relation with outsourcing
i $HERFREV_j$	Herfindhal of revenues (sector concentration)	$\sum_t \left(\dfrac{REV_{ij}}{REV_j}\right)^2$	REV_{ij} = firm i's revenues in sector j; REV_j = sector j's revenues	$+/-$
ii $FIRMSIZE_t$	Firm size	$FIRMSIZE1_t = SIZE1,$ $SIZE2, SIZE3$ $FIRMSIZE2_t = \log EMP_t$	$SIZE1$ = dummy for firms with 100–249 employees; $SIZE2$ = dummy for firms with 250–499 employees; $SIZE3$ = dummy for firms with more than 500; EMP_t = n. of employees	$+/-$
iii $IN\ DREL_t$	Industrial relations (quality)	synthetic index of industrial relations	see Antonioli et al. (2004)	$+/-$

Market competition and output concentration (Table 8.3: i)

At the outset, it would be sensible to argue that the higher the degree of competition on the market, that is, the less concentrated its output is among few suppliers, the more outsourcing is used as an instrument of competition. However, when outsourcing is viewed as a special kind of 'governance differentiation' (Argyres and Liebeskind 1999, pp. 44–52), which is costly to implement in the presence of 'governance inseparability', a higher level of competition could hamper outsourcing by making the resulting welfare losses less bearable. In less competitive markets firms are, in fact, shielded from competition by the possession of unique resources or capabilities, so that the expected correlation would have a reverse sign: summing up, it is ambiguous.

Firm size (Table 8.3: ii)

If outsourcing is viewed as a special kind of division of labour – between the client and the provider – according to the Smithian argument, increasing returns from specialization emerge providing the outsourcing firm's demand (and output) is large enough. On the other hand, the outsourcing firm usually intends to benefit from the supplier's experience in provision of the relevant production input or service, as the supplier runs the inherent activity on a larger scale and thus with more specialized equipment and more competent skills. Once more, the sign of the relation between firm size and outsourcing depends on the relevant theoretical approach to the issue and is far from being conclusive (for example, Taymaz and Kilicaslan 2005).

Industrial relations (Table 8.3: iii)

The size of the firm also affects its outsourcing decisions via other channels. One important channel is the role which, typically in larger firms, is played by industrial relations (Hyman 2003), whose importance for outsourcing decisions is to be determined case by case. On the one hand, good industrial relations might entail a greater participation of the workforce representatives in the outsourcing decision, and thus increase its feasibility. Furthermore, outsourcing itself might be thought to improve the quality of industrial relations by transferring part of their responsibility outside the firm (Benson and Ieronimo 1996). On the other hand, good industrial relations might once more mean higher governance inseparability and thus less outsourcing.

8.2.4   The Outsourcing Firm as an 'Innovation' Unit of Analysis

The meaning attached to the firm as an 'innovation' unit of analysis stems from neo-Schumpeterian and evolutionary economics. Accordingly, it refers to the firm's capabilities of accumulating knowledge, learning and introducing relatively new products, production processes and organizational arrangements (for example, Dosi 1988). In the latter respect outsourcing represents an extremely sensitive variable for the firm, for the following set of reasons (Table 8.4).

Technological uncertainty and technological regimes (Table 8.4: i, ii)
At the outset, outsourcing could favour the firm's capabilities to deal with the inner uncertainty determined by a 'technological shock': the higher the costs of accommodating the effects of outsourcing through some kind of 'governance switch', the more vertically is integrated the firm (Argyres and Liebeskind 1999). More in general, outsourcing modifies the firm's fitness to the relevant 'technological regime' (TR): in brief, a specific combination of technological opportunity and appropriability conditions, cumulativeness of learning and nature of the knowledge base (Malerba and Orsenigo 1993). In a TR characterized by 'creative destruction' (that is, in a 'Schumpeter-Mark-I TR') outsourcing may be strategic and thus expected, in that it is crucial in upgrading the firm's knowledge and capabilities by tapping into the 'provider', even at the risk of a certain knowledge leakage (Pardo and Rama, Chapter 9 in this book). By contrast, the same kind of leakage does matter and makes outsourcing non-strategic, and thus not expected, in a TR where a competitive advantage is instead guaranteed by 'knowledge accumulation' (that is, in a 'Schumpeter-Mark-II TR') (Mahnke 2001; Malerba and Orsenigo 1993).

The firm's technological innovations (Table 8.4: iii)
At the outset, outsourcing could increase the firm's innovativeness for more than one reason (Robertson and Langlois 1995; Teece 1992). The 'conventional' wisdom which associates innovation exclusively with the advantages of vertical integration has been, in fact, seriously questioned by a 'relational view' (Mol 2005, p. 575). The latter also considers benefits obtained from establishing connections with outside suppliers, regarding such connections as crucial in terms of networking and learning-by-interacting (for example, Dyer and Singh 1998; Brusoni *et al.* 2001) and, in particular, in helping the firm to overcome the 'learning-traps' encountered when seeking to balance knowledge exploration and exploitation (Leonard-Barton 1992). On the other hand, outsourcing could make the firm excessively dependent on external suppliers (Benson and Ieronimo 1996; Dyer and Nobeoka 2000) and compromise its 'absorptive capacity' with regard to new, external knowledge (Cohen and Levinthal 1989) and thus its 'dynamic capabilities' (Teece *et al.* 1997). Once more, an ambiguous effect.

Table 8.4 Expected outsourcing correlations: innovation level

Label	Outsourcing variable	Definition	Positions	Relation with outsourcing
i $TECUNC_j$	technological uncertainty	$$\dfrac{\sum_t INNOK_{ij}}{n_j}$$	$INNOK_{ij}$ = innovation of kind K introduced by firm i in sector j $K = PROD$ (new product) $K = PROC$ (new process) $K = QUAL$ (improved product or process) n_j = n. of firms in sector j	+
ii	technological regime Schumpeter Mark I Schumpeter Mark II			+ −
$HERFINNO_j$	Herfindhal of innovations	$$\sum_t \left(\dfrac{INNOK_{ij}}{INNOK_j} \right)^2$$	$K = PROD, PROC, QUAL$ $INNOK_{ij}$ = firm i's innovations in sector j $INNOK_{ij}$ = sector j's innovations	
$SPEARINNO_j$	Spearman correlation in innovation rankings	$(SPEARINNO_{J1998-1999} +$ $SPEARINNO_{J1999-2000} +$ $SPEARINNO_{J2000-2001})/3$	$SPEARINNO_{ji,t+1} =$ $$1 - \dfrac{G \sum_t^n d_{ij}^2}{n \cdot (n^2 - 1)}$$ $d_{ij} = rank(INTASS_{ij+1}) - rank(INTASS_{ijt})$	

iii $TECINNO_t$	technological innovativeness	$INNO_{PROD_t} + INNO_{PROC_t} + INNO_{QUAL_t}$	$+/-$
iv $INNORAD_t$	innovation radicalness	$INNOK_{ij}$ = innovation K introduced by t $K = PROD, PROC, QUAL$ $INNORAD_t = 1$ if either $INNORAD_t = 0$ if and or $= 1$, or both; $INNORAD_t = 0$ if $INNO_{PROL_t}$ and $INNO_{PROG_t} = 0$ and $INNO_{QUAL_t} = 1$	$+/-$
v $ORGINNO_i$	organizational innovations	synthetic index of new organizational practices see Antonioli *et al.* (2004)	$+/-$
vi $FLEXINNO_t$	firm flexibility	synthetic index of flexibility indicators $INWORKt$ = index of workers' participation to production decisions $FLEXFUNt$ = index of plants and labour relations flexibility $FLEXWAGEt$ = index of wage related flexibility $INNOREWARDt$ = index of compensations linked to performances see Antonioli *et al.* (2004)	$+/-$

161

Innovation radicalness (Table 8.4: iv)
The innovative implications of outsourcing also depend on the kind of technological innovations the firm introduces. Radical innovations, for example, have been argued to be more 'suitable' for vertically integrated firms as they more successfully coordinate the interdependent development efforts required by a 'systemic innovation' (Teece 1986) and/or new 'disruptive' products (Christensen *et al.* 2002). However, when radicalness is due to the rearrangement of existing variables in an unknown framework (Henderson and Clark 1990), a decentralization process which creates an appreciable diversity in information signals and stimulates networking effects might be more suitable than vertical integration, and not only when faced with incremental innovations (Robertson and Langlois 1995). Accordingly, the sign of the present correlation sign is unpredictable unless a more precise meaning of innovation radicalness is referred to.

The firm's organizational innovations and its flexibility (Table 8.4: v, vi)
As outsourcing could be considered as a special kind of organizational change, one might expect to find it as a substitute for other kinds of organizational innovations directed to re-enforcing the efficacy and efficiency of the firm's production processes, or, alternatively, as complemented by other changes in the firm's organization (job rotation practices, quality circles and so on). The quest for higher flexibility, for example, could be carried out by decentralizing some of the firm's activities, in particular when these are regarded as peripheral to the firm. In this context a relationship between flexibility and outsourcing has been put forward with respect to all the different meanings in which the former can be understood (Benson and Ieronimo 1996).[3]

8.3   OUTSOURCING IN A LOCAL PRODUCTION SYSTEM: THE CASE OF REGGIO EMILIA (EMILIA-ROMAGNA)

As we argued at the outset, if we look at the outsourcing firm as an embedded firm, the theoretical correlations identified in the previous section will take on different specifications in different contexts of analysis. In order to illustrate this point, we here focus on the province of Reggio Emilia (RE) (in Emilia-Romagna, Italy), an area which shares the typical features of what have been called the 'local production systems' of the Italian North-East (Seravalli 2001) in terms of firm size and district-like, spatial organization of production. A recent survey, carried out on a population of 257 firms with at least 50 employees in 2002 (Pini 2004), confirms these features, in particular as far as production specialization is concerned (Table 8.5).[4]

The analysis of a representative sample of the same survey (described in the following) reveals that RE is characterized by extensive recourse to outsourcing. Nearly 87 per cent of the sample decentralized some of their activities between 1998 and 2001 (Antonioli and Tortia 2004, p. 68), and as many as 52.3 per cent of the sample decentralized to sub-contractors. On the other hand, differences in outsourcing decisions emerge by considering the number and the nature of the activities which are externalized. In this respect the survey distinguishes as many as 17 activities, which are here grouped into three classes according to a functional criterion: (i) 'ancillary activities', that is to say accessory to the production process as such, implying the transformation of production inputs into output (for example, janitorial services); (ii) 'production supporting activities', not primarily productive but contributing to the production process more directly than the former (for example, engineering); and (iii) 'production activities' (Table 8.6).

These and other specific patterns of outsourcing are related to the characteristics of the RE firms. We tested the validity of the outsourcing arguments put forward in Section 2 by carrying out an empirical analysis on a large sample of RE firms. As it constitutes the core of the empirical analysis, its representativeness is worth commenting on initially (Section 3.1). The methodology (Section 3.2) and the variables (Section 3.3) through which it has been applied will then be presented.

8.3.1 The Dataset

The sample of analysis refers to 166 firms drawn from a population of 257 companies located in the Italian province of Reggio Emilia – listed in both national (Intermediate Census 1996 of the National Institute of Statistics) and local (Camera di Commercio in Reggio Emilia 2001) databases – which were surveyed in 2002 (for a description of the survey, see Pini (2004)). The 257 firms in the population operate in 19 manufacturing sectors as classified by the ISTAT-ATECO 91 codes and are all firms with at least 50 employees.

Although the respondent firms numbered 199, economic performance indicators as well as variables concerning firm characteristics were available for only 166 of the respondents.

The firms in the sample constitute 64.59 per cent of the entire population. Their distribution by sector and size is characterized by a limited bias when comparing the 166 firms with all the firms surveyed. Both the textile sector and 'small-size' firms (50 to 99 employees) are slightly underrepresented. However, no significant statistical distortion emerges.[5]

Table 8.5   Reggio Emilia: industrial structure of the firm population
            (2001)

Istat Ateco91 Sectors (2 and 3 digit)	No. of firms (% of total)	No. of employees per establishment (% of total)	Average no. of employees per establishment
Food and beverage	5.45	6.65	170
Textiles	1.56	1.08	96
Clothing	4.67	6.74	201
Wood and wood products (excl. furniture)	0.78	0.61	109
Pulp, paper and paper products	1.56	1.69	152
Printing and publishing	1.17	1.10	131
Chemicals (excl. chemicals)	1.56	1.81	162
Rubber and plastic products	6.23	4.70	105
Non-metal mineral products:	21.79	20.94	134
Ceramic tiles	15.95	15.37	134
Other non-metal minerals	5.84	5.56	133
Iron and steel and other basic metals	1.95	1.86	133
Fabricated metal products (excl. machinery)	9.73	6.82	98
Machinery and equipments:	34.63	36.27	146
Machinery for mechanical energy	8.56	10.74	175
Other generic machinery	8.56	7.77	126
Agricultural machinery	4.67	6.19	185
Machinery for metal transformation	1.17	0.66	79
Other specific machinery	8.95	6.08	95
Machinery for domestic use	2.72	4.82	247
Office machinery	0.39	0.23	84
Electrical machinery	3.89	4.51	161
TV, radios and other comm.equipment	0.78	1.63	291
Medical, precision and optical instrument	0.39	0.39	141
Motor vehicles, trailer and semi-trailers)	1.56	1.88	169
Other transport equipment	1.17	0.76	91
Furniture and other manufacturing	0.78	0.33	59
Total	257 = 100	35798 = 100	139

Table 8.6   *Reggio Emilia: outsourcing firms of the sample by activity (1998–2001)*

Outsourced activities	Outsourcing firms (% of the total)
Ancillary activities	
1 Inventories management	14.45
2 Internal logistics	24.86
3 Distribution logistics	24.28
4 Cleaning services	85.55
5 Plants maintenance	77.46
6 Machinery maintenance	63.01
7 Data processing	31.79
Production supporting activities	
8 Marketing	11.56
9 Engineering	20.81
10 Research & Development	16.18
11 Labour consultancy	58.96
12 Human resource management	8.67
13 Quality control	8.09
Production activities	
14 Supply of intermediate products	52.52
15 Production stages	44.60
16 Products and trademarks	14.39
17 Other production activities	9.35

8.3.2   The Model

In general, the use of outsourcing as a dependent variable of any kind of empirical model poses several methodological problems in comparison to other kinds of organizational innovations. In particular, a shared reduced form equation to be used in dealing with outsourcing as an 'explanandum' is not yet available, in contrast to the case when outsourcing is considered as an explanatory variable, for example, of the different firms' performance (for example, Gorg and Hanley 2004; Reinstaller and Windrum, Chapter 7 in this book).

A robust and feasible way to proceed is, however, to refer to the idea of 'knowledge production function' (Griliches 1979), and define a reduced form which attempts to provide an explanation of outsourcing by exploiting a theoretically consistent set of covariates. In other words, we estimate a reduced form such as the following:

$$
\begin{aligned}
y_{OUTi,t} = \beta_0 &+ \beta_{1,t} \cdot x_{ORGi,t} + \beta_{2,t} \cdot x_{PRODi,t} + \beta_{3,t} \cdot x_{INDi,t} + \\
&\beta_{4,t} \cdot x_{INNOi,t} + \beta_{5,t} \cdot x_{STRUi,t} + e_i
\end{aligned} \quad (1)
$$

In Equation 1 $y_{OUTi,t}$ represents the outsourcing 'output' of firm i at time t. $x_{ki,t}$ is the set of outsourcing related variables identified with respect to a certain level of analysis k, out of the four presented in Section 2, that is: organizational ($k = ORG$), production ($k = PROD$), industrial ($k = IND$) and innovation ($k = INNO$). $x_{STRUi,t}$ is the set of control variables of structural nature, β_{1-5} the corresponding set of coefficients, θ_o the constant term and e_i the error term with usual properties.[6]

8.3.3 The Variables

Dependent variable
In order to capture the different implications of outsourcing depending on the activity involved (suffice it to think of contracting out R&D rather than janitorial services), in the present application we introduce an index of outsourcing complexity, $OUTCOM_i$. This index captures the number of activities outsourced by firm i – out of the 17 considered – by weighting differently, and increasingly, 'ancillary' activities, 'production-supporting' activities and 'production' activities as such (Table 8.6). In other words, our dependent variable is the following (for the sake of simplicity, the temporal index will be omitted):

$$
\begin{aligned}
y_{OUTi} = OUTCOM_i = OUTANC_i \cdot s_1 &+ OUTSUPROD_i \cdot s_2 + \\
&OUTPROD_i \cdot s_3
\end{aligned} \quad (2)
$$

In Equation 2 OUT_{ji} is the share of activities of a certain kind j outsourced by firm i. s_j 'weighs' the difficulties of outsourcing an activity of kind j, and takes on the entire values 1, 2 and 3 for, respectively, ancillary ($s_1 = 1$), production-supporting ($s_2 = 2$) and production activities as such ($s_3 = 3$). The rationale of these weights is both theoretical and empirical. From a theoretical point of view, production activities are the core (that is, the 'primary' activities) of the strategic idea of 'value chain' (Porter 1980), while ancillary and production-supporting activities mainly fit among those, still in the value chain framework, held to be 'support activities', whose function is to improve the effectiveness and efficiency of the production activities. What is more, production activities, intensive as they are of material assets, are those in which the core competences of the firm are actually embodied (Hamel and Prahalad 1990), and with respect to which outsourcing thus entails a higher risk of impoverishment.

These arguments are confirmed from an empirical point of view, as RE firms (on average, between 1998 and 2001) outsourced ancillary to a greater extent than production-supporting activities and, in turn, than production activities as such (Table 8.6).

The reference to a dependent variable such as $OUTCOM_i$, rather than to a standard discrete variable of outsourcing presence/absence, is prompted by the nature of our sample in which, as stated above, nearly all of the interviewed firms resort to some kind of outsourcing. On the other hand, although continuous, $OUTCOM_i$ likewise ranges from 0 to 1[7] and this makes the dependent variable fractional.

As is well known, this fact poses some econometric problems (Pindyck and Rubinfeld 1991). However, since the aim of the chapter is to detect significant correlations, rather than estimating any kind of elasticity, OLS corrected for heteroskedasticity can be used for estimating Equation 1 once Equation 2 is plugged into it.

Independent variables
The indicators used as independent variables are grouped into the four conceptual blocks identified in Section 2 and formally defined in the corresponding tables. Some of them deserve a few illustrative comments.

As far as the organizational level is concerned (see Table 8.1), $ASPEC_i$ tries to proxy (product) asset specificity at the firm level objectively, by capturing each firm i's involvement in products whose local market (here meant as regional) is made up by fewer rather than many competitors (Gonzalez-Diaz *et al.* 2000). In order to see how asset specificity interacts with governance inseparability, the former has been combined: first, with the firm's union density ($ASPEGOV1_i$), to check for outsourcing binding effects, and second, with the unions' role in the externalization process ($ASPEGOV2_i$), to check for governance enhancing effects.

An interesting comment can also be made with regard to $ORGPLA_i$, which tries to capture the outsourcing implications of what we earlier called 'interface knowledge' by estimating the degree of matching between the outsourced activities and the organizational divisions which are formally present within the firm. $PRODDIF_i$ is a rough proxy of the heterogeneity of the firm's products/activities, as it checks whether the firm is involved in the production of large volumes rather than of small series only (low 'differentiation') or, alternatively, in both kinds of production simultaneously (high 'differentiation'). Similarly, $GEODIV_i$ captures the extent to which geographical diversification is reflected in shares of total revenues that are distributed, rather than polarized, across different geographical markets, namely regional (*REG*), national (*NAT*), European (*EU*) and international (*INT*).

As far as the production level is concerned (see Table 8.2), the firm's relative wage ($RELWAGE_{ij}$) is proxied by working out the percentage deviation from the mean of sector j revealed by the unit labour cost of each of its firms i. As in other cases (for example, $INTASS_i$), contingent fluctuations have been smoothed by referring to average values over time for the available years (1998–2001). $FIRMUNC_i$ tries to capture the firm-specific effects of sectoral uncertainty by relating the standard deviation of firm's i revenues (on average in the 1998–2001 period) to the standard deviation of that branch j to which it can be related.

The indicators used at the industrial level (see Table 8.3) are quite standard. The degree of competition of a certain sector, for example, is captured by considering it to be inversely related to its concentration ratio, as it is measured by a common Herfindhal index of revenues ($HERFREV_j$).[8] The firm size is assessed by using, in addition to standard dummy variables applied as controls throughout the whole application ($FIRMSIZE1_i$), the log of the total number of employees of firm i ($FIRMSIZE2_i$). $INDREL_i$, on the other hand, is an original synthetic indicator of the intensity and quality of the relationships between managers, employees and trade unions within the firm, in particular as far as innovation strategies are concerned (see Antonioli *et al.* (2004) for its construction).

A more careful illustration is required for the innovation level of analysis (see Table 8.4). To start with, $TECUNC_j$ tries to proxy the degree of technological turbulence of firms' i business domain by counting the number of technological innovations which have been introduced in its reference branch j (that is, $TECINNO$)[9] and by checking for the differences in the relative firm populations. As far as the technological regimes are concerned, following Malerba and Orsenigo (1993), we have tried to identify them through two variables (to which the expected signs in Table 8.4 refer). $HERFINNO_j$ works out the concentration degree of a certain sector j through a standard Herfindhal index, but in terms of innovation rather than production. $SPEARINNO_j$ proxies the innovative turmoil of sector j over time by checking for the average degree of reshuffling in the ranking of its firms in terms of innovative activities, when different periods of time are considered.[10]

As far as the radicalness of the firms' innovations is concerned, $RADINNO_i$ classifies as radical those innovations which are either product or process innovations, regarding quality innovations as incremental.

Finally, the other variables of the innovation level ($ORGINNO_i$, $FLEXINNO_i$, $INWORK_i$, $FLEXFUN_i$, $FLEXWAGE_i$ and $INNORE-WARD_i$) are, like $INDREL$, synthetic indicators which have been built up in another study, based on the same RE survey as the present investigation, but aiming to capture the organizational innovations and the flexibility of the sampled firms (Antonioli *et al.* 2004).

Let us now turn to the main results of the application.[11]

8.4   THE PROFILE OF THE REGGIO EMILIA OUTSOURCING FIRM

We first present the results of the econometric estimates for each of the four levels of analysis separately (Table 8.7). Then a regression including only the variables associated with a statistically significant coefficient in the distinct four levels (Table 8.8), is presented. In such a way the risk of high correlations between factors belonging to the four different sets, which could affect estimated correlations, is mitigated.

8.4.1   The Organizational Level

At the outset, it seems that the firms' involvement in activities in which rent-seeking behaviour is unfavoured does not play a significant role for outsourcing (Table 8.7). Asset specificity (*ASPEC*) does not turn out to be significant at the outset. By contrast, *UNION* is indeed significant, having a negative sign, which supports the idea that the pervasiveness of the unions might counteract externalization decisions by increasing the firm's governance inseparability. On the other hand, governance inseparability is not fuelled by the firm's contractual history. The firm's age (*FIRMAGE*), although not very significant at the present level, reveals an unexpected positive sign. Furthermore, older firms show greater willingness to experience the opportunities of outsourcing than do younger firms, and their thicker contractual history does not work as a constraint. This result is reinforced when the four levels are pulled together.

Quite interestingly, while *ASPEGOV1* does not turn out to be significant, *ASPEGOV2* is instead significant and with a positive sign. In other words, if unions are enabled to enter the outsourcing decision-making process actively (being informed or consulted), the firm seems to become willing to externalize activities even if they are intensive of specific assets. Although apparently counter-intuitive, the result is quite interesting. While an increasing level of unionization could be thought to increase the governance inseparability of the firm, the union's participation in the outsourcing decision-making process actually turns governance inseparability into governance separability conditional on their involvement. And this would seem to set an organizational deterrence to the hold-up behaviour which is naturally associated with asset specificity. In this respect it is interesting to

Table 8.7 *Regression results: the four different levels of analysis*

Level:	Organizational		Production		Industrial			Innovation		
Dep. Variable:	OUTCOM		OUTCOM		OUTCOM			OUTCOM		
Covariates:	Version 1	Version 2	Covariates:		Covariates:	Version 1	Version 2	Covariates:	Version 1	Version 2
constant	2.739	2.751***	constant	2.933***	constant	2.404	-1.530	constant	2.833	3.185***
SIZE1	-2.521	-2.569	SIZE1	-2.477**	SIZE1	-1.728*	-1.728*	SIZE1	-2.284**	-2.261**
GROUP	-2.027**	-1.965**	RWSKILL	-2.387**	GROUP	-1.687*	-1.728*	SKILL	-2.155**	-2.161**
SKILL	-1.718*	-1.742*	UNION	-2.751***	RI		-2.490**	FIRMAGE	2.006**	2.210**
FIRMAGE	1.414	1.382	FIRMUNC	-1.204	SI		1.661	TECINNO	2.403**	
ASPECOV2	6.264***	7.258***			HERFREV	-1.006	-1.984**	SPEARINNO	-1.946*	-2.164**
PRODDIF	1.659*	1.808*			INDREL	-2.104**	-1.795*	ORGINNO	-2.435**	-2.163**
ORGPLA	1.785*	1.857*						INNOPROD		2.674***
ORGHIER	-3.265**	-2.281**								
MKTUNC		-2.569***								
UNION	-2.286**	-2.280**								
F test (prob)	3.29	3.17		2.58		2.06	3.28		3.02	3.19
	(0.0003)	(0.0003)		(0.0015)		(0.0042)	(0.0003)		(0.0001)	(0.0001)
adj-R-squared	0.142	0.146		0.062		0.048	0.088		0.099	0.106
N	166	166		106		166	166		166	166

notice that by checking, through dummy variables, for the outsourcing implications of firms which merely inform and firms which at least consult the workers' unions on their outsourcing decisions, none of them prove to be very significant. On the other hand, the interaction of outsourcing consultation with asset specificity makes the relative variable significant, thus supporting our interpretation.

As much as asset specificity, other basic insights of TCE find a partial confirmation in our application. On the one hand, the intensity of intangible assets (*INTASS*) shows an expected negative sign on the coefficient, but never reaches a sufficient significance threshold in several specifications (and it has thus been omitted from Table 8.7). As expected, the uncertainty related proxy (*MKTUNC*) is found to be poorly significant, confirming other empirical evidence on the issue (Gonzalez-Diaz *et al.* 2000). But its interaction with asset specificity (*MKTASPE*) is likewise non-significant, thus confirming that TCE might not be an appropriate theoretical explanation for outsourcing in the context of Reggio-Emilia. The only relevant confirmation seems to come from product differentiation (*PRODDIF*), which hampers vertical integration: its sign with respect to outsourcing is positive, although it is only moderately significant (10 per cent).

As far as the role of interface knowledge is concerned, its codification into the organizational relationship actually seems to be an enabling factor making it possible to 'detach' and externalize parts of the firm's value-chain: *ORGPLA* is positive, showing a 10 per cent significance level with respect to *OUTCOM* and a higher 5 per cent significance with respect to a simple, unweighted outsourcing index as a dependent variable. By contrast, hierachization, although possibly making interface knowledge more explicit and thus somehow favouring outsourcing, also makes the firm's activities dependent on a greater number of control centres and thus hampers interface knowledge. The latter effect apparently counteracts the former: the hierarchical ratio (*ORGHIER*) is significant (5 per cent to 10 per cent), but with a negative coefficient across different specifications.[12]

8.4.2 The Production Level

Although saving on labour costs is usually held to be an outsourcing argument, *RELWAGE* does not turn out to be significant in any of the different versions of the index used[13] (Table 8.7). On the other hand, *RWSKILL* is found to be significant and with a negative sign, a result which is 'pulled' by the significance and the negative sign of *SKILL*. This seems to corroborate a strategic interpretation of outsourcing, where high skills in-house possibly spur the firms to be more selective in resorting to outsourcing.

Out of the two possible effects of the firm's unionization degree (*UNION*) on outsourcing decisions, the negative effect, which passes through a possible increase in the firm's governance inseparability, seems to prevail over the positive effect, which instead passes through a possible increase in the firm's labour cost. The present result should, however, be read along with that obtained at the organizational level, where an outsourcing enabling role of the unions, rather than a binding role, also emerges when the nature of their intervention in the firm's decision is disentangled.

Finally, outsourcing seems to be neither a mere labour cost reduction strategy nor a way of smoothing the costs of adapting to firm-specific demand changes: *FIRMUNC* is in fact not significant.[14] Apparently, the problems induced by market uncertainty are dealt with by resorting to other internal organizational arrangements, possibly of a flexible nature, as will be argued in the following section.

8.4.3 The Industrial Level

That outsourcing would be more a competitive means in low concentrated sectors than a rent appropriating instrument in highly concentrated sectors cannot be taken as more than a suggestion (Table 8.7). *HERFREV* does not emerge as very significant, although its association with a negative sign is worth noting. Interestingly, such an argument appears also significant at 1 per cent when a probit regression concerning OUT_{PRO} is assessed.

When the size effects are examined, the only significant and negative sign (ranging over 1 per cent to 5 per cent statistical levels) is *SIZE1*, which refers to firms whose employees number between 100 and 249. The continuous size variable, when used alternatively, is also associated with a similar, from a significance perspective, negative coefficient, driven by the small-medium firm effect. In other words, it seems possible to conclude that compared to 'small' firms (between 50 and 99 employees), larger firms are possibly less involved in outsourcing activities.[15] In the context of RE, therefore, outsourcing does not appear as a 'dual' relationship, where the largest firms simply exploit and subordinate smaller firms to them, but rather a 'developmental' or equivalent kind of relationship, where even the smaller firms could benefit from the larger firms in terms of flexibility and specialization.

Finally, regarding the quality of industrial relations, *INDREL* is negatively related to outsourcing, and its significance depends on the variable capturing the skill intensity of the firm (*SKILL*): if the latter is omitted, the significance level is 1 per cent, otherwise it decreases to 10 per cent (the relative specification has thus not been chosen). Accordingly, we would argue that the more industrial relations are intensive and simultaneously involve qualified workers, the less outsourcing tends to characterize firm strategies, with a moderate correlation. This is another extremely interesting result, especially when read along with the results obtained at the organizational level. That is to say, on the basis of our findings it seems possible to interpret the outsourcing processes of the RE firms as two-fold. On a first level, the pervasiveness (captured by *UNION*) and the quality of the relations which involve the unions (proxied by *INDREL*) tend to determine a 'bargaining equilibrium' where outsourcing is less likely to occur. On a second level, once union representatives are more directly involved in the process, which thus occurs under their involvement, outsourcing becomes more possible, and may even counteract other organizational risks (such as those entailed by opportunistic behaviour in connection with specific assets, as captured by *ASPEGOV2*).

8.4.4   The Innovation Level

First of all, let us note that *TECUNC*, which proxies the degree of technological uncertainty, is not significant, although with some caveats to which we shall return later (Table 8.7). Quite interestingly, however, *SPEARINNO* is significant and with a negative sign. Although the non-significance of *HERFINNO* partly weakens this result, outsourcing seems a safer strategy to undertake in sectors characterized by the typical turmoil (here reshuffling) of Schumpeter-Mark-I technological regimes.

As far as the firm's innovativeness is concerned, *TECINNO* proves to be significant and positively correlated with *OUTCOM*, thus supporting the interpretation, recently put forward by Mol (2005), according to which vertical disintegration is not necessarily inconsistent with technological change, in contrast to the claim made by standard organizational theories (typically TCE based). The risks of diminishing the firm's innovativeness by impoverishing its absorptive capacity are apparently not confirmed. On the contrary, it seems that outsourcing may be important for RE firms to tap into the resources and competences of the provider and implement them into superior technological processes. This is an interpretation consistent with the technological regime which can be more typically associated with outsourcing in RE (that is, of the Schumpeter-Mark-I type).

Quite interestingly, *RADINNO* turns out to be significant and with a positive sign, although the significance level is relatively low. Despite a certain arbitrariness in measuring radical innovations, this would suggest that even relatively more radical innovations might benefit from the knowledge specialization induced by outsourcing. However, the significance of *TECINNO* is driven by that of $INNO_{PROD}$. In other words, rather than radicalness, it is the nature of the innovation itself which matters: more precisely, it is mainly the introduction of a new product, so that the selected specification has been chosen accordingly in Table 8.7.

As far as the organizational innovations are concerned, *ORGINNO* also presents a significant correlation with *OUTCOM*, but negative. Outsourcing therefore seems to be an organizational innovation which substitutes for other innovations the firm might adopt in trying to increase its flexibility and, in so doing, its dynamic capabilities and competitiveness. This may suggest that their inspiring rationale is actually quite different and amounts to a change in, respectively, the 'external governance' of the firm (outsourcing) and its 'internal' governance (the other organizational innovations).

8.4.5   The General Profile of the Outsourcing Firm

As a final stage, we present the results of a regression including only the aforementioned significant factors (Table 8.8). As expected, this final regression is associated with a high overall fit, regarding both adjusted *R* squared and *F* statistics.

The extended regression does not present sharply different outcomes with respect to coefficient significance, confirming that independent variables are exogenous and significant correlations between them are not present. The experience effects that a longer firm history exerts on its outsourcing decision is here reinforced by a higher significance level of *FIRMAGE*. The same holds true for the governance inseparability effects played by union density (*UNION*).

Among the controls, *GROUP*, *FIRMAGE* and *SIZE1* emerge among the others, while *SKILL* shows reduced significance here. The variables associated with the production, organizational and innovation level that we have detected above confirm their impact, while the industrial conceptual level is in the end the least relevant in terms of relative weight.

8.5   CONCLUSIONS

In trying to embed the outsourcing firm, in this chapter we have carried out a multi-level analysis in which not only are TCE and the resource-competence based explanations combined at the organizational level, but the organizational level is, in turn, combined with other levels of analysis at which important features emerge for qualifying the general profile of the outsourcing firm.

In a specific context, such as that of an Italian province (Reggio Emilia), with the typical traits of a local production system similar to that of North-

Table 8.8 Regression results: all levels of analysis

Level: Dependent variable:	All levels OUTCOM
Covariates:	
constant	3.079***
SIZE1	−2.556***
GROUP	−2.269**
SKILL	−1.616
FIRMAGE	2.036**
ASPEGOV2	3.213***
PRODDIF	1.909**
ORGPLA	1.758*
ORGHIER	−3.076***
UNION	−2.206**
HERFREV	−1.136
SPEARINNO	−1.067
ORGINNO	−1.959**
INNOPROD	3.288***
F test (prob)	3.11 (0.0001)
adj-*R*-squared	0.1868
N	166

Notes:
The following apply to tables 8.7 and 8.8.
1. *t* ratios only are shown since we do not emphasize elasticities. *: significant at 10 per cent significance level; **: at 5 per cent significance level; ***: at 1 per cent significance level. Non-relevant covariates (with t ratios lower than 1.645) are generally omitted.
2. All regressions adopt by default a White corrected robust estimator for the variance covariance matrix to address heteroskedasticity.
3. A part from the production level, two specifications are shown for each of the others by varying the regressors included. Only final specifications, consistent with a 'from general to particular' estimation procedure, are shown.
4. Controls are not shown except for size-related dummies and firm age. Other controls include: macro manufacturing sub-sectors (chemical, machinery, ceramic) or, alternatively, production orientation a' la Pavitt (Labour Intensive (LI), Resource Intensive (RI), Specialized Suppliers (SS), Scale Intensive (SI)), firm training coverage, international turnover market share, number of establishments per firm, firm performance and group membership. All control variables are not significant except for group membership (GROUP), which in some regressions arises with a negative sign and on average with a 5 per cent significance coefficient. They are nevertheless included to control for cross section heterogeneity. When highly insignificant they are omitted from final specifications and not shown.

East Italy, outsourcing is apparently not well accounted for by TCE. The majority of the variables which refer to the outsourcing explanations provided by TCE are either non-significant or have a non-expected sign. The interpretative power of TCE found by other studies (for example,

Gonzalez-Diaz *et al.* 2000) thus could depend on the specific sector and geographical context investigated (in the cited case the Spanish construction sector).

The institutional setting of RE may render TCE arguments not very relevant: in particular, the typical industrial relations of the area and the 'social capital' which is usually associated with a district kind of local production system could make the opportunism of the agents embodied by TCE less explicative. This is to some extent confirmed by the strong interpretative power of industrial relations, which seem to play an important role in affecting the outsourcing decisions of the RE firms. More specifically, it emerges that unions push the brake pedal at the outset, but when outsourcing occurs, they are involved or at least informed. Outsourcing, like other dynamics, springs from a bargaining arena including such key topics as labour related flexibility, wages, innovation dynamics (with outsourcing inside) and employment levels, which are typical historically and institutionally determined features of the industrial system under analysis.

In conclusion, our multi-level analysis suggests that the profile of the RE outsourcing firm seems to be more consistent with a 'network/cluster' than with a 'dualistic' approach (Taymaz and Kilicaslan 2005), strategic rather than operative. Essentially, the RE outsourcing firm has the following features: (i) it is relatively not very large and does not seem merely to 'exploit' smaller subcontractors; (ii) it conceives a hierarchical organizational structure and the organizational matching of outsourcing, respectively, as an obstacle and as an enabler; (iii) it does not appear to subcontract in order to save labour costs or to smooth unexpected demand peaks; (iv) it deals with outsourcing strategically, in particular, to tap into the resources and competences of its suppliers, which it then possibly implements into technological, product innovations, without crucial knowledge leakage; and (v) it uses outsourcing as a substitute, rather than as a complement, of other organizational innovations, distinguishing different paths of governance change (respectively, external and internal) towards flexibility.

NOTES

1.   A previous and more extended version of this chapter was published as DRUID Working Paper 20/2006. All the three authors contributed equally in the development of this chapter and share the attribution of Section 1 and Section 5. However, Section 2 and Section 4 should be attributed to Sandro Montresor, and Section 3 to Massimiliano Mazzanti and Paolo Pini. Correspondence on the chapter should be addressed to Sandro Montresor. We would like to thank Michael Best, David Gann and the other participants in the 2006 DRUID Summer Conference (Copenhagen, 17–20 June 2006), and Patrick Llerena and the other participants in the 2007 REF International Workshop (Lucca,

19–20 January 2007) for their comments. We are particularly indebted to Stefano Brusoni for his suggestions on an earlier version of the chapter. Sandro Montresor acknowledges funding from the Italian Ministry for Education University and Research (MIUR) PRIN 2005 on 'Fragmentation and local development'. The usual disclaimers apply.

2. However, the present section does not report the outsourcing arguments of the literature on 'strategic outsourcing' drawing on game-theory (for example, Kamien *et al.* 1989; Spiegel 1993; Baake *et al.* 1999). And neither those which have been put forward following a network/cluster approach (Taymaz and Kilicaslan 2005). Although quite important, they have been omitted as testing them would have required very detailed data on inter-firm relationships that the dataset of our application does not contemplate.

3. As argued by Benson and Ieronimo (1996, p. 60): 'outsourcing contributes to all three forms of flexibility [functional, wage and numerical]. Tasks undertaken are contract – not craft – related, payment is made only for work completed, and worker numbers can be adjusted to the production requirements of the plant.'

4. For a more detailed description, see Mazzanti *et al.* (2006).

5. On the representativeness of the sample, see *Ibid.*

6. From an econometric point of view, the estimation of Equation 1 poses some problems (for example, heteroskedasticity and potential endogeneity) which are, however, less crucial in the context of the present application. For an account of how they have been addressed, see *Ibid.* For a similar, but more circumscribed, application to outsourcing and delocalization in RE where the endogeneity problem has been overcome with a panel dataset, consisting of a cross with lagged terms for the set of explanatory variables, see Mazzanti *et al.* (2007).

7. Let us observe that we are prevented from transforming $OUTCOM_i$ into a fully continuous logarithmic form given the presence of values equal to 0.

8. The expected sign of the corresponding table thus refers to its reciprocal.

9. Innovations were distinguished into three categories by the managers interviewed. While product and process innovations were indicated to them as the introduction of relatively new products and production processes, respectively, quality innovations were defined as ameliorations on the quality of an existing product and/or process. According to this distinction, consistent dummies were also built up for each of the three categories, that is, $INNO_{PROD}$, $INNO_{PROC}$ and $INNO_{QUAL}$.

10. As usual, the closer the Spearman correlation index is to 1 (-1), the more similar (dissimilar) the two correspondent temporal firm rankings are in terms of asset intangibility, the more sector *j* resembles a Schumpeter-Mark-II (Mark I) regime.

11. The set of explanatory variables here presented and used as covariates in the analysis is the result of a preliminary selection of an extended full set of proxies deriving from the information sources related to the survey questionnaire. This first selection was carried out to reduce collinearity problems and assure the exogeneity of independent factors, mitigating biases. The final correlation matrix (not shown) highlights low figures concerning main independent variables, never exceeding a threshold fixed around 0.20.

12. As far as controls are concerned, sectoral effects seem of minor relevance. Among other controls, skill intensity (*SKILL*) and group membership of the firm (*GROUP*) emerge as quite robust factors, both with negative signs.

13. The cost of labour emerges as a weak outsourcing determinant also in other studies carried out at the firm level, such as Abraham and Taylor (1996) and Taymaz and Kilicaslan (2005).

14. Of course, more accurate proxies are needed to reach such a conclusion. Let us note that the interaction between *FIRMUNC* and asset specificity turns out to be significant and negative, thus apparently supporting a TCE kind of interpretation. However, the latter interactive variable turns out to be correlated with *ASPEGOV1*: the correlation between the two is around 0.25; not excessively high, but some suspicions may remain that the variable significance is driven by the latter.

15. The size effect we detected is also found by Abraham and Taylor (1996) for most outsourced activities, while Mol (2005) does not find significant size effects in a recent study on the relationship between outsourcing and innovation.

REFERENCES

Abraham, K. and S. Taylor (1996), 'Firms' use of outside contractors: theory and evidence', *Journal of Labor Economics*, **14** (3), 394–424.

Aghion, P. and J. Tirole (1997) 'Formal and real authority in organizations', *Journal of Political Economy*, **105** (1), 1–29.

Antonioli, Davide and Ermanno Tortia (2004), 'Caratteristiche delle imprese e delle rappresentanze', in P. Pini (ed.), *Innovazioni, Relazioni Industriali e Risultati d'Impresa. Un'analisi per il Sistema Industriale di Reggio Emilia*, Milan: Franco Angeli, pp. 57–83.

Antonioli, D., M. Mazzanti, P. Pini and E. Tortia (2004) 'Adoption of techno-organizational innovations and industrial relations in manufacturing firms: an analysis for a local industrial system', *Economia Politica*, **21** (1), 1–52.

Antras, P. and E. Helpman (2004), 'Global sourcing', *Journal of Political Economy*, **112** (3), 552–80.

Argyres, N. and J.P. Liebeskind (1999), 'Contractual commitments, bargaining power, and governance inseparability: introducing history into transaction cost theory', *Academy of Management Review*, **24** (1), 49–63.

Baake, P.J., J. Oechssler and C. Schenk (1999), 'Explaining cross-supplies', *Journal of Economics*, **70** (1), 37–60.

Bartel, A., S. Lach and N. Sicherman (2005), 'Outsourcing and technological change', working paper W11158, NBER, Cambridge, Massachusetts.

Benson, J. and N. Ieronimo (1996), 'Outsourcing decisions: evidence from Australia-based enterprises', *International Labour Review*, **135** (1), 59–73.

Brusoni, S., A. Prencipe and K. Pavitt (2001), 'Knowledge specialization, organizational coupling, and the boundaries of the firm: why do firms know more than they make?', *Administrative Science Quarterly*, **46** (4), 597–621.

Cacciatori, E. and M. Jacobides (2005), 'The dynamic limits of specialization: vertical integration reconsidered', *Organization Studies*, **26** (12), 1851–83.

Christensen, C.M., M. Verlinden and G. Westerman (2002), 'Disruption, disintegration and the dissipation of differentiability', *Industrial and Corporate Change*, **11** (5), 955–93.

Coase, R.H. (1937), 'The nature of the firm', *Economica*, **4** (16), 386–405. Reprint in, Coase, R.H. (1988), *The firm, the market and the law*, Chicago: University of Chicago Press, pp. 35–55.

Cohen, W. and D. Levinthal (1989), 'Innovation and learning: the two faces of R&D', *Economic Journal*, **99** (397), 569–96.

de Kok, T.G. (2000), 'Capacity allocation and outsourcing in a process industry', *International Journal of Production Economics*, **68** (3), 229–39.

Deavers, K. (1997), 'Outsourcing: a corporate competitiveness strategy, not a search for low wages', *Journal of Labor Research*, **18** (4), 503–19.

Domberger, Simon (1998), *The Contracting Organization: A Strategic Guide to Outsourcing*, Oxford, UK: Oxford University Press.

Dosi, G. (1988), 'Sources, procedures, and microeconomic effects of innovation', *Journal of Economic Literature*, **26** (September), 1120–71.

Dyer, G. and K. Nobeoka (2000), 'Creating knowledge and managing a high performance knowledge-sharing network: the Toyota case', *Strategic Management Journal*, **21** (3), 345–467.

Dyer, J. and H. Singh (1998), 'The relational view: cooperative strategy and sources of interorganizational competitive advantage', *Academy of Management Review*, **23** (4), 660–79.

Foss, N.J. (2000), 'The theory of the firm: an introduction to themes and contributions', in N.J. Foss (ed.), *The Theory of the Firm: Critical Perspectives in Economic Organization*, London: Routledge, pp. 15–56.

Gonzalez-Diaz, M., B. Arruada and A. Fernandez (2000), 'Causes of subcontracting: evidence from panel data on construction firms', *Journal of Economic Behavior and Organization*, **42** (2), 167–87.

Gorg, H. and A. Hanley (2004), 'Does outsourcing increase profitability', *Economic and Social Review*, **35** (3), 267–88.

Granovetter, M. (1985), 'Economic action and social structure: a theory of embeddedness', *American Journal of Sociology*, **19** (3), 481–510.

Griliches, S. (1979), 'Issues in assessing the contribution of R&D to productivity growth', *Bell Journal of Economics*, **10** (1), 92–116.

Grossman, G.M. and E. Helpman (2002), 'Integration versus outsourcing in industry equilibrium', *Quarterly Journal of Economics*, **117** (1), 85–120.

Grossman, S. and O. Hart (1986), 'The costs and benefits of ownership: a theory of vertical and lateral integration', *Journal of Political Economy*, **94**, 85–120.

Hamel, G. and C.K. Prahalad (1990), 'The core competence of the corporation', *Harvard Business Review*, **68** (3), 79–93.

Henderson, R.M. and K.B. Clark (1990), 'Architectural innovation: the reconfiguration of existing product technologies and the failure of established firms', *Administrative Science Quarterly*, **35** (1), 9–30.

Houseman, S.N. (2001), 'Why employers use flexible staffing arrangements: evidence from an establishment survey', *Industrial and Labor Relations Review*, **55** (1), 149–70.

Hyman, Richard (2003), 'Industrial relations', in Kuper Adam and Jessica Kuper (eds), *The Social Science Encyclopedia*, 2nd edn, London: Routledge, pp. 411–23.

Jacobides, M.J. and S.G. Winter (2005), 'The co-evolution of capabilities and transaction costs: explaining the institutional structure of production', *Strategic Management Journal*, **26** (5), 395–413.

Kamien, M., L. Li and D. Samet (1989), 'Bertrand competition with subcontracting', *RAND Journal of Economics*, **20** (4), 553–67.

Kelley, M. and B. Harrison (1990), 'The subcontracting behavior of single vs. multiplant enterprises in US manufacturing: implications for economic development', *World Development*, **18** (9), 1273–94.

Langlois, R. (1992), 'Transaction cost economics in real time', *Industrial and Corporate Change*, **1** (1), 99–127.

Langlois, R. and N. Foss (1999), 'Capabilities and governance: the rebirth of production in the theory of economic organization', *Kyklos*, **52** (2), 201–18.

Leonard-Barton, D. (1992), 'Core capabilities and core rigidities: a paradox in managing new product development', *Strategic Management Journal*, **12** (Summer), 111–25.

Mahnke, V. (2001), 'The process of vertical dis-integration: an evolutionary perspective on outsourcing', *Journal of Management and Governance*, **5** (3–4), 353–79.

Malerba, F. and L. Orsenigo (1993), 'Technological regimes and firm behavior', *Industrial and Corporate Change*, **2** (1), 45–71.

Mazzanti, M., S. Montresor and P. Pini (2006), 'The general profile of the outsourcing firm: evidence for a local production system of Emilia Romagna', working paper 20–06, DRUID, Copenhagen.

Mazzanti, M., S. Montresor and P. Pini (2007), 'Outsourcing, delocalization and firm organization: transaction costs vs. industrial relations in a local production system of Emilia Romagna', mimeo, paper presented at the 2007 EAEPE Conference, Porto, Portugal, 1–3 November 2007.

Mol, M.J. (2005), 'Does being R&D intensive still discourage outsourcing? Evidence from Dutch manufacturing', *Research Policy*, **34** (4), 571–82.

Montresor, S. (2004), 'Resources, capabilities, competences and the theory of the firm', *Journal of Economic Studies*, **31** (5), 409–34.

Nellore, R. and K. Soderquist (2000), 'Strategic outsourcing through specifications', *Omega*, **28** (5), 525–40.

Nooteboom, B. (2004), 'Governance and competence: how can they be combined?', *Cambridge Journal of Economics*, **28** (4), 505–25.

Pindyck, Robert S. and Daniel L. Rubinfeld (1991), *Econometric Models and Economic Forecasts*, New York: McGraw-Hill.

Pini, Paolo (ed.) (2004), *Innovazione, Relazioni Industriali e Risultati d'Impresa*, Milan: Franco Angeli.

Porter, Michael J. (1980), *Competitive Strategy*, New York: The Free Press.

Robertson, P.L. and R.N. Langlois (1995), 'Innovation, networks, and vertical integration', *Research Policy*, **24** (4), 543–62.

Seravalli, G. (2001), 'Sviluppo economico e mercato del lavoro a Reggio Emilia', working paper, CGIL, Reggio Emilia.

Shya, O. and R. Stenbacka (2003), 'Strategic outsourcing', *Journal of Economic Behavior and Organization*, **50** (2), 203–24.

Spencer, B.J. (2005), 'International outsourcing and incomplete contracts', working paper 11418, NBER, Cambridge, Massachusetts.

Spiegel, Y. (1993), 'Horizontal subcontracting', *RAND Journal of Economics*, **24** (4), 570–90.

Taymaz, E. and Y. Kilicaslan (2005), 'Determinants of subcontracting and regional development: an empirical study on Turkish textile and engineering Industries', *Regional Studies*, **39** (5), 633–45.

Teece, D.J. (1986), 'Profiting from technological innovation: implications for integration, collaboration, licensing, and public policy', *Research Policy*, **15** (6), 285–305.

Teece, D.J. (1992), 'Competition, cooperation, and innovation – organizational arrangements for regimes of rapid technological-progress', *Journal of Economic Behavior and Organization*, **18** (1), 1–25.

Teece, D.J., G. Pisano and A. Shuen (1997), 'Dynamic capabilities and strategic management', *Strategic Management Journal*, **18** (7), 509–33.

Williamson, Oliver E. (1975), *Markets and Hierarchies*, New York: The Free Press.

Williamson, O.E. (1999), 'Strategy research: governance and competence perspectives', *Strategic Management Journal*, **20** (12), 1087–108.

9. Technical capital and social capital in outsourcing networks: complements or substitutes?[1]

Rafael Pardo and Ruth Rama

9.1 INTRODUCTION

Research founded on the resource-based view (RBV) of companies is beginning to investigate whether the establishment of inter-company linkages (Lavie 2006) is one method that firms use to obtain the resources they require. Given that participation in inter-firm linkages is often considered as an indication of the social capital available to companies (Gulati *et al.* 2000; Vanhaverbeke *et al.* 2001), this question can be formulated, from a theoretical approach, in the following way: Do the social capital and the technical capital available to firms substitute or complement each other?

The issue is also important from a practical point of view, since the academic and policy literature sometimes argues that promoting entrepreneurial linkages (such as outsourcing networks) between companies may improve company competitiveness. If firms lack specific competitive resources, it is claimed, they may compensate for this deficiency by forming external networks with other companies. This viewpoint assumes that the social and technical capital available to businesses can be mutual substitutes.

However, sharing knowledge with partners may produce heavy risks for companies, such as involuntary spillovers of knowledge (de Laat 1999); technologically advanced firms might be reluctant to network with other enterprises, meaning that potential sources of knowledge within an industry remain isolated. On the other hand, firms lacking technical capital may also find themselves isolated, and consequently deprived of the spillovers and transfers of technology which networking with more advanced businesses could provide. Previous research suggests that firms engaging in inter-company linkages are likely to have some technical capital at their disposal, as this makes them more attractive to potential partners (Ahuja 2000). This view implies that firms must 'buy a ticket' before potential partners allow them to participate in networks. If this is true, the efficiency of networking policies becomes controversial.

Which aspects of companies' technical capital really matter? It could be argued that firms with adequate financial resources can purchase state-of-the-art equipment to improve their technological level, even if they are not themselves innovators. Does a company's purchase of high quality equipment make it more attractive to potential networking partners? To answer these questions, the different aspects of firms' technical capital must be carefully investigated.

As Faems *et al.* (2005) note, most previous research into innovation and inter-firm relationships has measured technical capital by the number of patents granted to a company and the corresponding citations received. In our view, however, such indicators often neglect the importance of incremental industrial innovation and, even more importantly, are virtually irrelevant to the measurement of innovation in smaller companies.

Both technical capital and social capital are complex concepts, and we believe they cannot be accurately analysed using single approximations or one-dimensional indicators. We argue that their inter-relationship is better understood by examining a variety of facets which define them at the company level. Using a random representative sample of 162 medium-sized and large companies in the Spanish automobile and electronics industries, this chapter investigates the relationship between technical capital, as measured by seven different indicators, and social capital, proxied by four indicators. A description of the sample is provided in Section 3.

Our study makes a further contribution to the literature by the introduction of attitudinal variables, or views about technology, into the model; these control for the possible influence of company strategy upon the likelihood of networking. In concrete terms, does managerial awareness of the strategic importance of innovation make plants more likely to network? Most of the empirical literature on networking responds affirmatively to this question (Pittaway *et al.* 2004). In recent years, however, it has been extensively debated whether inter-firm linkages are actually the result of company intentions or, alternatively, due to structural or environmental variables. Analyses of this question have been based almost exclusively on case studies and theoretical models (see, for instance, Kogut 2000; Wilkinson and Young 2002); by contrast, few statistical analyses of representative empirical evidence have been conducted. The main hypothesis of the present study is that inter-firm matching processes are more closely related to the technical endowment of companies than to their intentions; a hypothesis open to empirical corroboration or falsification using data collected in the course of our research.

The chapter is organized as follows: Section 2 presents the theoretical background of our research, Section 3 describes the data and methodology and Section 4 lists the results. Finally, we discuss the results and present our conclusions.

9.2 THEORETICAL BACKGROUND

9.2.1 The Concepts of Social Capital and Technical Capital

Conceptually, social capital is multidimensional and the literature interprets it in many different ways. As Anderson and Jack (2002) note, for some research lines it is a structure (see, for instance, Coleman 1988), while others equate it with 'weak social ties' (Granovetter 1985), relationships of trust, and value and normative systems that facilitate cooperation between individuals and firms embedded in specific social contexts; see, for instance, the literature on Italian industrial districts (Becattini 2002; Brusco 1999).

While analyses of firm embeddedness in these specific contexts consider the implicit rules and social values prevalent within, say, regions or among ethnic groups, to give just two examples, the rational choice perspective views social capital as a resource: 'as a capital it is locked into the network and becomes an integral part of that structure', as argued by Anderson and Jack (2002, p. 196). These authors maintain that firms' social capital (as generally understood by economic and management literature) is equivalent to their 'networking capital'.

In an attempt to combine sociological and economic approaches, Coleman (1988) defines social capital as a resource available to actors, whether people or organizations. Unlike other forms of capital, he argues, 'social capital inheres in the structure of relations between actors and among actors' (p. 98). He claims that physical capital (such as machinery) is wholly tangible, human capital is less tangible (because it is embodied in the skills and knowledge of people) and social capital is the most intangible, since it exists in the relations among actors, including corporate actors. In spite of its relative intangibility, social capital is likely to be economically valuable for companies. Neoinstitutionalist and, more specifically, transaction cost literature (Williamson 1985) have made particularly important contributions to explaining the value of social capital for networked companies. Such literature contends that trust reduces the transactional costs in economic relations produced by uncertainty about contract performance (that is, each party to a transaction lacks complete information about the other party or parties and their true intentions, especially in non-recurrent operations). The existence of trust between the parties, it is argued, significantly reduces the cognitive or informational requirements for an agreement to be reached. One definition of the stock of trust within a specific society is the total time agents save by not having to check what others are doing (Zack and Knack 2001). Most studies of inter-firm link-ages assume that recurrent ('repeated games') or long-term relations increase trust between partners, a situation which presumably helps to reduce 'free rider' and opportunistic behaviour among actors and, conse-quently, the legal expenses of contract enforcement faced by companies. Trust facilitates the exchange of new ideas and information between part-ners, a particularly important consideration for innovators who envisage R&D cooperation with other companies (Häusler *et al.* 1994). Trust between partners is also essential when clients and subcontractors collabo-rate to implement new industrial processes, launch new products or improve old ones. However, a reduction of transaction costs is not the only advantage which companies obtain by the possession of social capital. Based on the analysis of entrepreneurial ethnographies, Andersen and Jack (2002) find that entrepreneurs value their social capital as a relational arte-fact which helps them to find opportunities for new business, tap into exter-nal resources or knowledge, obtain information and so on. Networks are also considered to be an important mechanism for increased manufactur-ing flexibility and a tool which enables firms to respond quickly to changes in demand (Hagedoorn 1994). Following their extensive review of the lit-erature on networks, Pittaway *et al.* (2004) report that networkers are more likely than isolated firms to reduce business risks, access new markets and pool complementary skills.

Management and organizational studies often consider the number of partnerships (for example, alliances or R&D collaborations) in which a company is involved to be an indicator of the social capital available to the firm. Ahuja (2000, p. 319), for instance, uses companies' previous relation-ships with other firms as a measure of their social capital, which he views as a resource available to companies. Similarly, we consider the networking resources of companies to be an indicator of their social capital.

Several types of business networks exist: networks of innovators, or R&D collaboration (Freeman 1991); networks of manufacturers and dis-tributors, or marketing channels; and networks of producers, including co-production arrangements among producers who pool their technological, human or financial resources, and so on (Fischer and Varga 2002). The present study analyses outsourcing arrangements between client compa-nies and their suppliers of intermediate production inputs and parts (sub-contractors).

The second concept discussed in this section, technical capital, is more straightforward. For classical economists, the principal technical capital of a company is its physical capital (equipment, buildings and infrastructure, for example). Contemporary authors include, in this category, either the equipment of the firm ('technical capital equipment'), its investment in R&D, its 'technological knowledge' (including tacit knowledge) or, as noted in the introduction to this chapter, its stock of patents.

As stated earlier, previous research into the association between technical capital and inter-firm linkages has generally employed a single technological variable, typically patents or patent citations, which are seldom important in medium-sized companies, like many of the firms we sample. Other studies only consider the contribution to turnover of new products and new technology, as a measure of the commercial success of innovation (Faems *et al.* 2005).

An alternative approach is provided by Kotabe *et al.* (2003), in their study of vertical partnerships and technology in the US and Japanese automobile industries; they emphasize the need to distinguish between the various aspects of technology. However, and probably as a result of insufficient data, few of the authors who analyse networking resources have considered the different elements which comprise the technical capital of companies, although there are some exceptions (Fischer and Varga 2002, Petroni 2000).

As stated above, we consider that a multiplicity of aspects should be taken into account when analysing firms' technical capital. Variables measuring the quality of company equipment, for instance, approximate the new technology embodied in the capital goods used by manufacturers. The literature views the proclivity of firms to implement technical advances as an important aspect of their innovativeness (Garcia and Calantone 2002). R&D variables approximate the innovative effort made by firms and their capacity to absorb knowledge and information generated elsewhere (Cohen and Levinthal 1989). Nevertheless, not all innovations produced by firms originate in their R&D laboratories. The upgrading and customization of existing products and the imitation or adaptation of products produced elsewhere may take place primarily at the shop floor level. On the other hand, an invention produced in a laboratory does not become an innovation until it is diffused in the marketplace (Garcia and Calantone 2002). If we wish to understand the technical endowment of firms, we must also take into consideration their capacity to launch new products onto the market.

This chapter studies the technical capital equipment (the physical element of technology) and the technological capabilities of companies, or 'those capabilities directly associated with the development, acquisition and use of technology' (Rush *et al.* 2007, p. 222), focusing on aspects such as companies' R&D intensity and their capacity to launch marketable products.

9.2.2   Are Technical Capital and Social Capital Related?

In conventional RBV theory the internal development of resources (such as technological resources) enables companies to improve their profitability by gaining competitive advantages over other firms, and thus innovating companies prefer a degree of isolation from possible competitors; in other words, innovators are unlikely to enter into many partnerships. By contrast, recent research maintains that this traditional view ignores the fact that the benefits of innovation can be jointly generated by partners via inter-firm relationships (Lavie 2006). In Lavie's theoretical model the possession of technical capital and social capital is associated at company level, as firms are willing to network in order to share combined resources and generate innovations. Furthermore, according to Gulati *et al.* (2000), firms can encounter value-creating resources and capabilities beyond their own boundaries, through the formation of business networks.

Other authors point to a different cause for the possible association between technical and social capital. They argue that firms engaging in inter-firm linkages are likely to have technical capital at their disposal; in a linkage 'market', it is claimed, such companies are more attractive to potential partners (Ahuja 2000). A homogeneous distribution of R&D resources seems to be especially important, for instance, in inter-firm R&D collaborations; weaker contenders are not considered to be worthwhile partners by potential collaborators (Häusler *et al.* 1994).

The results of empirical studies dealing with the association between technical capital and social capital are mixed. Following a review of 179 selected papers, Pittaway *et al.* (2004) report that firms commonly engage in networking to gain access to new technology and skills. Although most of the literature reviewed focuses on the UK, the USA and Germany, studies of other countries confirm the relationships between networking and innovativeness. An analysis of a sample of Belgian manufacturing firms finds a positive relationship between inter-firm collaborations and company innovation (Faems *et al.* 2005). In a sample of Spanish electronics firms Holl and Rama (2008 forthcoming) demonstrate a positive relationship between networking and innovativeness at the plant level. In their sample networking firms were more likely than their non-networking counterparts to have launched new products, which in addition made a greater contribution to turnover. They found that subcontractors had also implemented a significantly greater number of new industrial processes in the previous three years. In general, networking firms were found to be more efficient than non-networking companies when employing financial and human resources allocated to innovation, a result which confirms that of Suárez-Villa and Rama (1996), in their study of the Madrid electronics industry. An analysis of 58 Spanish automotive suppliers shows that the principal motivation for networking is to access new technology and know-how (Pérez and Sánchez 2002).

Although part of this literature refers to innovator networks (R&D collaboration), outsourcing networks also entail knowledge exchange, often face-to face tacit knowledge, even when no specific arrangements to transfer technology are made by the partners (Holl and Rama 2008 forthcoming); moreover, collaboration in outsourcing networks can enable the partners to specialize and save human and financial resources, which can then be redirected towards plant-level innovation (Suárez-Villa and Rama 1996).

Alternatively, other researchers point to a possible trade-off between networking activities and technical capital. Love and Roper (2001) find that in-house R&D and technology cooperation with other companies are substitutes in UK, German and Irish plants (they also control for market factors, location factors and other variables in their model). They argue that firms manage their portfolios of external relationships concurrently with the development of in-house innovative capabilities. Suárez-Villa (2002) observes that the most R&D-intensive electronics plants in the metropolitan area of Los Angeles avoid clustering with other companies because, he claims, these innovators value privacy more than the sharing of knowledge. Privacy, he argues, is becoming increasingly important in high-tech industries, given the role played by innovation in inter-firm competition. In an investigation of approximately 200 manufacturing plants in metropolitan Vienna, Fischer and Varga (2002) find that technological resources, as measured by four variables (size, age and other variables are also checked), are not a significant determinant of the likelihood of networking. In their study of US metalworking and machinery manufacturing, Kelley and Harrison (1990) find no statistically significant association between plant equipment age and the likelihood of subcontracting out part of their production (level of product diversification, hourly wages and other variables are also controlled). An analysis of small Japanese firms suggests that the probability of working as a subcontractor is negatively related to size, foreign sales and technological capabilities (Kimura 2005).

Furthermore, flexible specialization theory assumes that one reason for firms to outsource part of their production is their lack of in-house skills or specialized machinery. In our opinion this assumption also implies a trade-off between companies' proclivity to outsource and their technical capital; in other words, firms which outsource some of their production are less technologically advanced than vertically integrated firms, whose production is undertaken completely in-house.

The present chapter tests whether firms participating in outsourcing networks are likely to have significant technical capital at their disposal.

9.2.3   Differences Within Networks

In their study of a high-tech sector Vanverbeke *et al.* (2001) find that technical capital and social capital, as measured by the number of technological alliances a company has, act as mutual reinforcements. They note, however, that both types of capital could become substitutes if a company is involved in extensive networks and already has a substantial patent portfolio. Consequently, they find two equilibria which guide two different types of strategy. Some firms develop strong internal capabilities, supported by a small network of companies, while others focus on technology acquisition through networking but seldom develop their internal technological capabilities. This result suggests that different situations must be analysed in order to understand the relationship between technical capital and social capital.

Networked firms, for instance, may have competing visions and strategies (Kogut 2000). In outsourcing networks the technological role of clients and subcontractors may differ (Holl and Rama 2008 forthcoming; Petroni and Panciroli 2002; Sako 1994). Consequently, we argue, the association between networking resources and technical capital may vary between companies which occupy different positions within a business network.

In order to detect differences in the association between technical capital and social capital, we distinguish between clients and subcontractors (suppliers) in outsourcing networks.

9.2.4   Strategy and Companies' Awareness of Their Technical Resources

In the last two decades academic research has assumed that the strategy process begins with the firm's awareness of its own critical resources, such as technology (Foss 1998). The resource-based perspective of strategy, Foss claims, has also been influential in managerial practice. The present study tests whether a positive appraisal of the dimension of technological change at the plant level makes firms less likely to network (our model checks real company innovativeness and technological level). This exercise helps us to understand whether firms which perceive themselves as having made technical advances are reluctant to engage in networking, as various authors claim.

Management literature suggests that the starting point for the measurement of companies' technological capabilities is to assess the initial awareness by senior management of 'the role of technology in competitiveness and the dangers of "standing still" in today's highly competitive environment' (Rush *et al.* 2007, p. 227). Logically enough, managerial awareness may be a particularly important element in industries, such as those studied here (automobiles and electronics), due to the rapid pace of technological change in these sectors and the substantial role played by innovation in competitiveness. According to Granovetter (1998), one reason why firms might connect with other companies, instead of operating in isolation, is their need to obtain resources, such as technology; furthermore, he opines, companies may federate in order to adapt to technological advances. Empirical literature often assumes that, given the variety of technology and know-how now required to manufacture certain products, firms intentionally build a portfolio of partners in order to acquire innovative capacities through networking (Pittaway *et al.* 2004; Vanhaverbeke *et al.* 2001). According to the literature review performed by Pitttaway *et al.* (2004), most studies conclude that firms are induced to network as a way of obtaining access to the technology they lack. Such literature suggests that firms are not 'chosen' by others in a linkage 'market', as maintained by Ahuja (2000), but instead actively search for a variety of partnerships which may supply many different new techniques.

The study by Love and Roper (2001) is one of the few to provide empirical evidence of how managerial perception of a company's technological resources affects its networking behaviour. These authors find very weak coefficients for the association of attitudinal variables and variables measuring networking resources (real technological resources are also checked in their model). Other authors go further and argue that companies have only limited control over their relationship portfolios, since business networks are, to a large extent, complex self-organizing systems (Wilkinson and Young 2002).

The present study tests whether those plants which are strongly aware of the strategic importance of product innovation are more likely to network. Given that our model controls for the real innovativeness of the establishment and other objective measures of technological level, the introduction of this attitudinal variable will help us to better understand the role of strategy per se in network structures.

9.3   DATA AND METHODOLOGY

The study population consists of large and medium-sized establishments operating in the Spanish automobile and electronics industries. In both sectors outsourcing is quite important in developed countries and, more specifically, in Spain (Dyer 1996; Dyer and Nobeoka 2000; European Commission 1992; European Commission 1997a; European Commission 1997b; Sako 2004; Suárez-Villa and Fischer 1995; Suárez-Villa and Rama 1996).

Table 9.1   Characteristics of the sample (N = 162)

Variable *No. of employees (plant size)*	% of plants
50–99	26.5
100–499	58.0
500–1000	12.3
1001–5000	2.5
> 5000	0.6
Ownership	
Domestic plants	48.8
Subsidiaries and joint ventures	51.2
Sector	
Automobiles	69.1
Electronics	24.7
Auxiliary industries	6.2
Region	
Catalonia	38.9
Madrid	10.5
Aragon	9.3
Basque Country	9.3
Navarre	9.3
Other regions	22.7

The 162 firms in the sample, surveyed in 2003, have more than 50 employees each;[2] their distribution in the sample is proportional to the geographic and size distribution of companies in these Spanish industries. The definition of industrial activities followed that of the National Classification of Economic Activities. A pre-test of the questionnaire was conducted before launching the survey. Within companies the majority of the respondents were directors of production.

Table 9.1 presents some of the characteristics of the sample and shows that it takes a variety of firms into account, in terms of size, ownership and other relevant features.

The objects of study are industrial plants[3] and their relationships with their outsourcing partners. We analyse clients and their relationships with their subcontractors (suppliers), as well as subcontractors and their relationships with their clients.

Most previous research models the determinants of company networking behaviour; in these models the likelihood of networking is often a dependent variable and the set of independent variables may include one or more technical variables. Logit regression methods are commonly used; the dependent variable is the decision to network or the decision to subcontract out, and the responses are Yes or No. Other analyses measure inter-firm linkages at the company level by the number of partnerships in which the focal firm is engaged. However, even if a company has many partnerships, interactions may be weak or sporadic. Moreover, a Yes or No response is unlikely to capture important information which defines the networking resources of a company, such as its previous partnership experience and the affect of outsourcing upon sales. In order to define more accurately such resources, we take into consideration the intensity of interactions and their degree of stability in recent years. A company which largely depends on outsourcing and has had an increasing number of partnerships is likely to cooperate with other companies, and thus we adopted a multivariate method of analysis.

Unlike the majority of the studies cited in the theoretical background section, we do not model the determinants of company networking behaviour. Instead, we attempt to improve our understanding of the relationship between technical capital and networking behaviour (as an approximation of social capital). To do so, we perform a canonical correlation between a set of variables representing the technical capital of companies and another set approximating their social capital.

Canonical correlation is used to investigate the linear relationships between two sets of variables, in this case the set indicating the importance of vertical inter-firm linkages and the set denoting companies' technical capital. The purpose of canonical correlation analysis is to find two linear combinations of the variables, one for the 'exogenous' or the predictor set and one for the 'endogeneous' or criterion set, such as their product-moment correlation is as large as possible, and not to model individual variables (Dillon and Goldstein 1984).

We use four variables aimed at assessing company networking resources. The distinction between two different company roles (clients and subcontractors) within outsourcing networks helps us to provide an in-depth analysis of the interactions of networking resources and technical capital.

9.3.1 Set 1

The four variables approximating company networking resources are:

Clients:

1. *OUTDIR.* Outsourcing direction (client). The firms surveyed were requested to rate the importance of outsourcing part of their production, as compared to three years previously. This is a time-varying

measure of the relationships of clients with their subcontractors (suppliers). This question employed a six point Likert-type scale.

2. *INCOUT.* Incidence of outsourced production (clients). The firms sur-
    veyed were asked to indicate the current percentage of sales accounted
    for by outsourced production. This variable approximates the eco-
    nomic importance of outsourcing for the firms sampled. There were
    four possible responses: 0 per cent of total sales (that is, the firm is not
    a client in outsourcing networks), 1 per cent to 25 per cent, 25 per cent
    to 50 per cent or over 50 per cent.

Subcontractors (suppliers):

3. *SUBDIR.* Evolution of subcontracting (subcontractors). The firms
    surveyed were asked to rate the importance of work subcontracted by
    clients as compared to three years previously. This is a time-varying
    measure of the relationships which subcontractors (suppliers) main-
    tain with their clients. This question used a six point Likert-type scale.
4. *INCSUB.* Importance of subcontracted work for subcontractors.
    Companies were requested to indicate the value of the work performed
    for clients, as a percentage of total sales. This variable provides an
    approximation of the economic importance of subcontracted work in
    the firms sampled. This question permitted four responses: 0 per cent
    of total sales (that is, the company is not a subcontractor in outsourc-
    ing networks), from 1 per cent to 25 per cent, from 25 per cent to 50 per
    cent or over 50 per cent.

9.3.2   Set 2

Here, we measure the technical capital of a plant by studying, as stated
earlier, two crucial aspects: (i) technical capital equipment (the quality of
industrial machinery) and (ii) the availability of various technological
capabilities at the plant level, as indicated by company involvement in
formal R&D, R&D intensity, product innovation and design capabilities.
We take into account the following five variables:

1. *AGE.* Quality of the equipment, as measured by its age: under 2 years,
    2–4 years, 5–10 years and over 10 years. We calculated a new variable
    with four categories ranging from 'new equipment' (1) to 'old equip-
    ment' (4).
2. *NEW_PROD.* New products. The firms surveyed were asked to report
    whether they had launched new or technologically improved products
    onto the market in the last two years. Products were considered 'new'

when they were either new to the industry or to the company surveyed. It was operationalized as a dichotomical variable (Yes = 1, No = 0).

3. *AESTHETIC.* Aesthetic changes. The companies surveyed were requested to provide information about their non-technological innovations. This question used a five point Likert-type scale (1 = the company has not introduced this type of innovation).

4. *R&D.* This variable indicates whether the firm performs formal R&D. Operationalized as a dichotomical variable (Yes = 1, No = 0).

5. *R&D_PERSON.* Share of personnel involved in R&D. This is a composite variable and consists of the number of employees (as a percentage of total employees) involved in full-time R&D activities; it also includes a calculation of the time devoted to R&D by personnel only involved in such activities part time. It approximates the R&D intensity of the plant and in-house research skills.

AGE attempts to measure technological change in capital goods: newer capital equipment has suffered less wear and tear and embodies the latest technology, while vintage capital equipment often implies low efficiency. Thus, the variable provides an approximation of technological change embodied at the plant level. *R&D* and *R&D_PERSON* provide an approximation of companies' accumulated internal knowledge and their capacity to absorb knowledge generated externally (Cohen and Levinthal 1989). *NEW_PROD* measures firms' ability to transform inventions into marketable products; the source of the new ideas may be either formal R&D or improvements produced on the shop floor. We include aesthetic improvements (*AESTHETIC*) in this set, since innovation other than the technological type may increase companies' technical capital.

In addition, the second set includes two variables which reflect managers' perception of technological change and their awareness of the strategic importance of innovation as a key factor in company competitiveness. These two additional variables facilitate our understanding of the driving forces behind relationships and, more specifically, the role of technical capital. The variables are as follows:

6. *STRATEGY.* Perceived strategic importance of product innovation for the firm, on a scale of 1 to 100 (as compared to cost, quality and variety).

7. *TECH_CHANGE.* Self-assessment of technological change at the plant level. This question used a five point Likert-type scale, ranging from 'no changes' (1) to 'total change' (5) in the previous three years.

In our statistical analysis, the percentage of non-missing values exceeded 96 per cent for all the variables.

9.4   RESULTS

We now attempt to determine whether the variables representing networking activities are related in any way to the technical capital variables. As stated earlier, a canonical correlation analysis examines the association between the two sets of variables.

Table 9.2 displays the correlation matrices between the original variables, and no serious problems of multicollinearity are detected. Correlations between the variables of the technical set are moderate, a result which justifies the inclusion of several variables to define the technical capital of companies; the result shows that each of them supplies some additional information. For instance, the correlation coefficient between *R&D* and *R&D_PERSON* is only 0.38, which suggests that skilled personnel perform part-time R&D activities even in plants with no formal R&D laboratory. *NEW_PROD* is very weakly (albeit positively) correlated to *R&D_PERSON* (0.12). This result may indicate that some new products originate through *R&D* performed by the parent company rather than in-house efforts at plant level, and thus a range of variables in this set must be considered. Curiously, *STRATEGY* is very weakly correlated to *R&D_PERSON* (0.02), which indicates the proportion of skilled personnel hired by the plant. Although some managers rate product innovation highly among strategic priorities, this is not necessarily reflected in the proportion of skilled workers in the plant in question. According to the correlation matrix, the one-to-one correlations between the networking variables and the technical capital variables are moderate, the strongest being between *R&D* and *OUTDIR* (0.32). In other words, those companies which have increasingly outsourced production in recent years are more likely to undertake in-house R&D. There exist some larger within-set correlations in the first set, between *SUBDIR* and *INCSUB* (0.37); in the second these occur between *TYPE_EQU* and *TECH_CHANGE* (0.41) and between *STRATEGY* and *NEW_PROD* (0.49). In sum, the two variables representing managerial perception (*TECH_CHANGE* and *STRATEGY*) are moderately correlated with those indicating actual technological change in the plant; we shall return to this question below. As expected, *AESTHETIC* has a positive (albeit weak) association with the remaining technical variables; the only exception is the correlation coefficient with *NEW_PROD*, which is negative. This result suggests that aesthetic innovations are used to improve old products, although the negative coefficient is very low.

The first canonical correlation is 0.40, which is larger than the between-set correlations (Table 9.3). The shared variance is approximately 16 per cent, denoting a moderate relationship between the two sets.[4] However, the

Table 9.2   Correlations among the original variables

Correlations among the *VAR* variables

	OUTDIR	*SUBDIR*	*INCOUT*	*INCSUB*
OUTDIR	1.0000	0.3134	−0.0718	−0.2026
SUBDIR	0.3134	1.0000	−0.0823	−0.0703
INCOUT	−0.0718	−0.0823	1.0000	0.3699
INCSUB	−0.2026	−0.0703	0.3699	1.0000

Correlations among the *WITH* variables

	STRATEGY	*AGE*	*TECH_CHANGE*	*NEW_PROD*
STRATEGY	1.0000	0.1818	0.2174	0.4915
AGE	0.1818	1.0000	0.4147	0.2927
TECH_CHANGE	0.2174	0.4147	1.0000	0.3178
NEW_PROD	0.4915	0.2927	0.3178	1.0000
AESTHETIC	0.0385	0.0039	0.0579	−0.0203
R&D	0.1673	0.0031	0.1252	0.1993
R&D_PERSON	0.0224	0.1868	0.1430	0.1231

Correlations among the *WITH* variables

	AESTHETIC	*R&D*	*R&D_PERSON*
STRATEGY	0.0385	0.1673	0.0224
AGE	0.0039	0.0031	0.1868
TECH_CHANGE	0.0579	0.1252	0.1430
NEW_PROD	−0.0203	0.1993	0.1231
AESTHETIC	1.0000	0.0779	0.0112
R&D	0.0779	1.0000	0.3774
R&D_PERSON	0.0112	0.3774	1.0000

Correlations between the *VAR* variables and the *WITH* variables

	STRATEGY	*AGE*	*TECH_CHANGE*	*NEW_PROD*
OUTDIR	0.0768	−0.1587	−0.0286	0.0604
SUBDIR	0.0071	−0.0083	0.0700	0.1321
INCOUT	0.0538	−0.0211	−0.0050	−0.2332
INCSUB	−0.0500	0.0295	0.0708	−0.0226

Correlations between the *VAR* variables and the *WITH* variables

	AESTHETIC	*R&D*	*R&D_PERSON*
OUTDIR	0.0291	0.3204	0.1393
SUBDIR	−0.0252	0.1497	0.2170
INCOUT	0.0321	−0.0986	−0.0688
INCSUB	0.0124	−0.1024	−0.0833

Applied analyses

*Table 9.3 Association between variables denoting networking activities
and variables denoting technical capital*

Canonical correlation analysis

	Canonical correlation	Adjusted canonical correlation	Approximated standard error	Squared canonical correlation
1	0.399 136	0.292 332	0.073 733	0.159 309
2	0.333 343		0.077 960	0.111 118
3	0.167 787		0.085 237	0.028 152
4	0.096 978		0.086 881	0.009 405

Eigenvalues of Inv(E)*H
= CanRsq/(1-CanRsq)

	Eigenvalues	Difference	Proportion	Cumulative
1	0.1895	0.0645	0.5369	0.5369
2	0.1250	0.0960	0.3542	0.8910
3	0.0290	0.0195	0.0821	0.9731
4	0.0095		0.0269	1.0000

	Likelihood ratio	Approximate F-value	DF	Den DF	Pr > F
1	0.71 940 741	1.48	28	434.09	0.0558
2	0.85 573 368	1.08	18	342.72	0.3727
3	0.96 270 757	0.47	10	244	0.9096
4	0.99 059 521	0.29	4	123	0.8827

Multivariate statistics and F approximations
S = 4   M = 1   N = 59

Statistic	Value	F-Value	DF	Den DF	Pr > F
Wilks' Lambda	0.71 940 741	1.48	28	434.09	0.0558
Pillai's Trace	0.30 798 417	1.47	28	492	0.0603
Hotelling-Lawley Trace	0.35 296 841	1.50	28	290.39	0.0549
Roy's Greatest Root	0.18 949 801	3.33	7	123	0.0028

first canonical variable accounts for most of the data variability (54 per cent) and the F-test demonstrates that only the first component is significant (0.05). The remaining canonical variables are not worthy of consideration, as the probability levels in Table 9.3 show.

We now examine the first canonical variable in detail. As the variables are measured in different units, we analyse the standardized coefficients rather

Table 9.4   Canonical correlation analysis

Standardized canonical coefficients for the *VAR* variable

	adepend1
OUTDIR	0.6189
INCOUT	0.3507
SUBDIR	−0.5925
INCSUB	0.1317

Standardized canonical coefficients for the *WITH* variables

	aindepend1
STRATEGY	−0.3301
AGE	−0.3875
TECH_CHANGE	−0.0467
NEW_PROD	0.6921
ASTHETIC	−0.0368
R&D	0.5664
R&D_PERSON	0.2691

than the raw coefficients (Table 9.4). The first canonical variable for the networking set is a weighted difference of *OUTDIR* (0.62) and *SUBDIR* (0.59), with greater emphasis on *OUTDIR*. The variables display opposing signs, and the coefficients for *INCOUT* (0.35) and, especially, *INCSUB* (0.13) are quite low, although positive.

The first canonical variable for the technological set also displays opposing signs, with *NEW_PROD* and *R&D* having the greatest weight. Nearly 70 per cent of the information in the *NEW_PROD* variable and 56.6 per cent of that in the *R&D* variable can be accounted for by the remaining technological variables. This finding indicates that these two variables are the best predictors of companies' technical capital and are to be preferred for analysis if complete information is not available. By contrast, *TECH_CHANGE*, which indicates managers' perceptions of in-house technological change, has a very low (negative) coefficient of correlation with the objective measurements. In other words, there is some inconsistency between managerial perceptions and the actual technical endowment of plants. This result suggests that this variable is the least useful indicator to characterize actual technical capital.

Finally, *STRATEGY* displays a moderate (negative) association with the other technical variables. This indicates that some firms, despite having limited technical capital at their disposal, may be aware of the strategic importance of innovation in their industry. In sum, our results suggest that the variables characterizing managers' perceptions, although often used as

Table 9.5   Correlations between the VAR *variables and the canonical variables of the* WITH *variables, and between the* WITH *variables and the canonical variables of the* VAR *variables*

Correlations between the *VAR* variables and the canonical variables of the *WITH* variables

	aindepend1
OUTDIR	0.2972
INCOUT	0.2331
SUBDIR	−0.2463
INCSUB	−0.0948

Correlations between the *WITH* variables and the canonical variables of the *VAR* variables

	adepend1
STRATEGY	0.0115
AGE	−0.0848
TECH_CHANGE	0.0192
NEW_PROD	0.2189
AESTHETIC	−0.0082
R&D	0.2957
R&D_PERSON	0.1921

indicators in the literature, provide only a weak reflection of the true technological level of companies.

Table 9.5 shows the correlation of the variables in the first set with the first canonical variable of the second set, and the correlation of the variables in the second set with the first canonical variable of the first set. *OUTDIR, INCOUT* and *SUBDIR* are moderately associated with the first canonical variable for technical capital, although *SUBDIR* has a negative sign. This result suggests that clients who have more technical capital at their disposal are increasingly involved in partnerships and obtain a larger share of their sales from outsourced production. For subcontractors, by contrast, the relationships between the variables denoting networking activities and the canonical variable for technology are negative or negligible. Subcontractors who have less technical capital available tend to have an increasing number of partnerships.

Conversely, subcontractors who possess greater technical capital tend to participate, over time, in fewer relationships, and probably network with only a small group of selected clients. In other words, there is a trade-off between social capital and technical capital among subcontractors.

Company size influences the relationship between networking and inno-vation (Holl and Rama 2008 forthcoming; Torbett 2001); one possible explanation is that subcontractors are smaller than their clients. To further test this hypothesis, we compare the sizes of clients and subcontractors. Thus, we test for size differences between both types of firms. In our sample, the size of clients (X = 291; σ = 279) and subcontractors (X = 243; σ = 260), as measured by the average number of employees at the plant level, is quite similar. Thus, differences cannot be attributed to the different sizes of client companies and subcontracting firms.

We now identify the elements of companies' technical capital which are most closely related to their networking resources (the model checks for the remaining technical variables). *R&D* is moderately associated with the first canonical variable for networking resources, while *NEW_PROD* and *R&D_PERSON* are weakly associated with it. The remaining technical variables display very low coefficients. *AGE* has a negative sign, suggesting that companies with relatively old equipment are less attractive to potential partners and less likely to network with other firms. However, given the low value of the *AGE* coefficient, we conclude that equipment quality does not influence networking. *AESTHETIC* also has a very low (negative) coeffi-cient; in other words, the greater the design capabilities of a firm, the less likely it is to network (although this effect is also negligible). In conclusion, company possession of a *R&D* laboratory is the element of technical capital most closely associated with the availability of networking resources.

The attitudinal variables display positive (although low) coefficients. Notably, *STRATEGY* per se does not accurately predict whether a firm possesses networking resources.

9.5 DISCUSSION AND CONCLUSIONS

In this chapter we investigate the relation between the technical and social capital of companies in a sample of 162 medium-size and large Spanish plants. Overall, the full model was significant. First, we found that the tech-nical capital of a company and its participation in vertical linkages with other firms are associated. This result corroborates the findings of most previous studies on this topic (Ahuja 2000; Faems *et al.* 2005; Holl and Rama 2008 forthcoming; Pittaway *et al.* 2004).

Does this mean that the social and technical capital available to a company complement each other? Not necessarily. Second, a closer look at our data shows two different types of statistical association, one positive and the other negative, between technical capital and social capital. For clients (companies which outsource some of their production), the more technical capital they have, the more likely they are to network with other firms. In this case social capital and technical capital complement each other. Backward linkages are more likely to be generated in firms which possess some technical capital; this may prevent technologically endowed companies from becoming isolated, a situation which would deprive other firms in their sector from a potential source of new knowledge.

By contrast, for subcontractors, the less technical capital the company has, the more it will engage in outsourcing networks. In this case social capital appears to compensate for the lack of technical capital. Our results are in line with Kimura's (2002) for small and medium-sized Japanese subcontractors.

Our findings suggest that subcontractors do not need to 'buy a ticket', in terms of technological endowment, in order to be accepted as partners by other firms (clients). In other words, insufficient technological capital does not condemn a potential supplier to isolation.

In one of the Spanish industries analysed in this chapter, namely automobiles, the main motivation for suppliers engaging in networks is to access new technology (Pérez Pérez and Sánchez 2002). Conversely, subcontractors with greater capabilities perform less work for other firms. This interpretation is coherent with previous research indicating that, in the electronics and automobile industries, as subcontractors become more skilled they may evolve into independent firms and prefer to market their own products, instead of participating in the manufacture of clients' products (Baba *et al.* 1995; Rama and Calatrava 2002; Sako 1994). This implies that highly skilled subcontractors tend to enter into fewer and fewer partnerships in the medium run. It may also be true that clients collaborate closely with their highly skilled suppliers and are understandably reluctant to see them collaborate with their competitors. Our result is coherent with analyses of specialized, first-tier suppliers to the automobile industry which invest in customized equipment (as opposed to standard equipment) and co-specialize with a reduced number of clients in innovation (Dyer 1996).

Briefly, two distinct strategies (social capital-intensive and technical capital-intensive) are apparent among the suppliers in our sample, as in the case of the networked innovators analysed by Vanhaverbeke and colleagues (2001).

The differences detected in our study regarding the two different types of firms, clients and subcontractors, may explain the conflicting results of previous studies of this subject. Our research indicates the need to take into account the position of firms within networks when studying the relationship between social capital and technical capital.

Third, the multivariate analysis shows that not all aspects of companies' technical capital are equally influential. The technical variables most closely associated with the likelihood of networking are those which indicate the development of internal company capabilities; by contrast, the technological quality of equipment is very weakly associated with the variables indicating company involvement in inter-firm linkages. This result suggests that providing firms with cheap credit for purchasing new equipment is clearly insufficient to stimulate inter-firm linkages.

Fourth, our findings suggest that even if managers are well aware of the strategic importance of innovation, company propensity to network may nevertheless be weak or non-existent. Our empirical results are coherent with those of Love and Roper (2001), who show that attitudinal factors exert only a weak influence upon companies' networking resources. Our research also implies that a company's technical capital is a key factor in determining whether other firms accept or reject it as a partner. As Wilkinson and Young (2002) note, firms have only limited control over their relationship portfolios. This may imply that the technical capital available to companies plays a substantial role in the formation of relationship portfolios. The opportunities offered by technical endowment may influence inter-firm matching processes more than company intentions. While technological strategy plays a certain role in the shaping of network structures, technical resource endowment is more important. Our findings support the views of those researchers who maintain that business networks involve a significant degree of self-organization (Kogut 2000; Ritter and Gemünden 2003), meaning that some limits are imposed on the efficiency of both management and policies.

Our results support the view that policies which encourage vertical inter-firm linkages may be effective in promoting the technological upgrading of industries and regions. Firms well endowed with technical capital are neither isolated nor lacking in social capital.

Nevertheless, our results indicate that the efficacy of such policies is hindered by certain limitations. First, policies aimed at fostering networks of technologically impoverished companies are unlikely to promote industrial development; at least some of the would-be-partners should possess modern machinery and, more importantly, some in-house skills and expertise. Second, the effects of networking stimuli are likely to differ according to company type. Unskilled companies benefit most from such policies, which may help them to participate in vertical linkages as subcontractors. By contrast, even if stimuli to networking exist, less well endowed companies cannot operate as clients; as they have little to offer in terms of knowledge and new technology, they encounter difficulties in attracting partners (subcontractors). Furthermore, even if policies to encourage networking are implemented, skilled subcontractors are unlikely to be interested in expanding their client portfolios.

Our research work is not free from limitations. It must be remembered that it studies the association of technical and social capital rather than any causality between the two factors.

NOTES

1. The authors are grateful to the BBVA Foundation (Spain) for its financial support (Project: 'Innovation in Spanish industry', CSIC-BBVA Foundation) and to Mario Furlotti for his comments on a previous version. Any errors are entirely the responsibility of the authors.
2. The European Commission defines small firms as those with fewer than 50 employees. Although we adopt this cut-off point, our unit of analysis is plants, and thus the companies to which they belong may be larger.
3. A plant is a functional unit located at a single physical location.
4. Usually, authors consider that an association between two sets of variables exists when the shared variance of these sets exceeds 10 per cent.

REFERENCES

Ahuja, G. (2000), 'The duality of collaboration: inducements and opportunities in the formation of interfirm linkages', *Strategic Management Journal*, **21**, 317–43.

Anderson, A.R. and S.L. Jack (2002), 'The articulation of social capital in entrepreneurial networks: a glue or a lubricant?', *Entrepreneurship and Regional Development*, **14**, 193–210.

Baba, Y., S. Takai and Y. Mizuta (1995), 'The Japanese software industry: the "hub structure" approach', *Research Policy*, **24**, 473–86.

Becattini, G. (2002), 'Industrial sectors and industrial districts: tools for industrial analysis', *European Planning Studies*, **10**, 483–93.

Brusco, S. (1999), 'The rules of the game in industrial districts', in A. Grandori (ed.), *Interfirm Networks. Organization and Industrial Competiveness*, London and New York: Routledge, pp. 17–40.

Cohen, W.M. and D.A. Levinthal (1989), 'Innovation and learning: the two faces of R&D', *Economic Journal*, **99**, 569–96.

Coleman, J.S. (1988), 'Social capital in the creation of human capital', *American Journal of Sociology*, **94**, Supplement: Organizations and Institutions: Sociological and Economic Approaches to the Analysis of Social Structure, S 95–120.

de Laat, P.B. (1999), 'Dangerous liaisons. Sharing knowledge within research and development alliances', in A. Grandori (ed.), *Interfirm Networks*, London and New York: Routledge, pp. 208–33.

Dillon, W.R. and M. Goldstein (1984), *Multivariate Analysis. Methods and Applications*, New York, Chichester, Brisbane and Toronto: John Wiley & Sons.

Dyer, J.H. (1996), 'Specialized supplier networks as a source of competitive advantage: evidence from the auto industry', *Strategic Management Journal*, **17**, 271–91.

Dyer, J.H. and K. Nobeoka (2000), 'Creating and managing a high-performance knowledge-sharing network: the Toyota case', *Strategic Management Journal*, **21**, 345–67.

European Commission (1992), 'Estudio sobre el peso económico y la evolución de la subcontratación en la Comunidad', ESP, Dirección General Política de Empresa, Comercio, Turismo y Economia Social, pp. 1–54.

European Commission (1997a), 'La nouvelle sous-traitance industrielle en Europe. Premiers résultats chiffrés avec une définition actualisée', Luxembourg.

European Commission (1997b), 'La sous-traitance dans le secteur électronique', pp. 1–50.

Faems, D., B. Van Looy and K. Debackere (2005), 'Interorganizational collaboration and innovation: towards a portfolio approach', *Journal of Product Innovation Management*, **22**, 238–50.

Fischer, M.M. and A. Varga (2002), 'Technological innovation and inter-firm cooperation: an exploratory analysis using survey data from manufacturing firms in the metropolitan region of Vienna', *International Journal of Technology Management*, **24** (7/8), 724–42.

Foss, N.J. (1998), 'The resource-based perspective: an assessment and diagnosis of problems', *Scandinavian Journal of Management*, **14**, 133–49.

Freeman, C. (1991), 'Networks of innovators: a synthesis of research issues', *Research Policy*, **20**, 499–514.

Garcia, R. and R. Calantone (2002), 'A critical look at the technological innovation typology and innovativeness terminology: a literature review', *Journal of Product Innovation Management*, **19**, 110–32.

Granovetter, M. (1985), 'Economic action and social structure. The problem of embeddedness', *American Journal of Sociology*, **91** (3), 481–510.

Granovetter, M. (1998), 'Coase revisited: business groups in the modern economy', in G. Dosi, D. Teece and J. Chytry (eds), *Technology, Organization, and Competitiveness. Perspectives on Industrial and Corporate Change*, Oxford, UK: Oxford University Press, pp. 67–103.

Gulati, R., N. Nohria and A. Zaheer (2000), 'Strategic networks', *Strategic Management Journal*, **21**, 203–15.

Hagedoorn, J. (1994), 'Internationalization of companies: the evolution of organizational complexity, flexibility and networks of innovation', MERIT Research Memorandum 2794-008.

Häusler, J., H.-W. Hohn and S. Lütz (1994), 'Contingencies of innovative networks: a case study of successful interfirm R&D collaboration', *Research Policy*, **23**, 47–66.

Holl, A. and R. Rama (2008 forthcoming), 'An exploratory analysis of networking, R&D and innovativeness in the Spanish electronics sector', *International Journal of Technology Management* (Special issue on 'Innovation Networks and Knowledge Clusters in the Global Knowledge Economy and Society: Insights and Implications for Theory and Practice').

Kelley, M.R. and B. Harrison (1990), 'The subcontracting behaviour of single vs. multiplant enterprises in US manufacturing: implications for economic development', *World Development*, **18**, 1273–94.

Kimura, F. (2005), *The globalisation of production networks, a view from Asia*, http://www.oecd.org/dataoecd/43/10/35650284.pdf, pp. 1–22, Faculty of Economics, Keio University.

Kogut, B. (2000), 'The network as knowledge: generative rules and the emergence of strucuture', *Strategic Management Journal*, **21**, 405–25.

Kotabe, M., X. Martin and H. Domoto (2003), 'Gaining from vertical partnerships: knowledge, relationship duration and supplier performance improvement in the US and Japanese automotive industries', *Strategic Management Journal*, **24**, 293–316.

Lavie, D. (2006), 'The competitive advantage of interconnected firms: and extension of the resource-based view', *Academy of Management Journal*, **31**, 638–58.

Love, J.H. and S. Roper (2001), 'Outsourcing in the innovation process: locational and strategic determinants', *Papers in Regional Science*, **80**, 317–36.

Pérez, C. and A.M. Sánchez (2000), 'Lean production and supplier relations: a survey of practices in the Aragonese automotive industry', *Technovation*, **20**, 665–76.

Petroni, A. (2000), 'Patterns of technological innovation in subcontracting firms: an empirical study in the food machinery industry', *European Journal of Innovation Management*, **3**, 15–26.

Petroni, A. and B. Panciroli (2002), 'Innovation as a determinant of suppliers' roles and performances: an empirical study in the food machinery industry', *European Journal of Purchasing and Supply Management*, **8**, 135–49.

Pittaway, L., M. Robertson, K. Munir, D. Denyer and A. Neely (2004), 'Networking and innovation: a systematic review of the evidence', *International Journal of Management Reviews*, **5/6**, 137–38.

Rama, R. and A. Calatrava (2002), 'The advantages of clustering: the case of Spanish electronics subcontractors', *International Journal of Technology Management*, **24**, 764–91.

Ritter, T. and H.G. Gemünden (2003), 'Interorganizational relationships and networks: an overview', *Journal of Business Research*, **56**, 691–7.

Rush, H., J. Bessant and M. Hobday (2007), 'Assessing the technological capabilities of firms: developing a policy tool', *R&D Management*, **37**, 221–36.

Sako, M. (1994), 'Supplier relationships and innovation', in M. Dodgson and R. Rothwell (eds), *The Handbook of Industrial Innovation*, Aldershot, UK and Brookfield, USA: Edward Elgar, pp. 268–83.

Sako, M. (2004), 'Supplier development at Honda, Nissan and Toyota: comparative case studies of organizational capability enhancement', *Industrial and Corporate Change*, **13**, 281–308.

Suárez-Villa, L. (2002), 'High technology clustering in the polycentric metropolis: a view from the Los Angeles metropolitan region', *International Journal of Technology Management*, **24**, 818–42.

Suárez-Villa, L. and M.M. Fischer (1995), 'Technology, organization and export-driven R&D in Austria's electronics industry', *Regional Studies*, **29**, 19–42.

Suárez-Villa, L. and R. Rama (1996), 'Outsourcing, R&D and the pattern of intra-metropolitan location: the electronics industries of Madrid', *Urban Studies*, **33**, 1155–97.

Torbett, R. (2001), 'Technological collaboration, firm size and innovation: a study of UK manufacturing firms', in OECD (ed.), *Innovative Networks: Co-operation in National Innovation Systems*, Paris: OECD, pp. 100–22.

Vanhaverbeke, W., G. Duysters and B. Beerkens (2001), 'Technological capability building through networking strategies within high-tech industries', in ECIS Working Papers, Eindhoven University of Technology, Eindhoven, the Netherlands, pp. 1–33.

Wilkinson, I. and L. Young (2002), 'On cooperating firms, relations and networks', *Journal of Business Research*, **55**, 123–32.

Williamson, O.E. (1985), *The Economic Institutions of Capitalism*, New York and London: The Free Press.

Zack, P. and S. Knack (2001), 'Trust and growth', *Economic Journal*, **111** (1), 295–321.

10. Manufacturing abroad while making profits at home: the Veneto footwear and clothing industry

Carlo Gianelle and Giuseppe Tattara

10.1 INTRODUCTION

Globalization has brought about a sharp increase in the real and financial integration of the worldwide economy. In this closely knit context the outsourcing of some of the productive and trade activities abroad becomes the focal point of the policies followed by firms in order to face competition on international markets.

The shift of manufacturers towards countries with lower labour costs was underlined by some experts at the beginning of the 1970s, and especially involved countries with relatively high labour costs such as the USA, Germany, Sweden, Denmark and UK (Ádám 1971; Finger 1976, 1977).

Over the past decades the capacity of manufacturing firms to slice the production cycle without incurring high diseconomies has given large impetus to production globalization and has driven firms in countries, like Italy, with salaries lower than those in the USA and Northern Europe, to look for lower production costs abroad. Additionally the participation of Eastern European countries, Russia and China in the international consumption market has provided a further incentive to transfer the manufacturing processes abroad by locating outposts in areas close to markets with high sales potential.

To determine the degree of internationalization of a firm is not an easy task: the usual measure is the value of the direct overseas investments made to set up a new company abroad, or to purchase one already in existence. Italian overseas investments are modest, and Italian businesses seem to be lagging behind compared to other industrialized countries of a similar size and comparable degree of development. Some scholars who have acquired information from the study of inter-industrial trade flow (Schiattarella 1999; Kaminski and Ng 2001; Corò and Volpe 2003) and from studies on individual companies have reached the conclusion that the process of internationalization is much wider and detailed than what appears from the data regarding direct investments. A conspicuous part of firms' overseas activities is, in fact, based on intermediary procedures, that is, trade agreements and subcontracting, particularly important in the case of Italian small and medium-size firms (Bigarelli and Ginzburg 2004). These forms of 'light' integration involve reduced capital flows and temporary commodity flows, as commodities are sent abroad in order to be processed and are subsequently re imported. But intermediate commodity flows blend with the 'normal' transit of goods at customs, they are not separately recorded, therefore they are difficult to identify. For this reason and not because 'light' integration is unimportant, international trade experts have devoted relatively little attention to it (Bugamelli *et al.* 2000).

In Italy the few analyses available seem to show the traditional sectors and the sectors characterized by important economies of scale as being less present in overseas markets and holding less investments compared with the high-tech sectors. This result contrasts with anecdotal evidence according to which the delocalization of textile, clothing and footwear sectors is highly relevant (CEPS-WIIW 2005; Gomirato 2004; Graziani 1998, 2001), but occurs in the mild forms mentioned before. For example, within traditional sectors there has been a steady and substantial increase of the number of firms that have established trade agreements with overseas partners (Bugamelli *et al.* 2000). A broad study regarding Italian manufacturers with more than ten employees, for the period 2000–03, reveals the well known fact that the large majority of Italian firms export abroad (70 per cent of the total) and the majority of them have maintained or started trade operations or overseas trade agreements with foreign correspondents, with a marked increase over the previous period (Capitalia 2005). Direct investment involves a limited number of businesses, while many more firms have set up technical collaboration agreements with overseas companies (Capitalia 2005, Tables D16bis and D30).

This work aims at investigating production outsourcing abroad of the Veneto footwear and clothing industries. It is based on information available from a direct survey combined with individual budget data. The survey takes into account outsourcing carried out both through direct investments and subcontracting and partnerships, and measures outsourcing with respect to the quota of the final product manufactured abroad. The various forms in which the value chain is organized is taken into account, but it is not considered of direct relevance to the present investigation.

The decision to outsource part of the production abroad is reflected in a positive variation in the level of activity and in gross profits. This analysis shows the importance of relocation on a global scale in order to give new competitivity to Veneto firms in a sector that in the 1980s resorted to domestic subcontracting and since the mid 1990s, after the abandonment of the lira's traditional weak rate of exchange, has sought new competitive strength through the delocalization of production to countries with low labour costs.

The first section of the chapter reviews the recent trends of the clothing industry on a global scale, introducing some basic concepts about international organization of production. The following section focuses on the dynamics of the clothing and footwear sector in Italy and in the Veneto region in the last 30 years. The third section highlights the possible consequences of relocating abroad part of the production process for firms that adopt this strategy, introducing the empirical analysis. The fourth section is dedicated to the econometric analysis. Finally, the fifth section gives an interpretation of the estimates' results, while the sixth section offers a conclusion.

10.2 THE INTERNATIONAL ORGANIZATION OF MANUFACTURING IN THE CLOTHING INDUSTRY

Since the 1990s various industrial sectors have been characterized by an increase in the international fragmentation of production. This is the result of the gradual reorganization of the production sequence on an international basis promoted by an ever-increasing number of businesses which extend their production processes outside their country of origin. International segmentation allows a higher degree of specialization within the value chain, and shows in an increase in trade, since many intermediate or semi-manufactured products obtained from manufacturing abroad are then re imported to be completed or distributed by the final producers, increasing international trade flows.[1] Over the past 15 years many European businesses have moved part of their productive processes to East Europe and China whose markets are well on the way towards development. This has opened up new and interesting markets, and in addition has offered production locations at a particularly low cost.[2]

In East Europe, in clothing and footwear in particular, the management of the value chains based on subcontracting prevails over direct investments because of the relatively simple processes which could be carried out abroad, the low transport costs and the skills available in many of these countries. Small and medium Italian manufacturers in traditional sectors are not able (from an organizational and financial point of view) to undertake complex operations, such as setting up agreements regarding new products and production technologies, few of them have made direct investments in overseas markets, but the majority have created a dense network of sub contracting relations with foreign companies in order to manufacture slices of the value chain under their surveillance and at a low cost.

In the 1990s the gradual elimination of trade barriers encouraged the reorganization of the productive cycle of clothing and footwear firms on an international basis and fostered investments between industrialized and developing countries (Baden 2002). As far as Europe is concerned, we should mention the ATC agreement (Agreement on Textiles and Clothing), signed in 1995 by countries in the EU belonging to the World Trade Organization, which stipulated gradual total liberalization of restricted imports, completed in January 2005 with the end of the Multifiber Agreement which had controlled the international market of textile products since 1974. Since the 1990s more and more European companies have exploited the outward processing trade tariff regime, negotiated in 1986, 1992, 1994 and 1995 by the European Union with central Eastern Europe and the Mediterranean, which allowed EU countries to export raw materials, subsequently re importing the finished products as compensation at no cost. The interest of companies in this type of trade has gradually slackened off following the growth of the EU, which now includes many of the countries involved.

Most Italian clothing manufacturers have relocated abroad using international subcontractors. These companies had already delegated many production phases to Italian outworkers, often located near the final producers in a territorial network of specialized suppliers, the district. This form of industrial organization is centred on the exploitation of phase economies (Brusco [1975] 1989), based on domestic fragmentation of the productive cycle. For example, in the clothing sector cutting, sewing, stitching and pressing are often outsourced, while in the footwear sector stitching is typically subcontracted. Setting up a workshop is relatively easy and inexpensive since the initial requirements (a simple technology and availability of skilled workers) are low, but they gradually increase as other production phases are included in the outsourcing flows. Phases at the beginning or at the end of the production chain sometimes require sophisticated machinery for cutting, washing, dyeing and printing and, in footwear, for the production of uppers and moulded soles.[3]

The choice made to produce in a low-wage country – but maintaining fixed quality standards – is a function of the ability of the available workforce and of the technological level of the production procedures. Initially the least complex phases of production are outsourced and resources concentrate on the training necessary for a few specific tasks. In most cases international production is set up by the leading firms of the industrial countries that have no direct production activity – brand-driven commodity chains, according to Gereffi (1999). These are well established brands or trading companies which build up and coordinate sometimes huge international production networks that cover a large number of countries with low labour costs. However the leading Italian clothing and footwear industries that have delocalized in recent years have not abandoned domestic production and usually keep a sometimes relevant quota of production at home (weaving, dyeing, flash collections and re orders, high quality leather shoes).[4]

A production cycle already segmented domestically is easily relocated abroad. In some cases production is exclusively focused on agreements with local manufacturers which foresee the purchase by the Italian company of a final product made with raw materials acquired in the place of production, a full-package relation. This relation is used in dealing with Asian suppliers due to the fact that good quality raw materials and top quality accessories are locally available, and efficient production networks organized by local intermediaries take care of production coordination (Gereffi 1999, 2002). In all those situations where low-wage countries are not far away from the location of the industrial brand, as happens with central Eastern Europe and North Africa, they have a relatively weak industrial structure and do not possess the necessary elements to complete all the parts of the productive process, production outsourcing develops into a semi-manufacturing relation: the brand supplies fabric, leather and accessories and subcontracts some production phases on its detailed specifications, then reimports the finished product (Crestanello and Dalla Libera 2003).

The brand manages the complex relations with each unit of the process, coordinates to a greater or lesser degree the people involved and often performs the necessary checks with its own personnel (Gereffi *et al.* 2005).

10.3 DEVERTICALIZATION OF THE VENETO CLOTHING INDUSTRY, DOMESTIC SUBCONTRACTING AND INTERNATIONAL RELOCATION

Veneto is a region of the Italian North-East of 4.6 million inhabitants, specialized in manufacturing production, mainly in light mechanics, textile-clothing, furniture and footwear production. In the year 2001 100 000 employees worked in the textile-clothing-footwear sector: 24 per cent of the total employment in manufacturing; the sector's maximum expansion dates from the 1970s and was accompanied by the creation of a large number of small and medium-size firms. In the following decade growth continued at a slower pace and there was a general reorganization; large businesses faced increasing economic difficulties and many firms outsourced domestically significant phases of the productive process that in the more recent years had been transferred abroad. The biggest and well-known clothing firm in Veneto, the Benetton Group, is a clear example of the strategy set in motion by many Veneto firms during the last 30 years. The Benetton Group can be considered an extreme case of vertical integration as it included, from the very beginning, retailing side by side with manufacturing and, at the same time, has been characterized by a strong tendency towards outsourcing, initially involving a large number of small local domestic producers (Nardin 1987), but in recent years turning rapidly towards foreign subcontractors (Crestanello and Tattara 2007).

The alternative phases of product outsourcing domestically and abroad can be clearly described by looking at the employment variations in clothing firms, brands and small laboratories during the last three decades. The situation regarding employment in the Veneto clothing sector is detailed on the basis of VWH data (Veneto Worker Histories) processed by Venice University, although it should be kept in mind that – besides registered employment – the sector is characterized by a large number of workers 'under the table', estimated to be one-fifth of total employment.[5]

The clothing sector (Figure 10.1), studied in the four principal provinces, Verona, Vicenza, Padova and Treviso, strictly limited to garment manufacture (csc[6]: 10801, 10803, 10805) and to knitwear (csc: 10713), had about 65 000 employees in 1980. During the following decade employment increased rapidly, reaching a total of 78 000 in 1990, but the increase was concentrated in local, small artisan units which doubled their employment (plus 93 per cent) with 17 000 additional workers. In large firms employment declined by more than 12 per cent, corresponding to a loss of 5500 jobs. According to a national survey carried out in 1993 by Confartigianato, two-thirds of clothing companies worked as subcontractors, thus employing more than half of the workers in the sector. The national clothing industry is characterized by major regional differences and Veneto has a particularly dense network of subcontractors consisting of small firms (ten workers on average) working almost exclusively for the final producers that have their headquarters in the region (Crestanello 1999). In the mid 1990s subcontracting in clothing in Italy employed a third of all subcontracting workers in the sector in Europe (European Commission 1996, Table 1). The fall in employment by bigger firms has brought about a process of disintegration of the final product to such an extent that 'now many large firms have delocalized all production processes keeping only planning and marketing in the main firms' (Crestanello 1999, p. 18).

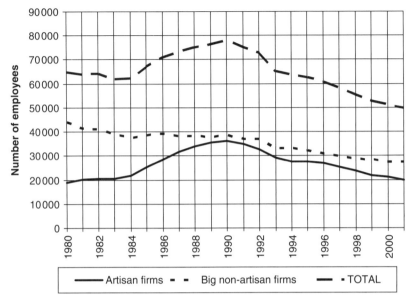

Source: VWH, DBVeneto, regional account data for 1980–95 and Istat 1996–2003.

Figure 10.1   Employment in clothing according to firm type in Veneto

In 1991–2001 the situation was reversed. Small artisan firms lost nearly all the workers they had acquired in the previous decade. Moreover final producers lost a further 11 000 jobs. In 2001 people employed in this sector in our territory totalled only 49 600, 36 per cent less than 11 years earlier. This was the result of the fact that most production was taking place abroad.[7]

However, the Veneto textile-clothing-footwear sector made steady progress over time, at least until the year 2000: the regional value added, together with exports, increased considerably in real terms during the 1990s even if at a lower average rate compared to the previous decade (Figure 10.2). Faced with the job loss which hit the sector starting from 1991, the value added continued to rise with an unchanging trend until 1997, then remaining more or less unchanged until 2001, and finally fell sharply in 2002, due to a general crisis in the sector.[8] Productivity measured by value added per capita increased notably: this was because part of production moved abroad with a drastic drop in domestic employment while the value of production did not significantly diminish. In fact, in those years the profits of final producers – in particular medium-size firms – showed a steady improvement.[9]

Source: VWH, DBVeneto, regional account data for 1980–95 and Istat 1996–2003.

Figure 10.2   Value added at constant prices in textile-clothing-footwear and employment in Veneto

Summing up, three periods can be quite clearly outlined. The first period involved the growth of the sector with an increase in small and medium-size firms and the creation of the Veneto clothing industrial district (the 1960s and first half of the1970s). In the second period the development of subcontractors prevailed, mostly localized within the district (1980s): the number of small laboratories rapidly increased and employment grew. In the third period, on the other hand, subcontracting shifted abroad, either through direct investments or foreign firms, and many domestic laboratories were forced to close down. This last move brought about a drop in employment and a notable increase in per capita value added at a regional level (1990s).

10.4   THE EFFECTS OF OUTSOURCING

The significant change that occurred in the structure of the firm, similar to what has been noted here with regard to the previous decades, can be illustrated by way of a simple numeric example. The three possibilities examined are: integrated production processes, a final firm with national

Table 10.1 *Structure of the production in an integrated and in a*
              deverticalized firm

	Integrated producer	National subcontracting		Foreign subcontracting	
		Final Firm	Sub contractor	Final Firm	Sub contractor
Turnover	1000	1000	500	1000	410
Cost of labour	650	300	280	300	100
Raw materials	200	–	200	–	300
Semi manufactured	–	500		410	–
Gross profits	150	200	20	290	10
Unit cost of labour	1	1	0.8	1	0.2
Employees	650	300	350	300	500
Value added	800	500	300	590	110

subcontracting and a final firm with overseas subcontracting (see also
Gordon 2004). The example shows values which reflect the average magnitude occurring in the Veneto clothing sector around 2003, while foreign
subcontracting refers to Romania. The per capita labour cost equals 1 for
the final producer, drops to 0.8 for a national subcontractor and goes down
to 0.2 in the case of an overseas subcontractor.[10] The value of the turnover
of an Italian subcontractor is divided into 50 per cent for salaries and 50
per cent for expenses in order to purchase intermediate materials which the
subcontractor buys or receives from its customer. In the case of the
Romanian subcontractor the ratio is 25 per cent for salaries and 75 per cent
for intermediate materials (for footwear the proportion for raw materials is
slightly higher, see Crestanello and Tattara 2007). Let us assume for the
sake of simplicity that the final producer relocates abroad by sending materials of the same value as those used previously in Italy. The structure of
the production processes is shown in its basic terms in Table 10.1.

From a value chain perspective we can consider the domestic and the
overseas units as separate plants belonging to the final producer. How the
overall profit is shared between the final producer and the subcontractors
depends on the price at which semi-manufactured goods are transferred (in
the case of FDI) or purchased (subcontracting), hence on the final firm's
relative power, on its targets and on various fiscal regimes. The experience
resulting from several visits to subcontractors working in Romania in the

clothing sector leads us to believe that the final producer is able to keep the subcontractors' profit to a minimum, owing to some guarantees concerning quality and reliability.[11] In synthesis in Table 10.1 we end up with a profit of 150 in the case of integrated production, 200 in the case of national fragmentation and 290 in the case of overseas fragmentation.

Relocation abroad is usually carried out by firms which had already fragmented their production by delegating some parts to local subcontractors, so that moving abroad involves fewer risks and doubts (for a theoretical example, see Melitz 2003). In this case the impact of relocation on the final producer is obtained by comparing the values in column three to that in column five: the lower cost of overseas subcontractors compared to the national equivalent increases profits. The increase shows the benefits gained by the final producer in utilizing this new corporate strategy.[12]

Many firms transferred abroad part of the machines used domestically; several Italian subcontractors in clothing and footwear productions were pressed to move abroad by their customers in order to reduce costs, particularly in Hungary and Romania but also in Tunisia. The large number of Veneto small firms that have been set up in Romania, in Timisoara, prompt economic commentators to currently refer to Timisoara as to the eighth Veneto province.

The impact of overseas delocalization should be evident in the budget data of firms producing final products, although the shift from a numerical example to enterprise balance sheet figures cannot be direct and is not without risks. But one may expect the delocalized processes to have a positive effect on turnover and gross earning (EBITDA[13]) for final producers. The gross operative earning of the final producer increases when shifting from integrated production to domestic subcontracting and then to overseas subcontracting, owing to reduced labour costs. In the majority of cases examined in our study the decision to carry out part of production abroad is associated with an increase in the level of activity. Production increases both because the decision to govern a value chain with productive units operating in different countries is feasible only in the presence of larger productive volumes, and because the decision to outsource abroad is expected to reduce unit costs, promoting a more aggressive policy and larger sale volumes.

The definition of a new corporate strategy that brings about important changes regarding the value chain, such as those we are discussing, is often combined with a firm's repositioning at the higher levels of the chain; this involves new management roles and an increase in qualified staff responsible for the governance of the more complex strategy. The overall analysis may thus become more complicated, and new variables may be introduced which can so far only partially be accounted for.

Figures 10.3 and 10.4 graphically represent the trend over time of turnover and EBITDA of four Italian companies with reference to the main relocation event (dotted line). If overseas outsourcing were a pure substitution effect (from domestic to overseas), turnover would not be affected while the effect on EBITDA might be positive, reflecting the decline in the labour cost of production. A positive result for both turnover and EBITDA means a large volume of activity and larger profits as well.

10.5   THE ESTIMATES

In order to verify if the delocalized process has a positive effect on gross profits and turnover in the final firm, and if the effect turns out to be higher according to the quota of goods which a firm produces abroad (out of the overall total), we have estimated a linear regression model using panel data referring to a group of firms.

The analysis was carried out on a self-selected group of 70 limited and joint stock companies based in Veneto involved in the clothing and footwear sector on 31 December 2003. They are mainly medium-sized companies (110 employees on average) which have delocalized some important production phases abroad. They represent more than 25 per cent of the total employment of the companies with more than 50 employees operating in the textile, clothing and footwear sector in Veneto in 2001, according to the Industrial Census. Less than a half of these internationalized production through direct investments (and possible subcontracting), while the majority resorted to subcontracting to foreign firms (see Appendix for descriptive statistics). The model's estimate is built on budget data from the Veneto Provincial Chamber of Commerce collection, employment data from the VWH database and data on outsourcing obtained from a questionnaire delivered to each company and supplemented by several telephone interviews. Keeping in mind that overseas production is a phenomenon which started in the mid 1980s, we extended the data collection from 1982 to 2003. Some companies included in the analysis began their activity after 1982 and therefore the panel is unbalanced.

Information on outsourcing for each company was acquired from a direct survey carried out at the beginning of 2004 and refers to the previous year (Gianelle 2005). For each delocalization (direct investments, subcontracting to foreign firm and so on) the starting year, the country involved and the type and intensity of the relation are known.[14] The latter is computed as the ratio of goods produced abroad to those made at home, and is taken into account if it is larger than 10 per cent of the overall pro-

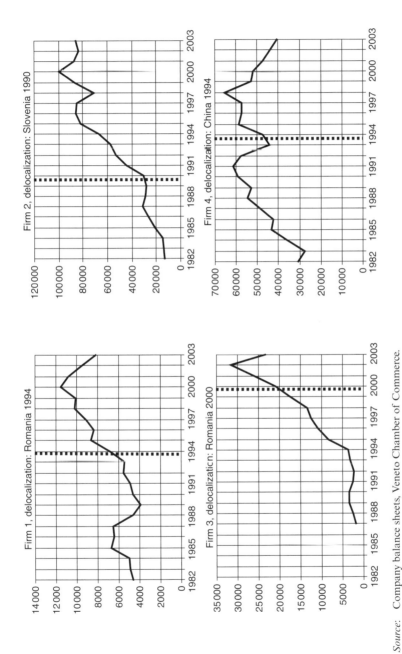

Source: Company balance sheets, Veneto Chamber of Commerce.

Figure 10.3 Turnover in four companies (in thousands of euros, current prices)

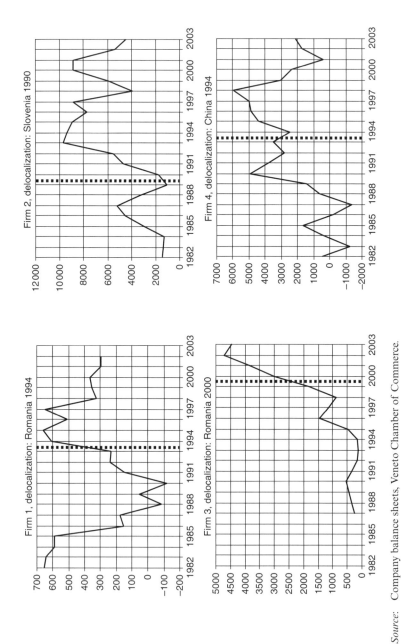

Source: Company balance sheets, Veneto Chamber of Commerce.

Figure 10.4 EBITDA in four companies (thousands of euros, current prices)

duction. Outsourcing is limited to one episode for each company, the most significant in terms of number of delocalized commodities.[15]

The companies making up the panel vary in size, type of market involved, export trends, type of production phases carried out domestically and individual background. Diversity is considered as represented by a group of omitted structural variables, specific for every company and constant over time, and the effect of diversity is taken into account by estimating a fixed effect regression (Hsiao 2003).

The dependent variable of the model is alternately the turnover at current prices and the gross earning before taxation (EBITDA), both expressed in logarithms.[16] The latter is provided by the difference between the operative value added and labour costs in current terms.

The impact of outsourcing abroad can be estimated by means of a dummy variable which splits the time period referring to each company into two sub-periods: before and after the event. Delocalization occurs, for various companies, in different years within the time span studied and this allows the impact of the variable to be identified. The estimation equation also includes a linear trend, which shows the average company growth throughout the period. The delocalization dummy, which estimates the average effect of relocation, can interact with the trend, resulting in a delocalization variable that captures the growth effect of relocation. The impact of outsourcing is therefore estimated, on average, by the coefficient of these two delocalization dummies, henceforth 'average effect' and 'growth effect'.

In Figure 10.5 the horizontal axis measures the distance in years in relation to the year of delocalization t_d, which is labelled zero. The drift of the continuous function represents the average impact effect, while the difference in the slope of the dotted line represents the growth effect.

The constant delocalization dummy Dc (average effect) is defined as follows:

$$Dc_{it} = \begin{cases} 0 & \text{for } t < t_{d(i)} \\ 1 & \text{for } t \geq t_{d(i)} \end{cases}$$

where $t_{d(i)}$ is the year of relocation for firm i. The trend delocalization dummy (growth effect), which is assumed to be linear, is defined by making the variable trend (T) interact with the preceding dummy, obtaining the variable TDc. Hence the regression estimated with reference to turnover is:

$$logTurn_{it} = \beta_0 + \beta_1 Dc_{it} + \beta_2 TDc_{it} + \beta_3 T_{it} + \beta_4 Emp_{it} +$$
$$\beta_5 Ord_{it} + \gamma_t + u_i + \varepsilon_{it} \tag{1}$$

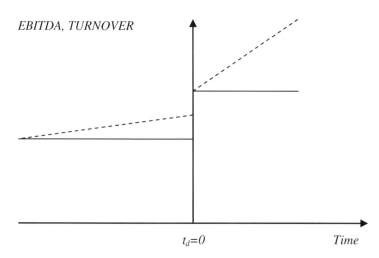

Figure 10.5   Impact of relocation

Turnover and EBITDA are regressed on the firm's employment level, *Emp* and a set of other controls in order to take into account cyclical factors, demand, price and technological progress, provided they involve all firms to the same extent in the same years. With the aim of taking into account cyclical trends[17] we have included among the independent variables an index of sector orders at the international level, calculated by Istat on a monthly basis,[18] *Ord.* The year variables γ are year dummies, that is, variables which include events involving all companies in the same way in a specific year and therefore show the influence of sector-specific shocks (inflation, average growth in the sector and so on) on the dependent variable. They do not prevent the identification of the delocalization dummy because the relocation events occur in different years.

Some caution is necessary: available data do not allow consideration of firm-specific effects like those deriving from a change in the type of product or market trends, nor the evolution of productive organization and changes in relation to other companies in the production sequence; as these elements are possibly correlated with outsourcing, the results can be blurred.

A visual presentation of the outsourcing impact is obtained by reproducing Figure 10.5 through our data. A regression of the two dependent variables *logTurn* and *logEBITDA* on control variables (year dummies, firm dummies, temporal trend, employment, sector orders) is estimated in order to eliminate them. In Figure 10.6 the vertical axis measures the yearly average residues of the regression in relation to time, and represents the net effects of relocation clear of yearly, company, sector-specific shocks. Time

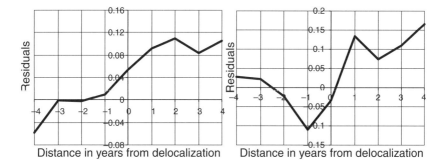

Figure 10.6   Residuals of the regression of logTurnover *(left) and*
logEBITDA *(right) over controls*

is centred on the delocalization event and Figure 10.6 is immediately comparable with Figure 10.5.

Figure 10.6 makes it clear that some firms have delocalized abroad after a drop in EBITDA. This is a rather reasonable result, which explains the firm's decision for a new strategy while nonetheless requiring caution in interpreting the coefficient estimates. In effect, firms self-select into treatment: some firms delocalize abroad after a negative profit shock and this cause the average delocalization result – measured by the coefficient of the dummy variable of interest – to be overestimated if referring to the entire population (it can also be considered a case of omitted variables, as firms' heterogeneity cannot be depicted: Heckman and Smith 1999). In the present work a self-selected sample of firms is used – only firms which delocalized abroad are considered – but, in the last decade, delocalization has been a strategy extensively pursued by the main clothing and footwear medium-size Veneto firms and firms that have not delocalized are very rare; consequently we believe the estimates we are presenting provide a reliable measure of the 'general' impact effect of delocalization.

The results of estimates (Equation 1, Tables 10.2 and 10.3, Column 2) show a remarkable average effect both on the value of turnover and on the EBITDA. On average, the delocalization impact is 15 per cent on turnover and nearly 17 per cent on EBITDA: the larger volume of activity is paralleled by larger profits. The growth effect is declining and very small in the case of turnover, suggesting a possible set back shortly after the outsourcing decision, and it is not significant in the case of EBITDA.

Using the information contained in the survey regarding the proportion of goods produced abroad by each firm when delocalization takes place, a different 'intensity' can be attributed to the delocalization process. The

Table 10.2   Effects of outsourcing on turnover (Equation 1)

| | | logTurnover | | | |
		1	2	3	4
Average impact	Dc	0.1623***	0.1517***		
		(0.0419)	(0.0418)		
Growth impact	TDc		−0.0238***		
			(0.0091)		
Average impact through quota	QDc			0.2423***	0.2842***
				(0.0733)	(0.0743)
Growth impact through quota	$QTDc$				−0.0361***
					(0.0131)
Employment	Emp	0.0019***	0.0019***	0.0019***	0.0019***
		(0.0003)	(0.0003)	(0.0003)	(0.0003)
Sector orders	Ord	0.0168***	0.0169***	0.0167***	0.0172***
		(0.0023)	(0.0023)	(0.0023)	(0.0023)
Trend	T	Yes	Yes	Yes	Yes
Yearly dummies	γ	Yes	Yes	Yes	Yes
Firm's specific effects	u	Yes	Yes	Yes	Yes
N. of observations		1138	1138	1138	1138
N. of firms		70	70	70	70
R-squared within		0.5641	0.5672	0.5639	0.5673

Note: Period of observation 1982–2003. All the regressions include specific firm intercept for each company and year dummies. Robust standard errors in brackets. ***: significance 1 per cent, **: significance 5 per cent,   *: significance 10 per cent.

information on delocalized quota refers to year 2003 and it is assumed that this firm quota has remained the same over the years, so that the 2003 values give an estimate of the extent of outsourcing over the whole period.[19] This assumption loses any information regarding the gradualism of the process and the estimate results provide a rough indication of the strength of the delocalization process.

Two further outsourcing variables are constructed, which take into account the different productive volumes involved in the event. The quota of goods produced abroad by each company is represented by Q_i, which varies between zero and one, that multiplied by Dc represents the average delocalization effect through the quotas, QDc. The variable $QTDc$ represents the growth effect of delocalization through the quotas.

Table 10.3   Effects of outsourcing on EBITDA (Equation 1)

		logEBITDA			
		1	*2*	*3*	*4*
Average impact	*Dc*	0.1650**	0.1663**		
		(0.0769)	(0.0766)		
Growth impact	*TDc*		0.0032		
			(0.0158)		
Average impact through quota	*QDc*			0.1648	0.1568
				(0.1262)	(0.1226)
Growth impact through quota	*QTDc*				0.0061
					(0.0256)
Employment	*Emp*	0.0016***	0.0016***	0.0016***	0.0016***
		(0.0005)	(0.0005)	(0.0005)	(0.0005)
Sector orders	*Ord*	0.0178***	0.0178***	0.0175***	0.0174***
		(0.0038)	(0.0038)	(0.0038)	(0.0038)
Trend	*T*	Yes	Yes	Yes	Yes
Yearly dummies	*γ*	Yes	Yes	Yes	Yes
Firm's specific effects	*u*	Yes	Yes	Yes	Yes
N. of observations		1096	1096	1096	1096
N. of firms		70	70	70	70
R-squared within		0.2868	0.2869	0.2851	0.2852

Note: Period of observation 1982–2003. All the regressions include specific firm intercept for each company and year dummies. Robust standard errors in brackets. ***: significance 1 per cent, **: significance 5 per cent, *: significance 10 per cent.

These variables replicate the pattern of the variables *Dc* and *TDc*, with the difference that in the presence of active outsourcing the delocalized dummy interacts with the quota of goods actually produced abroad. If, as a first approximation, the relationship between the productive volumes obtained abroad and the dependent variables is linear, the coefficient of the outsourcing variable interacting with the quota indicates how much turnover and EBITDA vary for each percentage point of production delocalized abroad by a delocalizing company. The effect through the quotas (Tables 10.2 and 10.3, Column 4) indicates that for one additional point of the product manufactured abroad, the turnover increases on average by 0.28 per cent, with a negative growth effect of nearly 0.04 per cent per year, while the EBITDA is not significant.

The decision to delocalize implies moving abroad those phases which were once carried out within the company itself, or were delocalized domestically. In the first circumstance the decision to delocalize entails process fragmentation, while in the second circumstance phases already outsourced are moved beyond the national borders. If slicing production and allocating abroad are superimposed on one another, the estimate blurs the effect attributed to outsourcing with the effect of fragmentation. It is therefore appropriate to disentangle fragmentation from delocalization so as to evaluate the net impact of the offshore alternative. To do so we split the sample into two sub-samples, made by treated and untreated firms:

- Treated firms are firms that delocalize abroad and at the same time fragment production.
- Non-treated firms are firms that delocalize abroad production phases previously outsourced in the domestic market.

In order to tackle the problem we define the variable *Fra*, which is zero for firms which delocalize abroad phases already outsourced domestically, and is one for firms which transfer abroad phases previously processed within the company, and a variable *Nfra*, which is zero for companies that outsource production previously processed directly, and one for the remaining. The delocalization dummies interact with the fragmentation dummies, giving rise to *FraDc*, *NfraDc* and *FraTDc*, *NfraTDc* variables. Equation 2 takes into account the delocalization and fragmentation processes:

$$logTurn_{it} = \beta_0 + \beta_1 FraDc_{it} + \beta_2 FraTDc_{it} + \beta_3 NfraDc_{it} +$$

$$\beta_4 NfraTDc_{it} + \beta_5 T_{it} + \beta_6 Emp_{it} + \beta_7 Ord_{it} + \gamma_t + u_i + \varepsilon_{it} \quad (2)$$

The splitting of the sample is made on the following assumption: if between the year that precedes and the year that follows the decision to outsource abroad, the firm's employment falls considerably (more than 10 per cent), while the turnover remains more or less the same or rises (we require that it does not drop more than 5 per cent), then the firm is defined as treated and the parameter estimate reflects both delocalization abroad and fragmentation. Fourteen firms out of 70 accomplish this assumption; the remaining firms are untreated and their estimate reflects only delocalization, as production was fragmented earlier in time.

Even in this case it is possible to show the interaction of delocalized variables, the variables referring to the fragmentation processes and the quota of goods produced abroad, in order to take into account different degrees of intensity with which outsourcing occurs. Thus the variables *QfraDc*, *QNfraDc* and *QfraTDc*, *QNfraTDc* are obtained.

The coefficients of the variables (Table 10.4, Columns 1 and 3) indicate that delocalization does increase turnover in firms which had already fragmented the production process domestically (plus almost 15 per cent). The average impact for firms that delocalize but had not previously outsourced to national subcontractors is larger (plus 18 per cent), as expected. The EBITDA increases by 23 per cent for firms which have already fragmented production, while firms that fragment and outsource abroad at the same time show a positive, gradual, profit increase (4 per cent per year) and a non-significant average impact effect.

Taking into account the quota (Table 10.4, columns 2 and 4), an additional percentage point of production shifted abroad increases the turnover and the EBITDA by 0.29 and 0.35 per cent, respectively, for firms which had already outsourced domestically. While in the case of firms that both delocalize and split the production process for the first time, the turnover reveals an average increase of 0.24 per cent and the EBITDA exhibits a positive and significant growth effect (close to plus 0.08 per cent per year).

10.6   INTERPRETING AND EMPIRICAL RESULTS

A crucial factor in influencing the decision to move part of the production process abroad is the cost of managing external suppliers. In the short run outsourcing may improve company focus and enables firms to reduce the wage cost by substituting internal labour with cheaper labour hired by the delocalized firms, particularly if located in a low-wage country: it is basically a labour cost driven process. However outsourcing abroad is accompanied by more complex logistics and increases the administrative overheads.

Many firms that move abroad had previously fragmented the production process domestically (no significant boundary change) and frequently rely on Italian subcontractors that have transferred their plants abroad: additional investments are limited, control and coordination routines have already been introduced, and need adaptation more than creation. The estimates show a sudden positive impact effect on profits due to the wage bill reduction (plus 23 per cent) and a turnover increase (plus 15 per cent), as moving abroad is associated with an increased competitive capacity and larger volumes. The positive impact is a one-off effect and the productivity trajectory does not improve or decline[20] (no positive growth effect). Firms that fragment the process and at the same time move abroad drastically change their market/boundary line: they 'slice' their production process. Domestic employment is consequently reduced and firms face considerable

Table 10.4   Net/gross effects of delocalization and fragmentation (Equation 2)

		logTurnover		logEBITDA	
		1	2	3	4
Average impact and fragmentation	FraDc	0.1799*** (0.0659)		0.0001 (0.1395)	
Growth impact and fragmentation	FraTDc	−0.0193** (0.0096)		0.0448** (0.0175)	
Average impact net of fragmentation	NfraDc	0.1453*** (0.0495)		0.2306*** (0.0875)	
Growth impact net of fragmentation	NfraTDc	−0.0273*** (0.0103)		−0.0193 (0.0187)	
Average impact and fragmentation through quotas	QFraDc		0.2367** (0.0997)		−0.2716 (0.2190)
Growth impact and fragmentation through quotas	QFraTDc		−0.0240* (0.0145)		0.0765*** (0.0290)
Average impact net of fragmentation through quotas	QNfraDc		0.2918*** (0.0947)		0.3496** (0.1507)
Growth impact net of fragmentation through quotas	QNfraTDc		−0.0323** (0.0148)		−0.0308 (0.0311)
Employment	Emp	0.0019*** (0.0003)	0.0019*** (0.0003)	0.0016*** (0.0006)	0.0015*** (0.0005)
Sector orders	Ord	0.0167*** (0.0024)	0.0172*** (0.0024)	0.0183*** (0.0038)	0.0189*** (0.0039)
Trend	T	Yes	Yes	Yes	Yes
Year dummies	γ	Yes	Yes	Yes	Yes
Firm's specific effects	u	Yes	Yes	Yes	Yes
N. of observations		1136	1136	1096	1096
N. of firms		70	70	70	70
R-squared within		0.5677	0.5664	0.2926	0.2918

Note: Period of observation 1982–2003. All the regressions include specific firm intercept for each company and year dummies. Robust standard errors in brackets. ***: significance 1 per cent, **: significance 5 per cent,   *: significance 10 per cent.

investments in logistics: new personal relations, process modularity and codification, a set of new organization routines that make the reward of moving abroad rather gradual. It is essentially a process of learning and experimentation and the volume increase (plus 18 per cent) is accompanied

Table 10.5   Delocalization and the boundary of the firm

Strategy	Firm/market boundary change	Value chain management (agency problem)	Profitability
Labour cost driven strategy	*No change:* outsource abroad a process already fragmented	Limited changes (more complex logistic)	Sudden impact effect(+22%), no long-run effects
Labour cost driven strategy	*Change:* outsource abroad a process previously vertically integrated	Considerable investment in personal relations, process modularity, codification, administration	Gradual impact effect (4% yearly growth) due to the required support for the new division of labour

by a gradual profit increase through time (4 per cent yearly growth). Our results are summarized in Table 10.5.

10.7   CONCLUSIONS

At the moment information on globalization of Italian firms is extensive but incomplete and bitty. We have analytical data relative to direct overseas investments and their effect on firms' profitability (Barba Navaretti and Castellani 2004; Barba Navaretti *et al.* 2006; Castellani *et al.* 2006). However, we are aware that globalization is a much vaster phenomenon.

This work estimates the effect of organizing production in a global value chain framework on the firm's turnover and gross earnings. Both subcontracting relations and direct investments abroad are considered. A database has been constructed on the basis of a direct survey, supplemented by information available from the firms' balance sheets and firm-level employment data. Both the turnover and the gross operative margin positively responds to the impact of relocation abroad.

The delocalization strategy, moving significant phases of production abroad and attaining significant unit cost reductions, seems to offer an important contribution in order to increase the level of activity and foster profitability. A higher profitability, in turn, means benefiting from additional opportunities for growth and development, and chances of survival for firms facing temporary difficulties.

Delocalization abroad is a measure which has a notable one-off effect both on margins and turnover. However it seems to have no effect on the rate of growth through time, and therefore one should not expect lasting aggregate effects when all the companies are delocalized. The rationale for this conclusion is that outsourcing, in the majority of cases, occurs with the transfer abroad of phases and processes previously carried out in Italy, and it is prompted by increased price competition at the international level, while the machinery and the production techniques remain substantially unchanged. A sequence of governance innovations (product modularization, export of knowledge and so on) is required which is likely to further increase productivity and encourage the use of new technologies in order to continue the positive run.

Working in a more and more complex international context encourages the final producers to improve managerial and organizational efficiency and increases domestic demand for skilled high value added services.[21] Nonetheless the choice to delocalize abroad has an immediate strong negative impact on employment in small artisan laboratories and on the related skills, particularly in a region where the number of people employed in manufacturing is high, as in Veneto in the clothing and footwear sectors, and where domestic outsourcing has been common practice (Tattara 2001). The negative consequence of the drastic reduction of domestic outsourcing in the region and the crisis of some major brands, which have been unable to manage the value chain at an international level, is evident.

In an area which has always been characterized by the presence of small firms, clustered in industrial districts, the destiny of the firm has often been considered in symbiosis with that of the workers: a mutual solidarity connects entrepreneurs, the surrounding areas and society towards the attainment of a mutual progress. Over the last decade, however, the firms of the Veneto clothing and footwear districts have embarked on a different trend. Profit realization is now farther and farther away from places where companies that lead the productive chains are located. Therefore a profit increase by the final producers no longer directly reflects positive corresponding variations in local employment and in local revenues and this inevitably corrodes some of the constituent characters of the industrial district.

NOTES

1.   Disintegration at the global level implies an upsurge in trade flows, as many intermediate commodities are exchanged across national borders (Feenstra 1998).

2. The cost is the highest priority element according to all surveys concerning firms in the traditional sector, but the tax benefits relative to setting up companies overseas also proves very important. On the latter point, see Stevanato (2004). See Bénassy-Quéré *et al.* (2005) on how different tax legislation directs the flow of direct investments.

3. Sometimes big brands, very soon after setting up delocalization, face bottlenecks in the sequence of phases into which the production process has been sliced and resort to direct investments in order to complete the process. On several occasions, Italian clothing brands have set up industrial laundries, cloth printing facilities and so on in order to manufacture the entire production cycle abroad. In this way a complex production can be entirely manufactured abroad with increased efficiency in the management of the value chain. See Crestanello and Tattara (2006).

4. Therefore the Veneto companies differ from the Gereffi type (2002) where the brands have delocalized almost the entire production. There are numerous examples, from Benetton to Stefanel, Diesel and Marzotto, to mention just a few. See Owen (2001) for a more complete view on this topic.

5. Referring to Italy in 1992, the European Commission estimated work 'under the table' in the clothing industry to be 21 per cent of overall employment (European Commission 1996, Table 2). Therefore, a widespread phenomenon.

6. Acronym for contributive statistic code.

7. The role of Veneto within the sphere of outsourcing in 'traditional' sectors was pointed out by Schiattarella in 1999 and subsequently has been widely confirmed. The Capitalia survey, referring to traditional sectors, shows that 61 per cent of companies based in the North-East completely delocalized production to countries with low labour costs over the past three years, compared to 46 per cent at a national level.

8. Istat and INPS data are similar regarding the fall in employment. In the 1990s in Veneto, the decline was above the national average.

9. Between the years 1996 and 2000 the value added of final producers of footwear and clothing in the North-East, calculated from average-size joint stock companies, went up by 12.5 per cent, compared to a much lower overall increase, while unemployment went down by 1.6 per cent (Mediobanca and Unioncamere 2003).

10. Labour costs in the clothing sector in Romania total about one-eighth of the cost in Italy, although this varies greatly. In the example we use a value of about 25 per cent, adding other costs relative to outsourcing (transport, training and so on).

11. The companies have strict control over their subcontractors in Romania and the sub-contractor functions as a delocalized sector of the client's factory. In the case of delocalization towards Asia, package relations are prevalent and the subcontractor acquires raw materials and accessories and produces the final product, accepting the risks involved.

12. In reality it is widely believed that productivity in Romania is lower than in the Veneto and this brings about an increase in employment which is, however, slight and does not alter the meaning of the example of Table 10.1. See also Crestanello and Tattara (2006).This measure has nothing to do with productivity calculated by relating the value of the product to the number of employees, which is often mentioned in international publications. This method is not a technical estimate of efficiency but the result of how production chains are organized and therefore of the proportion between the value imputed to semi-manufactured and to finished goods in the relations within the chain. In fact, productivity measured as the ratio between value added and number of employees regarding the Romanian clothing-textile sector hardly totals 14 per cent of the 15 EU countries' production, according to standard purchasing power. See CEPS-WIIW (2005, Table 4).

13. Earnings Before Interests, Taxes, Depreciation and Amortization.

14. Outsourcing can involve direct investments, subcontracting and so on, but here we make no distinction. Each example of delocalization defined by its first year and the country involved can also be characterized by a range of manufacturing links with different companies situated in the same country. This aspect is not relevant as far as our analysis is concerned because all the companies in the same country have similar costs. Therefore

we consider relations with each foreign country (for example, Romania, Tunisia and China) as a single occurrence.

15. Some companies have several delocalized activities in various countries, set up in different years, involving various productive volumes. In this survey we take into consideration the main delocalization event.

16. Negative values of the EBITDA, for which the logarithm does not exist, are treated as missing values.

17. See Heckman and Robb (1985) who suggests checking for the economic cycle.

18. The sales confidence index is sector specific. The sectors and corresponding indexes are based on the three digits Ateco 2002 classification (codes: DB177, DB182 and DC193).

19. It proved very difficult to obtain reliable information from the companies interviewed, concerning the gradualism through time involved in the delocalization process.

20. In the model presented by Reinstaller and Windrum (in Chapter 7 in this book) outsourcing has a possible long-run negative effect on productivity growth because managers might lose competences that are crucial in providing further quality and cost improvements. Closely reflecting our empirical results, they claim that short and long-run impacts of outsourcing can have the opposite sign and managers can, over the long run, be locked into low productivity growth trajectories.

21. Gereffi (1999) stresses that being part of a value chain at an international level means acquiring knowledge and therefore having a significant production upgrading.

APPENDIX

Table 10.A1   Descriptive statistics of the companies included in the sample (2003)

Firms in clothing sector	40 (10 knitwear)
Firms in footwear sector	30
Average n. of employees	110
Average turnover (thousands of euros)	36.3
Average EBITDA (thousands of euros)	2.6
Firms with FDI	34
Average n. of observations per firm in the panel	16.3
Average n. of observations before relocation	8.8
Average n. of observations after relocation	7.5

First ten countries of delocalization in order of importance:
  Romania
  China
  Tunisia
  Hungary
  Bulgaria
  Croatia
  Turkey
  Slovakia
  India
  Indonesia

Table 10.A2 Limited and joint stock companies

Employment class	Present sample (2003)						Veneto (2001)						Sample % over Veneto	
	Companies		Employees				Companies		Employees				Companies	Employees
1–19	6	(8%)	80	(1%)			858	(60%)	4971	(12%)			0.7	1.6
20–49	16	(23%)	577	(8%)			356	(25%)	10318	(24%)			4.5	5.6
50–99	21	(30%)	1472	(19%)			131	(9%)	8892	(21%)			16.0	16.6
100–249	21	(30%)	3108	(40%)			69	(5%)	10200	(24%)			30.4	30.5
250 and more	6	(9%)	2494	(32%)			16	(1%)	8340	(19%)			37.5	29.9
Total	70	(100%)	7731	(100%)			1430	(100%)	42721	(100%)			4.9	18.1

Source: Survey; Industrial Census, Istat, 2001.

REFERENCES

Ádám, G. (1971), 'New trends in international business: worldwide sourcing and dedomiciling', *Acta Oeconomica*, **7** (3–4), 349–67.

Baden, S. (2002), 'Trade policy, retail markets and value chain restructuring in the EU clothing sector', PRUS working paper, no. 9, university of susser, Bnghton, UK.

Barba Navaretti, G. and D. Castellani (2004), 'Investments abroad and performance at home: evidence from Italian multinationals', CEPR discussion paper, no. 4284, CEPR, London, UK.

Barba Navaretti, G., D. Castellani and A.C. Disdier (2006), 'How does investing in cheap countries affect performance at home? France and Italy', CEPR discussion paper, no. 5765, CEPR, London, UK.

Bénassy-Quéré, A., L. Fontagné and A. Lahréche-Révil (2005), 'How does FDI react to corporate taxation?', *International Tax and Public Finance*, **12** (5), 583–603.

Bigarelli, D. and A. Ginzburg (2004), *I Confini delle Imprese*, Reggio Emilia, Italy: Reggio Emilia Chamber of Commerce.

Brusco, Sebastiano (1975), 'Organizzazione del lavoro e decentramento produttivo nel settore metalmeccanico', reprinted in S. Brusco (1989), *Piccole Imprese e Distretti Industriali*, Turin, Italy: Rosemberg and Sellier, pp. 59–153.

Bugamelli, M., P. Cipollone and L. Infante (2000), 'L'internazionalizzazione produttiva delle imprese italiane negli anni novanta', *Rivista Italiana Degli Economisti*, **5** (3), 349–86.

Capitalia (2005), *Indagine Sulle Imprese Italiane. Tavole Statistiche Allegate al Rapporto sul Sistema Produttivo e la Politica Industriale*, Rome, Italy: Capitalia Gruppo Bancario.

Castellani, Davide, Ilaria Mariotti and Lucia Piscitello (2006), 'Attività estere delle imprese multinazionali italiane e "skill upgrading"', in S. Mariotti and L. Piscitello (eds) (2006), *Multinazionali, Innovazione e Strategie per la Competitività*, Bologna, Italy: Il Mulino, pp. 165–83.

CEPS-WIIW (2005), *The Textiles and Clothing Industries in an Enlarged Community and the Outlook in the Candidate States*, CEPS Project Final Report, Part 1,Vienna: The Vienna Institute for International Economic Studies.

Corò, G. and M. Volpe (2003), 'Frammentazione produttiva e apertura internazionale nei sistemi di piccola e media impresa', *Economia e Società Regionale*, **81** (1), 67–107.

Crestanello, P. (1999), *L'Industria Veneta dell'Abbigliamento: Internazionalizzazione Produttiva e Imprese di Subfornitura*, Milan, Italy: Franco Angeli.

Crestanello, P. and P.E. Dalla Libera (2003), 'La delocalizzazione produttiva all'estero nell'industria della moda: il caso di Vicenza', *Economia e Società Regionale*, **82** (2), 5–45.

Crestanello, P. and G. Tattara, 'Connessioni e competenze nei processi di delocalizzazione delle industrie venete di affligliamento-calzature in Romania', in G. Tattara, G. coro and M. Volpe (eds), *Andersene per continuane a crescere: la delocalizzazione internazionale come strategia competitivia*, Rome, Italy: carocci, pp. 191–224 reprinted from *Economia e Societa Regionale* (2005), **90** (2), 63–99.

Crestanello, P. and G. Tattara (2007), 'A global network and its local ties. Competition and restructuring of the Benetton Group', paper presented at the SASE Meeting, Copenhagen, 29 June 2007.

European Commission (1996), 'The competitiveness of subcontracting in the textile and clothing industry in the European Union', Communication no. 96.201, Brussels.

Feenstra, R. (1998), 'Integration of trade and disintegration of production in the global economy', *Journal of Economic Perspectives*, **12** (4), 31–50.

Finger, J.M. (1976), 'Trade and domestic effects of offshore assembly provision in the U.S. tariff', *American Economic Review*, **66** (4), 598–611

Finger, J.M. (1977), 'Offshore assembly provision in the West German and Netherlands tariffs: trade and domestic effects', *Weltwirtschaftliches Archiv*, **113** (2), 237–49.

Gereffi, G. (1999), 'International trade and industrial upgrading in the apparel commodity chain', *Journal of International Economics*, **48** (1), 37–70.

Gereffi, G. (2002), 'The international competitiveness of Asian economies in the apparel commodity chain', ERD working paper, no. 5, Manila, Philippines (World Development Bank).

Gereffi, G., J. Humphrey and T. Sturgeon (2005), 'The governance of global value chain', *Review of International Political Economy*, **12** (1), 78–104.

Gianelle, C. (2005), 'Il Veneto che produce all'estero: una ricerca empirica sulla delocalizzazione delle imprese di abbigliamento', *Economia e Società Regionale*, **90** (2), 37–62.

Gomirato, E. (2004), 'La delocalizzazione dell'abbigliamento in Romania: il caso Stefanel', *Economia e Società Regionale*, **86** (2), 63–91.

Gordon, M.J. (2004), 'How Third World contracting is transformed into First World productivity', *Challenge*, **47** (1), 78–85.

Graziani, G. (1998), 'Globalization of production in textile and clothing industries: the case of Italian foreign direct investment and outward processing in eastern Europe', in J. Zysman and A. Schwartz (eds), *Enlarging Europe: The Industrial Foundations of a New Political Reality*, Berkeley, CA: International and Area Studies Press, pp. 238–54.

Graziani, G. (2001), 'International subcontracting in the textile and clothing industry', in S.W. Arndt and H. Kierzkowski (eds), *Fragmentation. New Production Patterns in the World Economy*, Oxford, UK: Oxford University Press, pp. 209–30.

Heckman, James J. and Richard Robb Jr. (1985), 'Alternative methods for evaluating the impact of interventions', in J.J. Heckman and B. Singer (eds), *Longitudinal Analysis of Labour Market Data*, Cambridge, UK: Cambridge University Press, pp. 156–246.

Heckman, J.J. and J.A. Smith (1999), 'The pre-programme earnings dip and the determinants of participation in a social programme. Implications for simple programme evaluation strategies', *Economic Journal*, **109** (457), 313–48.

Hsiao, C. (2003), *Analysis of Panel Data*, Cambridge, UK: Cambridge University Press.

Kaminski, B. and F. Ng (2001), 'Trade and production fragmentation: Central European economies. EU networks of production and marketing', World Bank discussion paper, Washington.

Mediobanca and Unioncamere (2003), *Le Medie Imprese Industriali del Nord-Est (1996–2000)*, Milan and Rome, Italy: Mediobanca and Unioncamere.

Melitz, M. (2003), 'The impact of trade on intraindustry reallocations and aggregate industry productivity', *Econometrica*, **71** (6), 1695–725.

Nardin, Giuseppe (1987), *La Benetton. Strategia e Struttura di un'Impresa di Successo*, Rome, Italy: Edizioni lavoro.

Owen, G. (2001), 'Globalisation in textiles: corporate strategy and competitive advantage', The third annual Pasold lecture, 11 December 2001.

Schiattarella, R. (1999), 'La delocalizzazione internazionale: problemi di definizione e di misurazione. Un'analisi per il settore del "Made in Italy"', *Economia e Politica Industriale,* **103**, 207–39.

Stevanato, D. (2004*), '*Fisco e delocalizzazione', *Economia e Società Regionale,* **87** (3), 84–104.

Tattara, Giuseppe (ed.) (2001), *Il Piccolo che Nasce dal Grande*, Milan, Italy: Franco Angeli.

Tattara, Giuseppe (2007), 'Emerging hubs in Central-Eastern Europe, trade blocs and financial co-operation', in A.K. Bagchi and G.A. Dymski (eds), *Capture and Exclude: Developing Economies and the Poor in Global Finance*, New Delhi, India: Tulika Books, pp. 282–304.

Index